OF COUNSEL

A Guide for Law Firms and Practitioners

Fourth Edition

JEAN L. BATMAN

HAROLD G. WREN

BEVERLY J. GLASCOCK

Cover design by Jill Tedhams/ABA Publishing.

Printed in the United States of America.

17 16 15 14 13 5 4 3 2 1

Library of Congress Cataloging-in-Publication Data is on file.

Batman, Jean L.
Of counsel / Jean L. Batman, Senior Lawyers Division, American Bar Association.—4e.
pages cm
Previous editions by Harold G. Wren and Beverly J. Glascock.
ISBN 978-1-62722-143-6
1. "Of counsel" relationships (Practice of law)—United States. I. Wren, Harold G., 1921- Of counsel agreement II. American Bar Association. Senior Lawyers Division. III. Title.
KF310.O34W74 2013
347.73'504—dc23

2013026738

Discounts are available for books ordered in bulk. Special consideration is given to state bars, CLE programs, and other bar-related organizations. Inquire at Book Publishing, ABA Publishing, American Bar Association, 321 N. Clark Street, Chicago, Illinois 60654-7598.

www.ShopABA.org

Contents

Preface to the Fourth Edition

In the eight years since *The Of Counsel Agreement*, third edition, was published, important changes have been made to the Model Rules of Professional Conduct that benefit firms and attorneys engaged in "Of Counsel" arrangements, such as the recognition of screening as a method of avoiding the disqualification of an entire firm as the result of one attorney's conflict. The "Of Counsel" popularity also has continued to increase as law firms and attorneys discover the numerous benefits and flexibility of these arrangements. Although I agree with the authors of previous editions that a well-drafted "Of Counsel" agreement is indispensable for lawyers or law firms that want to establish and maintain a mutually rewarding "Of Counsel" relationship, only about half the "Of Counsel" attorneys I interviewed for this fourth edition had written "Of Counsel" agreements. For this reason, and because this book goes well beyond contract considerations, the title for this edition has been abbreviated to simply *Of Counsel.*

I am grateful to Corinne Cooper of Professional Presence and Richard G. Paszkiet at the American Bar Association for encouraging me to take on this project and supporting my efforts along the way, and to my husband, Alexander V. Choulos, and children, James, William, and Lauren, whose love, strength, good humor, and encouragement keep me going. Finally, I am grateful to my parents, Ruth and Jim Batman, who raised two young women to believe they could be whatever they wanted to be most in this world, and ended up with a doctor and a lawyer.

Jean L. Batman

Preface to the Third Edition

Seven years have passed since the publication of the Second Edition of *The Of Counsel Agreement*. The basic points that we emphasized in our Preface to the Second Edition remain unchanged, except that they have been greatly intensified by the increase in the number of Of Counsel arrangements throughout the country. We remain convinced that a well-drafted Of Counsel Agreement is essential for any lawyer who desires to maintain a happy and prosperous relationship with another lawyer or law firm.

We wish to express our thanks to all those listed in the Prefaces to the First and Second Editions; to Richard L. Thies, Chair of the Senior Lawyers Division of the American Bar Association; to Newton P. Allen, who read the manuscript for the Third Edition; and to Adrienne A. Cook of ABA Publishing, who assisted us with its publication. Most especially, we wish to thank Francis J. Mellen, Jr., who not only encouraged us in the publication of the Third Edition, but gave us an extensive hand in preparing the final draft.

Harold G. Wren and Beverly J. Glascock

Preface to the Second Edition

In the seven years that have passed since the First Edition of this book, there have been a number of developments in the law affecting the Of Counsel Agreement. Although we have no statistical data, anecdotal evidence indicates the following trends:

- The Of Counsel arrangement is being increasingly used for a variety of purposes other than retirement planning.
- The courts are more concerned than ever about the importance of conflicts and imputed disqualification.
- Legal malpractice suits are becoming far more common, with a corresponding increase in malpractice insurance rates.
- The fiduciary responsibility of lawyers toward their clients is being given greater consideration in legal malpractice cases.
- The possibility of lawyers being held liable to third parties for malpractice, either directly or vicariously, is on the increase.

A well-drafted Of Counsel Agreement becomes essential for any law firm or lawyer who chooses to enter into this arrangement. We have added some newer drafts of possible contracts, which the law firm or Of Counsel may find helpful in drafting its own contract to meet its particular needs.

In addition to those persons mentioned in the Preface to the First Edition, we wish to express our thanks to Leigh B. Middleditch, Jr., Chair of the Senior Lawyers Division of the American Bar Association; John H. Pickering, Immediate Past Chair of the Division; and George H. Cain, Chair, Book Committee. We do appreciate all the efforts of Richard G. Paszkiet, Executive Editor, Book Publishing, ABA Publishing, and his staff, for their assistance in the production of this Second Edition. We would also like to express our deep appreciation to John R. Glascock, Jr., Amy M. Thorpe, and Francis J. Mellen, Jr., who encouraged us in this second endeavor. Finally, thanks to all those readers of the First Edition who gave us encouragement and many helpful ideas.

Harold G. Wren and Beverly J. Glascock

Preface to the First Edition

In the not too distant past, it was common for law firms to list certain distinguished members of the community on their letterheads as being Of Counsel. One of the authors remembers how puzzled he was by this nomenclature when he was a young lawyer associated with what was then considered a fairly large firm. The firm listed a former governor of the state as being Of Counsel. He never saw this particular gentleman around the office, and he wondered just what his role would be. Someone suggested that he was the firm's lawyer. For example, if the firm ever needed representation in court, then this very distinguished gentleman would serve as its lawyer. This made little sense to him, since he felt that the firm would certainly be able to represent itself if such a situation should arise. More recently, he has asked a retired state supreme court justice what he thought the phrase meant, and the judge replied that this was a designation that a law firm commonly used for persons whom it might occasionally ask to do things for the firm for no compensation. Whatever the phrase means, it is highly ambiguous, and it may well mean a variety of things depending upon the manner in which it is used.

Today, we doubt that many law firms use the designation "Of Counsel" as a way of decorating their letterheads. But the legal profession has found a number of new uses of the designation that are consonant with both a word and a profession that are rapidly changing. As a result, the Senior Lawyers Division of the American Bar Association was called upon by lawyers all over the country for guidance and advice in establishing an Of Counsel relationship.

Most of their recommendations were based upon Formal Opinion 330—issued in 1972 by the Standing Committee on Ethics and Professional Responsibility of the American Bar Association—the first formal opinion to define what the relationship entails. That opinion remained unchanged until May 10, 1990, when the committee issued Formal Opinion 90-357. Formal Opinion 90-357 expressly superseded Formal Opinion 330 and a number of informal opinions upon which 330 were based. The principal effect of 90-357 was to give the legal profession freedom to contract for an Of Counsel relationship in a variety of different situations, without being forced onto a procrustean bed that neither side desired.

The purpose of this book is to guide lawyers and law firms that are contemplating entry into an Of Counsel relationship. We have sought to describe the fact situations that make this arrangement particularly desirable and the legal doctrines that may impose some limitations on the parties' complete freedom to contract as they desire.

For purposes of readability, where the term "Of Counsel" appears, we have chosen to capitalize the initial letters of the two words and to use neither a hyphen nor quotation marks. We have also chosen to use the masculine gender when singular personal pronouns are in order. We have made these choices solely for purposes of style and readability, and it is our fervent hope that no reader will be offended.

We would like to express our deep appreciation to Robert M. Ervin, Esq., Don M. Jackson, Esq., John W. Storer, Jr., Esq., E. Charles Eichenbaum, Esq., and F. William McCalpin, Esq., officers of the Senior Lawyers Division of the American Bar Association, who encouraged us in this endeavor; to Victor Futter, Esq., Chair, Publications Committee, Senior Lawyers Division of the American Bar Association, who read the manuscript with great care; to Susan Yessne and Joseph Weintraub of the ABA Press; and to Rina Moore, our resident word processor expert. Finally, we wish to thank those members of the bar who shared with us their experiences with the Of Counsel relationship.

About the Authors

Jean L. Batman

JEAN L. BATMAN founded Legal Venture Counsel, Inc. in 2004 to provide outside general counsel services to investors, entrepreneurs, and small businesses. Prior to forming Legal Venture Counsel, Ms. Batman was a partner in the San Francisco offices of Duane Morris LLP, one of the country's 100 largest law firms. As outside general counsel to a variety of companies and individuals, Ms. Batman provides business and financial legal services to privately held entities operating in a broad range of industries including real estate development, financial and professional services, manufacturing, software, retail, biotechnology/specialty pharmaceutical, and high technology. She has written and spoken on a number of topics of interest to the business community, such as choice of entity, venture financing, and finding practical solutions to common legal problems.

Ms. Batman chaired the ABA Business Law Section's Middle Market and Small Business Committee from 2001 to 2005, served as a Board Member of the ABA Business Law Section's Publications Board from 2001 to 2005, cofounded and co-chaired the ABA's Private Placement Broker-Dealer Task Force in 1999, and is a member of The State Bar of California. She is also the author of *Advising the Small Business: Forms and Advice for the Legal Practitioner 2nd Ed.*, American Bar Association, 2011, and *Letters for Small Business Lawyers,* American Bar Association, 2011.

Before becoming an attorney, Ms. Batman had an active career in the securities industry, culminating with her position in 1989 as president of Smith-Thomas Investment Services, Inc. (a registered broker-dealer). During her tenure in the securities industry, Ms. Batman held seven licenses from the National Association of Securities Dealers (now FINRA) ranging from general sales to finance and operations principal (Series 7, 6, 63, 39, 22, 24, and 27).

Ms. Batman earned an American Jurisprudence Award for excellent achievement in the study of commercial transactions in 1989 and served as a Judicial Extern in the California Court of Appeal for the late Hon. Justice J. Perley, 1st District in San Francisco in 1990.

Ms. Batman is a 1990 graduate of the University of California's Hastings College of Law (JD) and a 1985 graduate of The Paul Merage School of Business at UC Irvine (MBA). She also completed her undergraduate studies at the UC Irvine (BA).

Harold G. Wren

HAROLD G. WREN has been Of Counsel to James R. Voyles, Attorney, Louisville, Kentucky, since 1991. He holds his A.B. and LL.B. from Columbia, and his J.S.D. from Yale. He first practiced with Willkie Farr & Gallagher of New York, and then entered the academic world, where he was Dean of three law schools, and a teacher at four others. His books include *Creative Estate Planning* (1970) and *Tax Aspects of Marital Dissolution* (with Leon Cabinet) (2d ed. 1997). He is a past Chair of the Senior Lawyers Division of the American Bar Association.

Beverly J. Glascock

BEVERLY J. GLASCOCK is an attorney with Becker Law Office, in Louisville, Kentucky, where her practice concentrates on medical malpractice, pharmaceutical liability, and wrongful death. Ms. Glascock is a graduate of Indiana University at Bloomington and the University of Louisville School of Law.

CHAPTER 1

Of Counsel: An Overview

The term "Of Counsel" is used in connection with a variety of arrangements between attorneys and law firms and means different things to different people. In the past, the "Of Counsel" designation was commonly used to show that a law firm had powerful friends in high places. Listing a senator, congressional representative, or former judge as "Of Counsel" to a firm was a common practice and largely a marketing tool for firms with such connections.[1] This use of the designation is no longer appropriate unless the relationship between the firm and the "Of Counsel" attorney is a "close, regular, personal relationship."[2]

Aside from elevating a firm's prestige with elder statesmen, historically the phrase "Of Counsel" has been most commonly used for those partially or fully retired from the practice of law. A retired partner might use the designation to describe an honorary status with the firm whether or not the retired partner actually maintained a professional working relationship with it. Use of the "Of Counsel" designation for a retired partner is still appropriate, but care must be taken to ensure that the designation is not

---

1. A writer in the *Maryland Bar Journal* describes this type of "Of Counsel" as follows:

> They were the elder statesmen, the distinguished gentlemen of the old school, who functioned primarily as firms' goodwill ambassadors. They lent legitimacy and prestige to a firm, and in return they were given the benefits of firm membership without the pressure to perform and make a serious time commitment.

2. *See* ABA Comm. on Ethics & Prof'l Responsibility, Formal Op. 90-357 (1990), set forth in its entirety in Appendix G.

misleading under the circumstances, such as the attorney's availability for consultation, status with the bar, etc.

"Of Counsel" is used now in so many different contexts that it cannot be assigned a single meaning. Contracting parties use it in different ways depending upon what they wish to accomplish. The term might describe a relationship between a law firm and a lawyer who works part-time for the firm and devotes the balance of her time to an otherwise solo law practice, teaching law, or to an unrelated business endeavor. The term also might describe the relationship between a law firm and an expert in an area of law in which the firm does not specialize. In short, the precise meaning of "Of Counsel"—a vague term that for years was never formally defined—has in some ways become even more ambiguous. This book seeks to add a measure of definition and precision to it.

Principal Patterns of Relationships

Each "Of Counsel" arrangement is unique, yet distinct patterns can be identified. In practice, "Of Counsel" relationships follow four principal patterns: (1) part-time lawyers, including those who have recently changed careers; (2) retired partners who do not actively practice law full- or part-time, but occasionally consult with their former firm; (3) probationary partners-to-be, who view the "Of Counsel" status as a stepping-stone to full partnership; and (4) lawyers who have a permanent role within a firm but do not expect to become full partners. The term "Of Counsel" is also used as an alternative for attorneys who wish to maintain the autonomy of a solo practice while enjoying some of the resources of a larger firm, the so-called entrepreneurial lawyer.

The Part-Time Lawyer

Some lawyers are uninterested in practicing law full-time, yet want a relationship with a law firm that enables them to receive logistical support (secretarial service, telephone, computer services, law library) which would be expensive for someone practicing law part-time. The partners and associates of the law firm receive the benefit of the expertise and personal relationships the "Of Counsel" lawyer may have developed.

A lawyer might wish to practice law part-time for many reasons. A senior lawyer might choose an "Of Counsel" arrangement with his former firm as an alternative to full retirement.[3] A young lawyer may enter a part-time "Of Counsel" arrangement as a way of becoming affiliated with a firm. Part-time "Of Counsel" arrangements are ideal for lawyers who want to devote a fixed number of hours to a practice, while still being free to do other things. The arrangement also can be attractive to young lawyers familiar with modern technology (including LEXIS, Westlaw, photocopying, word processing, e-mail, Internet, fax, and modems, telephone answering, call-waiting, and call-forwarding systems) who want to carry on a highly effective law practice from home.

A lawyer may prefer to practice "Of Counsel" because it provides greater autonomy and control of time than she would have as a partner. As an "Of Counsel" lawyer, she can be selective about the cases she works on, pursue more pro bono work, or do whatever else she may wish. Such an arrangement can benefit the lawyer, the firm, and ultimately, the client, who has both the security of a general practice firm and the services of a specialist.[4]

Fay Hartog was once "Of Counsel" to the large Chicago firm Seyfarth Shaw LLP. Her experience was typical of the young mother who prefers "Of Counsel" status over the traditional associate-to-partner promotion track. After the birth of her second child, Hartog left the firm to accept a less demanding and more flexible position as in-house counsel with a suburban school district. The firm invited her to "drop in occasionally as an Of Counsel." She ended up working two jobs fifty to sixty hours a week.

Eventually Hartog formally became "Of Counsel" with the firm and was compensated according to her billings. Hartog says of the relationship:

---

3. Some firms use "Of Counsel" as a form of "disguised retirement, wherein older attorneys cut back their hours and responsibilities. They could be eased into receiving smaller draws or just earning a salary, instead of having to leave cold turkey." Buchholz, *Of Counsel: It's Not Just for Retiring Anymore,* 81 A.B.A. J. 70 (Oct. 1995) [hereinafter Buchholz].

4. *See* Buchholz, *supra* note 3.

> I direct my own activities and don't have to let anyone know. I also don't have to sit on committees, deal with promotional activities, or go to the firm retreats. I'm also not an economic burden on the firm. The most important thing I have is control over my life, which puts me in charge of the benefits and the risks.

From the standpoint of the law firm, such lawyers must offer something the firm needs—expertise, contacts, or the answer to some special need—before the parties will be able to reach a mutually satisfactory agreement.

The flexibility and control of Hartog's position allowed her to pursue a challenging and prestigious career that did not follow, as she has pointed out, "a linear progression." Her children are now grown and she is a grandmother. She is also now Ambassador Hartog Levin, having served the Obama administration as the U.S. Ambassador to the Kingdom of the Netherlands from 2009 to 2011. Hartog has also served as a senior consultant at Res Publica Group, assisting nonprofits, and as vice president for external affairs at Chicago's Field Museum, responsible for the museum's government relations and public funding, in addition to her twenty years of practicing law as a specialist in Education Law. Hartog's advice to young people today is to "embrace adventure and explore all of the possibilities." To many young lawyers this could mean maintaining control over their careers by practicing in an "Of Counsel" capacity.

A Washington D.C. attorney's situation provides another illustration of a synergistic relationship where both the "Of Counsel" lawyer and the firm profited from their relationship. The attorney founded a nonlegal services business outside his law practice and became "Of Counsel" to a law firm specializing in the same type of law he practiced. From the firm's perspective, the attorney was well known and respected in his practice area, which helped the firm with client development. The firm also got to service many of the lawyer's clients.[5] The firm paid for the attorney's malpractice insurance, bar memberships, and marketing costs, but not his health insurance.[6]

---

5. Quoted in Buchholz, *supra* note 3.
6. *Id.*

The Second Career

George H. Cain of the Senior Lawyers Division wrote an excellent book, *Turning Points*,[7] outlining situations in which lawyers have chosen a new direction in their lives. In some cases, these are younger people who select a completely new career. Other instances involve older lawyers leaving the academic world, corporate counsel positions, public office, the legislature, or the judiciary.[8] These lawyers can bring a high degree of expertise and wisdom to any law firm to which they might become "Of Counsel."

Lawyers active in these roles find being "Of Counsel" well suited to their needs. Experienced professionals can act in supervisory roles where expertise is required by reviewing briefs of partners and associates or serving the firm in other ways.

The "Of Counsel" arrangement is unique in that it allows a measure of independence for a lawyer to develop his own clients while continuing to work in conjunction with the firm on firm matters. One Maryland attorney was "Of Counsel" to a firm, working four days a week for the firm, to allow him to practice law while running his own insurance company.[9] Needless to say, the lawyer and the law firm must both pay close attention to potential conflicts of interest under such circumstances.[10]

A well-publicized situation in New York City illustrates a typical conflict. David Boies Jr., a prominent litigator and partner in the prestigious firm of Cravath Swaine & Moore, chose to represent George M. Steinbrenner Jr. in a suit against Major League Baseball. When the managing partner discovered that there was a conflict because of the firm's representation of Time Warner, Inc., owner of the Atlanta Braves, Boies left the firm. Steven Brill, publisher of the *American Lawyer* and founder of Court TV, described Cravath's loss: "[I]t's like it's 1956, and Mickey Mantle is suddenly a free agent."[11]

---

7. George H. Cain, *Turning Points* (ABA 1994).

8. Adler, *supra* note 2. Some state constitutions have mandatory retirement for judges, typically at age seventy. Through December 31, 1993, institutions of higher education were free to impose mandatory retirement on tenured law professors at age seventy. *See* 29 U.S.C. § 631(d), as amended by Pub. L. No. 99-592, § 6(a), as repealed effective Dec. 31, 1993, by Pub. L. No. 99-592, § 6(b).

9. *See* Buchholz, *supra* note 3.

10. *See* Chapters 7 and 8.

11. *See* Buchholz, *supra* note 3.

Had Boies been "Of Counsel" to the firm, rather than partner, his situation would have been no different. In representing Steinbrenner, he would still be faced with a conflict.

The Retired Partner

Many "Of Counsel" arrangements are based on a common pattern: After retirement from full-time practice with a firm, the former partner continues to consult and advise the firm on an occasional basis. While this arrangement is sometimes deemed a form of disguised retirement,[12] it remains a useful device in structuring a law firm. It provides the lawyer with a transition period without responsibility for the day-to-day problems of law practice. Rather than worry about deadlines, bottom lines, and productivity, the retiree may practice or not, and still have time to devote to other interests.

From the firm's standpoint, the former partner can be called on to help solve other problems that arise within the firm. The "Of Counsel" attorney can represent the firm at bar association and other professional meetings, make speeches before laypersons, or train new lawyers of the firm in the practice of law. Most importantly, the firm can rely on the former partner to continue contributing to the wisdom essential to any successful practice. Some former partners who become "Of Counsel" to their former firm may continue to draw a salary. While not determinative, this could be an indication that the "Of Counsel" attorney is an employee, and not an independent contractor. Others lend their expertise for no compensation at all. In either situation, the former partner may or may not be receiving payments from the firm's pension or other retirement plan. Whatever the former partner may receive as pension from the firm must be carefully coordinated with any other monetary arrangements made with the firm by reason of being "Of Counsel."[13]

The case of *Hempstead Video, Inc. v. Incorporated Village of Valley Stream*[14] involved another retirement scenario:

---

12. *See* Buchholz, *supra* note 3.

13. *See* discussion of problems of the "Of Counsel" attorney and retirement in Chapter 10.

14. 409 F.3d 127(2d Cir. 2005).

> Prior to July 2003, Englander was a solo practitioner, renting office space from the Jaspan firm. . . . Englander, who was in his mid-70s, decided to "semi-retire" and work fewer hours. He proposed to turn the representation of several of his clients, particularly a local school district, over to the Jaspan firm. He agreed to become "of counsel" to Jaspan effective July 1, 2003 "[i]n order to effect an orderly transition of those matters." As for the Englander clients not being transferred to Jaspan, which included . . . , Englander continued to represent them in his individual capacity.[15]

The Probationary Partner-to-Be

An "Of Counsel" arrangement is often used where a law firm wants to bring in a highly talented or experienced lawyer but is reluctant to immediately make such person a partner. This arrangement is advantageous both to the firm and the lawyer involved. Corporate counsel who have had extensive experience in the business world, labor lawyers who have worked in industrial relations, younger lawyers with specific professional skills, former partners of law firms that have been dissolved—all are welcome a tryout relationship before it becomes permanent.

A probationary partner-to-be often has too much experience and/or expertise to come into the firm as an associate, but not enough to warrant becoming a partner of the firm. Moreover, an associate designation may hamper an attorney's client development efforts and/or the lawyer's successful transition from another practice environment. For example:

> William W. Weisner's move to of counsel at the large New York City firm of Patterson, Belknap, Webb & Tyler was spurred by slightly different considerations. Although a partner at Graham and James' New York office, which is based in San Francisco, he wanted to be associated with a headquarters office rather than a branch. He also wished to remain in New York.

15. *Id.*

Finally, Weisner, 36, wanted to be part of a firm that was interested in expanding its real estate practice, yet one in which he could play an important role rather than just be "another cog in the wheel. . . . This isn't a forty-person department, but one with eight attorneys."

While Weisner brought real estate clients to his new firm, neither he nor Patterson, Belknap could value the amount of billings and decided on a look-see period. Thus the of counsel title offers firms an easier way to bring in experienced lawyers than through hiring lateral partners.[16]

A Permanent Status

While an "Of Counsel" arrangement is often useful as a stepping stone to full partner status, the term is also used to designate a permanent status, ranking between those of equity partner and associate. Although various terms are used to describe this post ("senior attorney,"[17] "resident counsel," "principal attorney," and the like), all have one unifying characteristic: Neither the law firm nor the lawyer has any expectation that the one so designated will be promoted to partner status. The advantage of this arrangement is that the lawyer's status has a quality of tenure coupled with a measure of independence.

Take the case of Madelyn Spatt Shulman, a seasoned attorney and active member of the American Bar Association, with both large firm and sole practitioner experience. In November 2006, Shulman became "Of Counsel" to Rosner & Napierala LLP, a six-attorney Manhattan-based boutique firm that she was working with on a project basis while maintaining her own practice on Long Island. The "Of Counsel" relationship expanded her work to a new set of clients, relationships and matters beyond what she could

16. Buchholz, *supra* note 3 at 71, quoting Weisner.

17. Barbara Buchholz reports that the use of this term is now passé. *See* Buchholz, *supra* note 3. Since Formal Opinion 90-357, the other terms mentioned in the text are also passing out of use. The term "Of Counsel" may replace the other terms mentioned in the text as it acquires a word-of-art meaning. In addition, many large law firms have now created a "non-equity partner" position. An attorney in this position has the title of partner but typically is compensated by a salary rather than a share of profits. This position can be a way station to equity partnership but often it is permanent.

service as a sole practitioner and brought her into the Manhattan market, beyond suburban Long Island. Shulman enjoyed the flexibility the relationship provided. In 2012, Rosner & Napierala LLP was acquired by Carlton Fields P.A. and Shulman became "Of Counsel" to the Carlton Fields firm, a 300-attorney Florida- and Atlanta-based firm expanding its practice into New York. Shulman anticipated that her "Of Counsel" work with Carlton Fields would eventually supplant her independent practice and become her sole, permanent legal employment. From Shulman's perspective:

> The ability to work on matters I enjoy with people I enjoy working with, while maintaining the flexibility to spend almost 25 percent of my time in Arizona and to control which days I make the hour plus commute into Manhattan, is a very attractive situation. Our office in New York currently has four shareholders and four attorneys (including myself) who are either Senior Counsel or Of Counsel. I am the only one with an outside practice, spending the bulk of my time working out of my office in Lake Success on Long Island. All of our "counsel" attorneys graduated from major law schools (three from NYU) and previously worked as associates at major U.S. firms (Shearman & Sterling, Stroock & Stroock & Lavan, Kellye Drye, Vinson & Elkins, Jones Day).

There are any number of situations in which the "Of Counsel" arrangement will be used to satisfy some special need of the firm or the "Of Counsel" attorney. In one case, a large law firm notified an associate that it was unlikely that he would "make partner," despite his excellent record. He had devoted his energies to one corporate client, who was completely satisfied and delighted with his services. Rather than run the risk of losing the client, or having the lawyer leave the firm, he was offered a permanent "Of Counsel" position with a high salary and excellent benefits. When the lawyer accepted, all parties were satisfied: The firm kept its client, the lawyer continued work that he enjoyed with complete financial security, and the client was happy that he would continue to represent it without having to retain additional counsel.

Perhaps surprisingly to some, not all young lawyers want partnership in a large firm because being a partner has a number of drawbacks. One drawback is that partnership usually puts additional demands on the lawyer's time, such as for partner meetings and hiring and training responsibilities, in addition to the practice group meetings and office meetings in which all firm members participate. Being a partner in a law firm also has financial drawbacks, such as self-employment taxes, being required to file tax returns in multiple states, having a committee determine the attorney's compensation, and lack of control over expenditures. These are some of the reasons an attorney might prefer not to be a partner in a law firm. An "Of Counsel" affiliation may be a good option for such an attorney, offering freedom from many of the time demands and financial burdens of partnership, while allowing the attorney to benefit from an affiliation with a firm that provides access to other attorneys and resources that complement the attorney's practice.

An "Of Counsel" arrangement may also be attractive to the lawyer with an entrepreneurial spirit, as an alternative to solo practice. For example, Elio F. Martinez Jr. wrote recently in *GP Solo Magazine*[18]:

> A year ago I was a partner at a twelve-attorney firm. I attended partners' meetings regularly, maintained a rigid work schedule based on the firm's established hours of operation, and limited my cases to matters consistent with the firm's practice.
>
> Today I am a solo with an asterisk. I no longer attend partners' meetings and have limited my dealings with firm bureaucracy. I have great flexibility in my schedule, which allows time to attend events for my 15-year-old twins. I am taking in more diversified cases and coordinating more creative payment arrangements for my clients. I have effectively become a firm of one, with one caveat: By negotiating an of counsel relationship with a local firm, I have mitigated the uncertainty and risk that often accompany solo practice. . . .[19]

18. *GP Solo Magazine*, American Bar Association, July/August 2006.
19. *Id.*

Martinez explains his objectives in forming the relationship as follows:

> I commenced looking for alternative arrangements for my practice not because of any dissatisfaction with my former firm and partners . . . but because of my desire to be more entrepreneurial, lessen my entanglement in red tape, and have greater control over my time and cases.

Martinez identified another small firm and worked out a mutually beneficial "Of Counsel" arrangement in which he maintains a separate, independent practice while occupying an office within the firm's office space. Martinez runs his own practice, keeping his own schedule and developing his own clients, but in exchange for office space and a percentage of fees collected for work on the firm's cases, he guarantees to work a certain number of hours each month on the firm's cases.

> The of counsel arrangement also provides me the added benefit of always having someone with whom to discuss issues and ideas, as well as assurance that, in my absence, someone will be there to step in and handle emergencies on my cases. . . .
>
> For me, the of counsel relationship is the best of both worlds. I have the independence and entrepreneurial aspects of the practice that I sought, but I never find myself alone. I have the freedom to seek new clients and varied matters, as well as the security of knowing that I will not be short of work. I am indeed a solo with an asterisk—and enjoying every minute of it.[20]

Other Relationships

Sometimes two or more law firms in different localities may enter into an "Of Counsel" relationship with each other. Law Firm A will become "Of Counsel" to Law Firm B, and vice versa. While these arrangements are perfectly appropriate,[21] they should be governed by carefully drafted agreements

20. *Id.*
21. ABA Comm. on Ethics & Prof'l Responsibility, Formal Op. 90-357 (1990), *reprinted*

if the parties are to avoid problems of malpractice, conflicts, and imputed disqualification.[22]

There are obvious risks in this arrangement. It may be impractical to list on their respective business cards, letterheads, and so forth the precise nature of the relationship. Arguably, one firm might be deemed to be an independent contractor in relation to the other and avoid vicarious liability for each other's torts; but most courts would probably be unwilling to adopt this view.

The merger of two or more law firms, often in two or more jurisdictions, is no longer an unusual event. When this occurs, the new firm must examine the client lists of the former firms, and avoid any representations that might result in conflicts or imputed disqualification.

When a lawyer moves from one partnership to another and brings a client along, the second firm and its lawyers may know little or nothing about the new lawyer's client, and yet risk exposure to potential malpractice liability.[23]

In 1985, Monon Corporation retained Henry Price, then with Barnes & Thornburg in Indianapolis, to represent it in a lawsuit against Wabash National Corporation and its employees, for patent infringement. Monon specifically instructed Price that in any formal agreement between the parties, he should not release Wabash from any patent infringement claims related to a specific patent application filed by Monon in 1985. Despite this instruction, Price released Wabash. When the patent was later issued in 1990, and Monon sued to enjoin Wabash for patent infringement and for damages, the release operated to bar Monon from relief.

Monon then brought suit against Price and the law firm, Townsend, Yosha, Cline & Price, with whom Price was connected at the time of the release. His precise role in the firm, his relationship with the other lawyers, and their relationships with one another were not clearly defined. One of the lawyers, Yosha, practiced law as Louis Buddy Yosha, Professional Corporation (LBYPC). Even within the firm, the principals were unsure of their

---

in Appendix G; *see* discussion in Chapter 4.

22. *See infra* Chapters 6, 7, and 8.

23. *See generally* Chapter 6, *infra.*

relationships with one another: Townsend claimed that he never heard of LBYPC until Monon filed its lawsuit; Yosha testified:

> Q: . . . Is it fair to describe Townsend, Yosha, Cline & Price as an association of lawyers?
>
> A: I don't know what I would put on it. No, I said I told you before I can't tell you the label. I can tell you what it's not. If you say: Is it fair to say it? Yeah, that doesn't bother me. An association of lawyers, I don't know. I couldn't dispute that and say, no, we weren't an association of lawyers.[24]

Cline was unaware of Price's role in the firm, at least so far as Monon was concerned:

> Nobody . . . other than Price interacted with this client or his case at all. . . . Henry really had his own operation within our firm. I didn't even know about this case or this client, and I ended up getting sued.
>
> I just think they took their shotgun out and decided to shoot everything in sight with their lawsuit.[25]

In the trial court, the lawyers moved for summary judgment, contending that they were employees of LBYPC[26] and thus were not liable for Price's

24. Monon Corp. v. Townsend, Yosha, Cline & Price, 678 N.E.2d 807 (Ind. Ct. App. 1997).

25. *See* Swiatek, *Ruling on Rule 27,* THE INDIANA LAWYER, v. 8, no. 1, at 1, 29.

26. It would be possible to organize a law firm so that lawyers in the firm would all be "Of Counsel" to the firm leader, whether the leader was a wholly owned professional corporation or simply an individual. Each lawyer, other than the firm leader, would be an independent contractor vis-à-vis the leader or the corporation. Such a form of business organization would not necessarily relieve the leader or the corporation from liability for the torts of the lawyers, but it would insulate each lawyer from liability for the torts of fellow lawyers. *See* discussion in Chapter 10. In the years since *Monon,* all U.S. jurisdictions have adopted statutes or rules that permit law firms to organize as limited liability entities (LLEs), such as limited liability partnerships or limited liability companies. Generally, the LLE itself and the individual lawyer(s) directly involved in the representation of a client remain liable for malpractice, but other lawyers in the LLE are not vicariously liable. *See, e.g.,* Lewis v. Rosenfield, 138 F. Supp. 2d 466, *dismissed on other grounds on reconsideration,* 145 F. Supp. 3d 341 (S.D.N.Y. 2001). An "Of Counsel" could have a relationship with an LLE, but would not be a partner or member of the LLE.

tort. In reversing the lower court's decision in their favor, the Indiana Court of Appeals ruled:

> [T]he record contains sufficient evidence and inferences from which the trier of fact could conclude that the firm of Townsend, Yosha, Cline & Price was a partnership. The firm here used the name of Townsend, Yosha, Cline & Price on its letterhead, cards, listings, pleadings, and agreements, without any language of limitation. Some of the attorneys referred to each other as partners, or may have done so, and signed documents as partners. . . . Further, the Attorneys would take "draws" and "bonuses" based upon the fees which came into the firm.[27]
>
> . . . [T]he evidence supports the view that they carried on as co-owners of a business for profit. . . . [A] genuine issue of fact exists about whether the firm really was a partnership for the purposes of vicarious liability.[28]

Monon dramatizes the importance of carefully drafted "Of Counsel" and partnership agreements. One of Monon's lawyers has commented:

> [Y]osha and those who claim to be employees thought they could shield themselves from liability, yet represent themselves to the public as partners. . . . This case holds now that you have to be very careful when you're representing to others whom you have an affiliation with.[29]

Had Price joined the Townsend firm as "Of Counsel" in an independent-contractor status, with a carefully drafted agreement, much of the vicarious liability might have been avoided.

A number of important principles are illustrated by *Monon:*

---

27. Monon Corp. v. Townsend, Yosha, Cline & Price, 678 N.E.2d 807, 812 (Ind. Ct. App. 1997). Monon sued not only the lawyers and the firm, but also any successor partnerships, such as those that Yosha and Cline created after the malpractice incident.

28. *Id.*

29. Swiatek, *supra* note 25.

- In the usual partnership, each partner is an agent and principal of the other, and each is vicariously liable for the other's torts.
- Under Indiana's Professional Corporation Act of 1983, the vicarious liability for legal malpractice is the same as would be the case if the firm were a partnership engaged in the practice of law.
- LBYPC was one of the partners of the Townsend, Yosha, Cline & Price partnership. The other partners were not "employees" of the professional corporation, as the lawyers contended.
- Even if the firm were not considered an actual partnership, the court might well find the lawyers to be a partnership by estoppel, since "the Attorneys held themselves out as a partnership and . . . Monon relied on their representations to its detriment."
- Monon was free to amend its complaint, adding LBYPC and various later partnerships in which the lawyers practiced as parties defendant.

Although *Monon* does not involve the "Of Counsel" law firm relationship, it illustrates how liability might be attributed to a law firm because of an "Of Counsel" attorney's torts. While a law firm may not be able to insulate itself from liability for the "Of Counsel" attorney's torts, the independent-contractor status of the "Of Counsel" attorney may well protect the "Of Counsel" attorney from liability for the torts of the firm or its members.

The "Of Counsel" designation can be affixed to a wide variety of relationships.[30] Sometimes "Of Counsel" is used to denote a reciprocal relationship between a law firm and an individual lawyer in another firm, a relationship that might be formed in an effort to expand the areas of specialty that the firm offers its clients. Or the relationship may be formed between out-of-state or foreign law firms in an effort to extend both firms' geographical reach in the market.

30. The Restatement of the Law Governing Lawyers takes a broad and practical approach: "A lawyer is of counsel if designated as having that relationship with a firm or when the relationship is regular and continuing although the lawyer is neither a partner in the firm nor employed by it on a full-time basis." RESTATEMENT (THIRD) OF THE LAW GOVERNING LAWYERS § 133 cmt. (c)(ii) (2001).

Because there are so many variations, the term resists a singular meaning. As the *California Lawyer* explained:

> "Of Counsel" is coming to mean a general kind of independent contractor, and it's a much more free-floating, entrepreneurial thing than it was fifteen or even ten years ago.[31]

Not all of these variants can appropriately be designated as "Of Counsel" relationships under Formal Opinion 90-357, which was based on the Model Rules of Professional Conduct and, to the extent indicated, the predecessor Model Code of Professional Responsibility of the American Bar Association. However, the laws, court rules, regulations, codes of professional responsibility, and opinions promulgated in the individual jurisdictions are controlling. Before establishing an "Of Counsel" relationship, the parties should familiarize themselves with this ABA Formal Opinion, other formal and informal opinions of the American Bar Association, and the rulings of their state bars to determine whether the parties' arrangement comes within the definitions set out in those opinions.

Summary

Formal Opinion 90-357, issued in May 1990, has superseded Formal Opinion 330 and six of the eight informal opinions of the American Bar Association that have dealt with this subject and have now been withdrawn. Two other informal opinions, issued after 330, are still in effect. Despite these withdrawals, Formal Opinion 90-357 relies on this background in articulating the current rules with respect to "Of Counsel." The next chapter considers this earlier background to lay a foundation for understanding the current status of the law with respect to "Of Counsel" relationships. Subsequent chapters will explore the primary issues to

31. Wagner, *Variations on the "Of Counsel" Theme*, 6 CAL. LAW. 59 (July 1986) (quoting Robert G. Gordon, law professor and legal historian at Stanford University Law School).

be considered in connection with the "Of Counsel" designation, including avoiding the appearance of partnership, choosing between employee and independent contractor status, legal malpractice, conflicts of interest, imputed disqualification, and advertising and solicitation. Final chapters will explore appropriate terms for the "Of Counsel" agreement and planning and drafting the same.

CHAPTER 2

Of Counsel: Legal Development

Despite its long history, the "Of Counsel" designation was not formally defined by the ABA until 1972, when the Standing Committee on Ethics and Professional Responsibility issued Formal Opinion 330.[1] Through that opinion, the ABA, relying on the ABA Model Code of Professional Responsibility and prior published informal opinions on the subject, adopted a restricted meaning of the phrase. Widespread disregard of Formal Opinion 330 led the ethics committee to issue subsequent informal opinions and to reconsider the subject formally in Formal Opinion 90-357.[2] This chapter explores Formal Opinion 330 as a background for Formal Opinion 90-357, in which Formal Opinion 330 is withdrawn.

The Model Code and ABA Informal Opinions

Most of the guidelines regarding the ethics committee's definition of the "Of Counsel" designation are based on a single passage contained in the ABA's Model Code of Professional Responsibility:

1. *See* ABA Comm. on Ethics & Prof'l Responsibility, Formal Op. 330 (1972), *reprinted in* Appendix K, withdrawn by Formal Op. 90-357 (1990).
2. ABA Comm. on Ethics & Prof'l Responsibility, Formal Op. 90-357 (1990), *reprinted in* Appendix G.

> A lawyer may be designated "Of Counsel" on a letterhead if he [or she] has *a continuing relationship* with a lawyer or law firm, other than as a partner or associate.[3] (Emphasis added.)

The Model Code emphasized that lawyers must be scrupulous in representing their professional relationships to the public.[4] Yet, despite ethical mandates that the relationship be "continuing," the Model Code failed to define precisely the *nature* of the relationship. That task was left to the Standing Committee on Ethics and Professional Responsibility, which issued several informal opinions in response to individual inquiries about proper use of the designation.[5]

In the first of these, Informal Opinion 678 (1963), the committee considered the propriety of using the "Of Counsel" designation to describe a prolonged relationship between a District of Columbia lawyer and a Washington State law firm for the purpose of only one case. In the opinion, the committee defined "of counsel" as the term had been customarily used:

> [The] term, "of counsel," shown on a firm's letterhead or shingle, is customarily used to indicate a former partner who is on a retirement or semi-retirement basis, or one who has retired from another partnership or the general private practice or from some public position, who remains or becomes available to the firm for consultation and advice, either generally or in a particular field.[6]

---

3. MODEL CODE OF PROF'L RESPONSIBILITY [hereinafter MODEL CODE] DR 2-102(A)(4) (1969, amended 1980).

4. MODEL CODE EC 2-13 (1969, amended 1980).

5. ABA Comm. on Professional Ethics, Informal Ops. 678 (1963), 710 (1964), 1134 (1969), 1173 (1971), and 1189 (1971). The ABA created a Standing Committee on Professional Ethics in 1913. The name of the Committee was changed to the Committee on Professional Ethics and Grievances in 1919, and it was separated into two committees in 1958, with the Committee on Professional Ethics retaining responsibility for opinions concerning proper professional conduct. The name of that Committee was changed to the Committee on Ethics and Professional Responsibility in 1971.

6. ABA Informal Op. 678 (1963).

The committee concluded that using the phrase to describe the relationship in question would be misleading, since the relationship was only temporary, even though it might exist over an extended period of time.[7]

By the mid-1960s, another common use of the phrase was to describe an ongoing relationship between a law firm and an inactive or retired public official, such as a retired judge. Informal Opinion 710 (1964) reflected the committee's approval of the use of the designation in such a situation. A retired judge had asked the committee whether the phrase could be used to describe his relationship with a firm that included his son. The committee approved the judge's use of the phrase, stating:

> [Y]ou are clearly within the area which with propriety would permit the firm to include your name "of counsel," inasmuch as you were a former partner of your son; you are on retirement from a public position and in semi-retirement from the general practice; and it is assumed that you would be available to the firm for consultation and advice either generally or in a particular field.[8]

There soon was a growing desire in law practice to expand the use of the "Of Counsel" designation to describe more unconventional legal relationships. A series of opinions issued by the committee reflected this desire. For example, in Informal Opinion 1134 (1969), the committee considered whether the phrase could be used to describe a relationship between a law firm and a lawyer who was a current, rather than inactive, public official.[9] The inquiring law firm wanted to list a U.S. senator as "Of Counsel." Although the senator had never been a member of the firm, a continuing relationship between the senator and the firm had existed for years before he was elected to office. Even after he became a senator, he occasionally continued to perform legal services for the firm and its clients. The committee permitted the senator to use the designation, provided he was actively and regularly practicing law in the offices of the firm and rendering legal

---

7. *Id.*
8. ABA Informal Op. 710 (1964).
9. ABA Informal Op. 1134 (1969).

advice to the clients of the firm. In reaching this conclusion, the committee relied on the implications of DR 2-102(B), which states:

> A lawyer who assumes a judicial, legislative, or public executive or administrative post or office shall not permit his [or her] name to remain in the name of a law firm or to be used in professional notices of the firm during any significant period in which he [or she] is not actively and regularly practicing law as a member of the firm, and during such period other members of the firm shall not use [the lawyer's] name on the firm name or in professional notices of the firm.[10]

In allowing the senator to be designated as "Of Counsel,"," the committee for the first time acknowledged that a continuing relationship could exist between a law firm and an individual lawyer other than a retired partner or an inactive public official.

With this newly expanded concept, practitioners began to question whether the designation could be further expanded to include other non-traditional relationships. The committee was first asked whether a *law firm,* as distinct from an individual lawyer, could be designated as Of Counsel to another law firm or individual lawyer. Relying on the literal language of DR 2-102(A)(4), the committee wrote:

> The Code, in our opinion, precludes the use by a law firm of such designation "Of Counsel" by the very omission of the words "law firm" in such privileged designation.[11]

The committee was then asked whether an "Of Counsel" relationship could exist simultaneously with more than one lawyer or law firm. Relying again on the language of DR 2-102(A)(4), the committee concluded that the Model Code prohibited multiple simultaneous "Of Counsel" relationships. In so doing, the committee added a new requirement to the designation:

---

10. Model Code DR 2-102(B) (1969, amended 1980).
11. ABA Informal Op. 1173 (1971).

> [I]t is not proper, in our opinion, for any lawyer or law firm to be designated "Of Counsel" to more than one lawyer or law firm . . . because the continuing relationship referred to in DR 2-102(A)(4) connotes a *close, daily, in-house association,* free and clear of problems of conflict.[12] (Emphasis added.)

In explaining why multiple Of Counsel relationships were impermissible, the committee, for the first time, stated that all "Of Counsel" relationships must encompass a "close, daily, in-house association." It soon became apparent that this added requirement was causing confusion in the practice, since a literal reading precluded even retired partners and inactive public officials from using the designation. The committee attempted to correct this result in a later informal opinion by carving out an exception for retired partners:

> It is our opinion that the continuing relationship necessary for the designation "Of Counsel" referred to in DR 2-102(A)(4) which we have defined as close, daily, in-house association is susceptible to one exception which permits such classification to the designee if he had a previous continuing relationship with such other lawyer or law firm and during such relationship was physically present in the same office and/or suite with such other lawyer or law firm but which association of many years has been interrupted by the designee's inability to come to the office or his removal from the city or geographical area of his prior practice providing he is not associated with or holding himself out as being associated with any other lawyer or law firm.[13]

Although this exception attempted to restore the flexible nature of the "Of Counsel" relationship as it pertained to retired partners, it was so specific that few of them fell within it. An "Of Counsel" relationship had to be one in which there was a "close, daily, in-house association" or a "previous continuing relationship." A "previous continuing relationship" was in turn defined as one in which the lawyer had been *physically present* in the office

12. *Id.*
13. ABA Informal Op. 1189 (1971).

of the lawyer or law firm but was now unable to go to the office because of some sort of "inability" or because the lawyer no longer resided in the area.

As a corollary, the committee, in the same opinion, considered whether firms should be allowed to list in legal directories the names of lawyers from other cities or states who were occasionally or regularly associated with the firm. The committee disallowed the "Of Counsel" designation to describe these relationships. Instead, it directed that nonresident counsel be designated only by terms such as "New York Counsel," "Correspondent," "European Counsel," or the like.[14]

Less than one year after these two informal opinions were issued, a professional corporation wrote the committee and asked whether it could be designated as "Of Counsel" or "In Association With" another firm, lawyer, or professional corporation. The committee determined that a formal opinion would be helpful in clarifying the many questions that had arisen in using the phrase "of counsel." The result was Formal Opinion 330.

Formal Opinion 330

From 1972 to 1990, Formal Opinion 330 represented the American Bar Association's official view of the "Of Counsel" relationship. This has now been superseded by Formal Opinion 90-357, but a knowledge of Formal Opinion 330 is essential to understanding the current view of the ABA committee, as well as the current views of many state ethics committees.

In Formal Opinion 330, the committee reexamined the nature of the "Of Counsel" relationship as it had come to be defined in previous informal opinions. The controlling guidelines for using the term "Of Counsel" appeared in the headnote of Formal Opinion 330:

> The relationship indicated by the term "Of Counsel" is a close, continuing, personal relationship between an individual lawyer and a law firm or lawyer, and the relationship is one that is not that of a partner, associate, or outside consultant. A law firm may not be "Of Counsel"

---

14. *Id.*

> to another lawyer or law firm. While a lawyer conceivably could be "Of Counsel" to two law firms or lawyers, one cannot simultaneously have more than a maximum of two "Of Counsel" relationships. The term "Of Counsel" may be used, if it correctly describes the existing relationship, on letterheads and professional announcement cards and in law lists and directories.[15]

Under Formal Opinion 330, the concept of the "Of Counsel" designation had two basic aspects: first, there had to be a "close, continuing, personal relationship" between the parties, and second, the relationship could not be one of partner, associate, or outside consultant.[16] A copy of the full text of Formal Opinion 330 appears in Appendix K.

A Close, Continuing, Personal Relationship

The Model Code stated that the "Of Counsel" relationship must be a "continuing" one.[17] Formal Opinion 330 added that the relationship had to be "close, continuing, and personal":

> Generally speaking, the close, personal relationship indicated by the term "Of Counsel" contemplates either that the lawyer practice in the offices of the lawyer or law firm to which he is "Of Counsel" or that his relationship, for example by virtue of past partnership of a retired partner that has led to continuing close association, be so close that he is in regular and frequent, if not daily, contact with the office of the lawyer or firm.[18]

The committee defined a close, continuing, and personal relationship by giving specific examples found in permissible "Of Counsel" relationships. Most of these examples involved the traditional "Of Counsel" relationship,

---

15. ABA Comm. on Ethics & Prof'l Responsibility, Formal Op. 330 (1972).
16. *Id.*
17. Model Code DR 2-102(A) (4) (1969, amended 1980) ("A lawyer may be designated 'Of Counsel' on a letterhead if he has a continuing relationship with a lawyer or law firm, other than as partner or associate").
18. ABA Comm. on Ethics & Prof'l Responsibility, Formal Op. 330, at 69 (1972).

viz., one involving a retired partner or public official. A "close, continuing, personal" relationship could exist, the committee wrote, between a firm and a retired or semiretired former partner who remains available to the firm for consultation and advice.[19] It might also exist between a firm and a retired public official who regularly and locally is available to the firm for consultation and advice.[20] The committee listed one type of arrangement to which the phrase could never apply: a relationship better described as a forwarder-receiver of legal business.[21]

Formal Opinion 330's definition of a "close, continuing, personal" relationship differed significantly from the "continuing relationship" as defined in prior informal opinions. A continuing relationship required a "close, daily, in-house association between the lawyer and other lawyer or law firm." Prior informal opinions permitted an exception to exist under certain circumstances.[22] The exception was permitted where (1) the designated lawyer and other lawyer or firm had a previous continuing relationship, (2) during which the lawyer was physically present in the offices of the firm or other lawyer and (3) the lawyer was now unable to come to the office or had moved from the city or state where the office was located, providing the lawyer was not associated with another law firm. Under this exception, a former partner who was not in daily contact with the firm could still use the designation if all of the above requirements were satisfied. By contrast, Formal Opinion 330 required "regular, frequent, if not daily, contact" with the firm even in the case of the retired partner.[23] There were no exceptions to this requirement.

"Not a Partner, Associate, or Outside Consultant" DR 2-102(A)(4) states:

> A lawyer may be designated "Of Counsel" on a letterhead if he or she has a continuing relationship with a lawyer or law firm, other than as a partner or associate.[24]

---

19. *Id.*
20. *Id.*
21. *Id.*
22. ABA Comm. on Ethics & Prof'l Responsibility, Informal Op. 1189 (1971).
23. *See* ABA Comm. on Ethics & Prof'l Responsibility, Formal Op. 330 (1972).
24. Model Code DR 2-102(A)(4) (1969, amended 1980).

This provision is based upon language found in ethical principles that require a lawyer to represent his or her professional status so as not to mislead third persons.[25] A lawyer's designated status as "Of Counsel" would mislead third persons if, in fact, the lawyer was a partner or an employee of the firm, such as an associate.

One of the many incongruities of Formal Opinion 330 was the inconsistent use of terms in the text of the opinion and the headnote. For instance, the *headnote* stated that "Of Counsel" must not be like a "partner, associate, or outside consultant."[26] But the *text* of the opinion did not specifically state the same requirement. The text stated that the relationship must be one that is not that of a partner or an *employee:*

> [T]he individual lawyer who properly may be shown to be "Of Counsel" to a lawyer or law firm is a member or component part of that law office, but his status is not that of a *partner or an employee* (nor that of a controlling member of a professional legal corporation).[27] (Emphasis added.)

There was no explanation why the committee used the term "employee" in the text but "associate" in the headnote.[28] This inconsistency became particularly cogent when one considered the differences between an employee and an associate.

The term "employee" has come to mean one who works under the control of another. Employees of the lawyer might be non-lawyers (secretaries, legal administrators, paralegals, and the like) or other lawyers. While the typical lawyer-employee has come to be regarded as an associate,[29] the presence of

---

25. Model Code EC 2-13 (1969, amended 1980).

26. ABA Comm. on Ethics & Prof'l Responsibility, Formal Op. 330, at 69 (1972).

27. *Id.* at 69–70.

28. The committee also used the phrase "outside consultant" in the headnote. The text, however, mentions that phrase only as an example of impermissible forms of compensation: "He is compensated as a sui *generis* member of that law office, however, and not as an outside consultant." It is also noted that "outside consultant" is not defined in the opinion or the Model Code. This issue is taken up in further detail in Chapter 4.

29. ABA Formal Op. 330, at 68 (relying on ABA Comm. on Prof'1 Ethics, Formal Op. 310 (1963)).

new categories of lawyers in practice today signifies that the term employee can include many types of lawyer-employees besides "associates."

The term associate may have been used in the headnote in keeping with the literal language of the Model Code. It might also be that the committee felt the two terms were synonymous, even though they are not.

The inconsistent use of these two terms in Formal Opinion 330 caused particularly troublesome questions for practitioners setting up the "Of Counsel" relationship. It was at least clear that the relationship should not be like that of an associate. But did it preclude any kind of employee relationship between the "Of Counsel" lawyer and the other lawyer or firm?

Methods of Compensation

The method of compensation is an important part of any working relationship. In Formal Opinion 330, the committee felt that it should address the problem of how "Of Counsel" attorneys should be compensated. Formal Opinion 330 provided:

> While it would be misleading to refer to a lawyer who shares in the profits and losses and general responsibility of a firm as being "Of Counsel," the lawyer who is "Of Counsel" may be compensated either on a basis of division of fees in particular cases or on a basis of consultation fees. [The lawyer] is compensated as *a sui generis* member of that law office, however, and not as an outside consultant.[30]

Formal Opinion 330 precluded "Of Counsel" from sharing in the gross profits of the firm. A literal reading of the opinion required that the method of compensation be directly related to the work performed. But it was not clear whether the opinion also precluded "Of Counsel" from being compensated on a regular salary basis, whether weekly, monthly, or yearly.

Despite this lack of clarity, many "Of Counsel" lawyers continue to be compensated on an hourly basis, with a percentage of the hourly rate charged for the actual work performed by "Of Counsel." Others are

---

30. ABA Formal Op. 330, at 69 (citations omitted).

compensated on a flat annualized rate without regard to work done, or on a flat salary or draw plus a percentage of the fees on work brought in.

In still other arrangements, "Of Counsel" opt for little or no compensation for legal work they perform. In these arrangements, they may already be receiving income from the firm in the form of a pension or other retirement benefit for past services. Formal Opinion 330 could be read as limiting use of the designation in these arrangements.

Multiple Of Counsel Relationships

Formal Opinion 330 limited to two the number of firms with which a lawyer might have an "Of Counsel" relationship. This limit appeared in the headnote as follows:

> While a lawyer conceivably could be "Of Counsel" to two law firms or lawyers, one cannot simultaneously have more than a maximum of two "Of Counsel" relationships.[31]

The actual text of the opinion varied somewhat from this summary. In describing the number of "Of Counsel" relationships that a lawyer might simultaneously maintain, the committee recognized that "there is no per se prohibition against one's being 'Of Counsel' to two law firms."[32] The committee noted that a lawyer might possibly be able to establish the requisite relationships with two lawyers or law firms simultaneously:

> Given this view of the relationship indicated by the term "Of Counsel," it follows that one lawyer possibly could have the requisite relationship with two firms simultaneously, for example, one with which he practiced many years before his retirement and another at a location to which he has moved after his retirement.[33]

31. *Id.* at 67.
32. *Id.* at 70.
33. *Id.*

But the committee was not willing to state the point at which the number of relationships would be too great to satisfy the necessary qualities of closeness and continuity:

> To the extent that one lawyer does in fact have the requisite relationships properly to be designated "Of Counsel" to more than one lawyer or law firm simultaneously, Informal Opinion 1189 is modified.[34]

Law Firms as Of Counsel

Formal Opinion 330 affirmed the view expressed in prior informal opinions that a *law firm* cannot be listed as "Of Counsel" to another lawyer or law firm:

> Without necessarily adopting the descriptive language in Informal Opinion 678, we recognize that DR 2-102(A)(4) uses "Of Counsel" in a manner not inconsistent with earlier usage and that the term relates to an individual lawyer. Thus the term cannot be used with regard to a law firm, whether it be a partnership or professional legal corporation.[35]

The reasoning here was that the literal language of the Model Code connoted an *individual* lawyer. Prior informal opinions had concluded that a law firm could not be "Of Counsel" because "the practice of law is personal in nature and a law firm as such is never admitted to practice in any state."[36]

Yet the committee, in a later opinion, approved of arrangements between law firms that closely resembled "Of Counsel" relationships, although it prohibited the firms from describing their relationship as anything other than "affiliated" or "associated."[37] In one instance, the committee permit-

34. *Id.*

35. *Id.* at 69.

36. *See* ABA Informal Op. 1173 (1971); *see also* ABA Informal Op. 1189 (1971).

37. These designations are allowed if the firms are "closely associated or connected with the other lawyer or firm in an ongoing and regular relationship." ABA Comm. on Ethics & Prof'l Responsibility, Formal Op. 84-351, at 4 (1984).

ted an arrangement between law firms located in different cities whereby the firms effectively became "Of Counsel" to each other. The arrangement provided for a partner in one firm to be "Of Counsel" to another law firm in another city, while a partner in the second firm was simultaneously "Of Counsel" to the first firm.[38]

Advertising the Of Counsel Relationship

The final consideration of Formal Opinion 330 was the ethical consequence implied by using the term "Of Counsel" in firm announcements and other public communications. As noted previously, DR 2-102(A)(4) permits the designation "Of Counsel" to be used in connection with letterheads, as long as the requisite relationship exists. In Formal Opinion 330, the committee considered whether the designation could ethically be used in connection with announcement cards, shingles, law lists, and directories. The text of the opinion stated:

> Where a relationship exists which may be described accurately as an "Of Counsel" relationship, we hold that the relationship may be designated on a professional announcement card, on a shingle, and in a law list or legal directory.[39]

But the opinion failed to consider other significant ethical considerations that arise by virtue of announcing the relationship in professional communications. Could the name of the lawyer who is "Of Counsel" be included in the firm name? Should an "Of Counsel" attorney's jurisdictional limitations be listed on professional announcement cards, letterheads, directories, and law lists?

---

38. ABA Comm. on Ethics & Prof'l Responsibility, Informal Op. 1315 (1975).
39. ABA Comm. on Ethics & Prof'l Responsibility, Formal Op. 330 (1972).

Summary

The guidelines controlling the "Of Counsel" relationship were originally set out in ABA Formal Opinion 330, under which the relationship had to satisfy two basic requirements: First, it had to be "close, continuing, personal." Second, it could not be like that of a partner, associate, or outside consultant.

A "close, continuing, personal" relationship differed significantly from a "continuing relationship" as it was described in prior informal opinions. A "continuing relationship" seemed to require nearly a "daily, in-house association" between "Of Counsel" and the other lawyer or firm. But there was an exception to this requirement if there had been a previous relationship in which "Of Counsel" had been physically present in the offices of the lawyer or firm but was now precluded from going to the office. Under Formal Opinion 330, "Of Counsel" had to have frequent, "if not daily," contact with the office of the lawyer or firm. This requirement posed unusual difficulties for many "Of Counsel" attorneys, particularly retired partners. Little justification was offered for it. It did not reflect the reality of present-day affairs, nor was it consonant with the purpose and intent of the traditional concept of the "Of Counsel" designation. Formal Opinion 330 also required that "Of Counsel" could not be a partner, associate, or outside consultant. But the text of the opinion stated that the relationship must not be that of partner or employee. We do not know why the committee chose to use the word "associate" in the headnote and "employee" in the text. Perhaps it felt that these terms were synonymous. The inconsistency raised many questions. Could a lawyer and a law firm set up the "Of Counsel" arrangement as an employer-employee relationship if they so desired? Formal Opinion 330 seemed to forbid such an arrangement.

By permitting "Of Counsel" to be compensated based on division of fees in particular cases or based on consultation fees, Opinion 330 implied that "Of Counsel" could be compensated only for work actually performed. This was read by some as restricting a retired partner from using the designation if his sole income was the firm's pension or other retirement benefits.

Formal Opinion 330 reaffirmed the view that a law firm could not be designated "Of Counsel." This view was based on the literal language of the Model Code. But the policy underlying this view was not clearly expressed.

In short, the ABA concept of the "Of Counsel" relationship, as evidenced by Formal Opinion 330, was unduly restrictive. And although the ABA concept seemed lucid, it was far from definitive. In practice, there was often diverse interpretation that seemed contrary to the existing definition. More important, the opinion contained no discussion of the essential nature of the contractual relationship that opens the door to a variety of arrangements. Under the circumstances, the ethics committee correctly felt that it was time to issue a new formal opinion to eliminate this unnecessary confusion. The next chapter analyzes Formal Opinion 90-357, the vehicle chosen by the committee to accomplish this task.

CHAPTER 3

ABA Formal Opinion 90-357

For eighteen years, Formal Opinion 330 remained the view of the American Bar Association with reference to the "Of Counsel" designation. By 1990, the Committee on Ethics and Professional Responsibility recognized that there had been so many changes in the profession that it was time to review and restate its opinion.[1]

In Formal Opinion 90-357, the committee reconsidered the subject for several reasons: First, there had been a proliferation of variants of the term and of arrangements designated by the term or one of these variants. Second, some of the committee's prior opinions had been unnecessarily restrictive on certain relationships commonly designated as "Of Counsel." Third, the replacement of the ABA Model Code of Professional Responsibility by the ABA Model Rules of Professional Conduct presented an opportune moment for such a review.

The committee addressed this last situation first and concluded that there was no substantive difference between the Model Code and the Model Rules:

1. The Model Rules of Professional Conduct ("Model Rules"), promulgated by the ABA in 1983, are now the basis for the ethics rules for lawyers in forty-nine states. More than two-thirds of the Model Rules were revised by the ABA in 2002, but most U.S. jurisdictions that have adopted the Model Rules use the version that includes the ABA amendments through 2000. Thus the terms "Model Rules" and "Model Rules of Professional Conduct" in this book refer to the 2000 version.

> [T]he textual basis in both the Model Rules and the Model Code for determining whether particular uses of the title are or are not ethically permissible is in substance the same — a prohibition against misleading representations although the particular provisions embodying this prohibition are different in form. . . . The essence of the ethical requirement under both the Model Rules and the Model Code is avoidance of misrepresentations as to the lawyer's status, and the relationship between lawyer and firm.[2]

Designations Governed by Formal Opinion 90-357

Formal Opinion 90-357 governs the designation "Of Counsel" and all variant titles that use the word "counsel," such as "special counsel," "tax [or other specialty] counsel," and "senior counsel." The opinion does not cover terms that do not employ the word "counsel," such as "consultant," "consulting attorney," or "corresponding attorney."[3]

Even though there are slight differences between the variant titles that employ the word counsel, the committee viewed these as sharing similar characteristics so that they should all be governed by the opinion.

The term "Of Counsel" is used in a wide variety of situations. For example, the "Of Counsel" agreement may be used to accomplish certain ends not otherwise obtainable under more traditional arrangements, as illustrated here:

A Law Firm, F, and two independent lawyers, L and M, wished to practice law, using the following letterhead:

[FIRM F, or L, or M]
A member Firm of the Law Offices at X Square

2. ABA Comm. on Ethics & Prof'l Responsibility, Formal Op. 90-357, at 2 (1990), *reprinted in* Appendix G.

3. *Id.* at 3.

In addition, they proposed to describe themselves in advertisements as follows:

The Law Offices at X Square
An Association of Independent Lawyers and Law Partnerships

Both the proposed letterhead and the proposed advertisement may violate the rule against the use of trade names, including locational trade names in some jurisdictions.[4] However, an alternative possible approach for law firm F and lawyers L and M, depending on the precise nature of their relationship, might be to enter into mutual "Of Counsel" relationships that are expressly named as such. Firm F may become "Of Counsel" to lawyers L and M and lawyers L and M may become "Of Counsel" to firm F, as long as the parties maintain the requisite ties to support the "Of Counsel" relationship. Such an arrangement would permit the group to advertise their affiliation with the requisite degree of specificity, and to list each other on their individual stationery while using a label with a known and therefore acceptable clear meaning.[5]

If Firm F becomes "Of Counsel" to L and M and vice versa, and the group maintains the requisite relationship to support that designation, the three entities will be able to advertise jointly and indicate an "Of Counsel" affiliation with each other and also identify themselves as "associated" or "affiliated" with each other, provided that the requisites for an "Of Counsel" relationship are met.[6]

4. For example, New York forbids a law firm or legal clinic from practicing under a trade name or other name that does not convey the identity of one or more of the lawyers practicing. New York Disciplinary Rule 2-102(B). However, the ABA Model Rules of Professional Conduct, Rule 7.5(a) permits the use of trade names with some restrictions, and many states now follow that model. *See, e.g.*, The State Bar of California, Standing Committee on Professional Responsibility and Conduct, Formal Opinion No. 1982-66.

5. New York City Ethical Op. 1995-8, 1995 WL 875457 (N.Y.C. Ass'n of the Bar Comm. Prof'l Ethics 1995), modifying New York City Ops. 891, 81-3, 81-71, 81-102, 82-28.

6. *Id.* at 6.

Permissible Patterns of Relationships

Formal Opinion 90-357 suggested four permissible patterns of relationships in the use of the term "Of Counsel":

(1) *The Part-Time Practitioner.* A part-time practitioner is one who practices law in association with a firm or other lawyer, but out of the mainstream of the other lawyers of the firm. This person's part-time practice might originate from a change from full-time practice to part-time practice, or a change from a salaried position, such as a government official, law professor, retired judge, or corporate lawyer, to the practice of law.[7]

(2) *The Retired Partner.* The retired partner is one who is not actively practicing law but remains associated with the firm and is available for occasional consultation.

(3) *The Probationary Partner.* The probationary partner-to-be is one who is hired into the firm with the expectation of becoming a partner within a relatively short period of time.

(4) *The Permanent Senior Attorney.* Although a variety of terms have been used to describe this particular lawyer, the common characteristic is that he does not expect to attain full partner status but has a permanent tenure-like status between partner and associate.[8]

In the committee's view, all of these relationships are proper "Of Counsel" relationships, even though prior informal and formal opinions may have

---

7. There is an infinite variety of personal situations in which the "Of Counsel" paradigm is appropriate. *See* Chapter 1.

8. For example, "senior attorney," "senior counsel," "special counsel," "senior associate," "counsel."

concluded that they were not.[9] They all contain "core characteristics" necessary for the requisite relationship.[10]

Impermissible Patterns of Relationships

Formal Opinion 90-357 cited four relationships that always fall outside the ambit of the "Of Counsel" relationship. These are:

(1) A single case.[11]
(2) The forwarding or receiving of legal business.[12]
(3) Collaborative efforts among otherwise unrelated lawyers or firms.[13]
(4) Outside consultants.[14]

Core Characteristics of an Of Counsel Relationship

Relationships that do not fall within one of these four inclusive or four exclusive categories must contain the "core characteristics" of an "Of Counsel" relationship before they can properly use the designation. The committee in 90-357 defined that characteristic just as it had previously defined a permissible "of counsel" relationship in Formal Opinion 330:

> That core characteristic properly denoted by the title "counsel" is, as stated in Formal Opinion 330, a "close, regular, personal relationship"; but a relationship which is neither that of a partner (or its equivalent, a principal of a professional corporation), with the shared liability and/

9. State and local bar associations have followed this four-part categorization, or something similar. *See, e.g.*, Ohio Adv. Op. 97-2, 1997 WL 188916 (Ohio Bd. Comm. Grievance Disputes 1997). New Jersey creates an additional category by differentiating the "permanent senior associate who is not on a partnership track" from the "'special' counsel who has developed an expertise in a particular field of law." *Cf.* New Jersey Atty. Advisory Op. 21, 147 N.J.L.J. 979, 6 N.J.L. 475, 1997 WL 104570 (N.J. Advisory Comm. Prof'l Ethics 1997).

10. *See* core characteristics listed below.

11. *See* Chapter 4.

12. *See* Illinois Adv. Op. 776, 1982 WL 198379 (Ill. St. Bar Assn.); *see also* Chapter 4.

13. *See* Chapter 4.

14. *See* Chapter 4.

> or managerial responsibility implied by that term; nor, on the other hand, the status ordinarily conveyed by the term "associate," which is to say a junior non-partner lawyer, regularly employed by the firm.[15]

A "core characteristic" can be separated into two distinct components. The first is the "close, regular, personal" relationship. The second is the requirement that the relationship not be like that of partner or associate.

A Close, Regular, Personal Relationship

Formal Opinion 330's interpretation of a "close, continuing, personal" relationship limited the kinds of permissible "Of Counsel" relationships.[16] Under the guidelines of 330, the lawyer had to practice "in the office" of the firm or other lawyer or had to be "regularly and locally" available for consultation and in "daily contact" with the firm.

Formal Opinion 330 was unduly restrictive even in the most common "Of Counsel" situation, *viz.*, the relationship between a retired partner and his or her firm.[17] Like 330, Formal opinion 90-357 requires a "close, regular, personal"[18] relationship between the parties, but the committee allowed for more flexibility in meeting this requirement.[19] The sections that follow consider how Formal Opinion 90-357 relaxed these restrictions.

One welcome change contained in Formal Opinion 90-357 was the elimination of any possible suggestion that "Of Counsel" had to be in daily contact with the firm or other lawyer. Formal Opinion 90-357 stated:

---

15. ABA Comm. on Ethics & Prof'l Responsibility, Formal Op. 90-357, at 3 (1990).

16. See Chapter 2.

17. *See* Chapter 2.

18. The committee in Formal Opinion 90-357 used the language as it is found in the test of Formal Opinion 330 in describing this aspect of the relationship. The headnote of Formal Opinion 330 used the language "close, continuing, personal" in describing this same aspect.

19. The ethics committee of the New York City Bar has noted that Formal Opinion 90-357 relies on Formal Opinion 330 for the definition of "Of Counsel" (New York City Ethical Op. 1995-8, 1995 WL 875457 (N.Y.C. Ass'n of the Bar Comm. Prof'l Ethics 1995)), citing New York City Ethical Op. 81-3 (1982) for the same test ("close, continuing, regular and personal relationship [or a] present day-to-day working familiarity with the affairs of the law firm in question").

> [I]nsofar as Formal Opinion 330 carries any implication that the contact must be so frequent as to verge on *daily*, the Committee now disavows it.[20] (Emphasis added.)

The committee's current view has important ramifications for many relationships that previously failed to satisfy this requirement. A lawyer may now maintain multiple relationships with several law firms without jeopardizing the "Of Counsel" status with any one firm or other lawyer.[21] But there remains the very practical limitation that multiple relationships may cause an increased risk of conflicts of interest with resulting instances of imputed disqualification.[22] Some states, such as California and Ohio, have specifically warned against the increase in the potential for imputed disqualification due to an increased number of relationships.[23]

Even though daily contact is no longer required, "frequent and continuing contact" is. But the committee failed to define this requirement affirmatively. At the minimum, it requires more than "merely an availability for occasional consultations."[24]

Law Firms Of Counsel to One Another

Formal Opinion 90-357 made it clear that law firms, as well as individuals, could be "Of Counsel" to one another. In 1994, the Ethics and Professional Responsibility Committee became concerned about the proliferation of a wide variety of business arrangements within the legal profession because of the potential of misleading the public by the use of such words as "affiliated,"

20. ABA Comm. on Ethics & Prof'l Responsibility, Formal Op. 90-357, at 4 (1990).

21. State and local bar associations have taken different views about the propriety of multiple "Of Counsel" relationships. Iowa allows only one. *See* Iowa State Bar Ass'n, Ops. 87-9 (1987) and 82-19 (1982). Texas permits two. *See* State Bar of Texas, Op. 402 (1982). Other states do not limit the number. *See* California Ethical Op. 1993-129 (1993); Connecticut Bar Ass'n, Op. 88-13 (1988); Bar Ass'n of Nassau County (N.Y.), Op. 88-46 (1988); Ass'n of the Bar of the City of New York, Op. 80-22 (undated); Ohio Adv. Op. 97-2 (1997); Philadelphia Bar Ass'n, Ops. 86-54 (1986) and 86-143 (1986).

22. *See infra* Chapter 7 (conflicts of interest) and Chapter 8 (imputed disqualification).

23. *See* California Ethical Op. 1993-129 (1993) and Ohio Adv. Op. 97-2, *supra* note 21.

24. ABA Comm. on Ethics & Prof'l Responsibility, Formal Op. 90-357, at 5 (1990).

"associated," "correspondent," or "network," without a "meaningful description of the nature of the relationship."[25]

The resulting Formal Opinion 94-388 emphasized the necessity of full disclosure of two fundamentals:

> The first [precept] is the obligation not to misstate what a law firm has to offer. The second is to assure that a client of one firm is aware of the relationship between that firm and any other firms with which it is involved insofar as the relationship may give rise to conflicts of interest, the sharing of fees, or certain other instructions that implicate the Model Rules of Professional Conduct. This opinion presumes that the actual formation of relationships between law firms will have occurred only where the law firms were able to comply with their obligations to existing clients with respect to all such matters.[26]

Formal Opinion 94-388 noted that the relationships between law firms ranged "from something very close to an actual partnership to one involving occasional referrals."[27] Because of the possibility of misleading the general public, the committee noted that where a law firm is described as being a "member of a 'network,' in an 'association' or is a 'correspondent' of another firm," clients and prospects should be provided with more detailed information.[28]

The Opinion emphasized that a client is "entitled to know of conflicting commitments where . . . the relationship between the firms is 'close, regular, continuing and semi-permanent, and not merely that of forwarder-receiver of legal business.' It then added:

---

25. ABA Comm. on Ethics & Prof'l Responsibility, Formal Op. 94-388 (1994), *Relationships among Law Firms*, at 1; *see* Appendix I.

26. *Id.*

27. ABA Comm. on Ethics & Prof'l Responsibility, Formal Op. 94-388, at 2 (1994).

28. *Id.* The committee listed five major points that should be disclosed: (1) participation of "professional personnel" from the other firm(s); (2) whether the client's fee would be shared; (3) whether there was a sharing of profits; (4) whether there were "common training pro-grams and/or strategies and/or expertise"; and (5) whether the firms "conduct any other common operations, or by contrast, the relationship is simply a marketing device." *Id.*

> [L]awyers of the "affiliated" or "associated" firm will not simultaneously represent persons whose interests conflict with the client's interests, just as would be true of lawyers who occupy an "Of Counsel" relationship with the firm. The same expectation necessarily exists when two firms are "Of Counsel" to each other. . . . In each case, of course, if the lawyer believes the representation will not be adversely affected, the client can be asked to consent to the representation.[29]

Specialty Counsel

Prior informal opinions indicated that a permissible "Of Counsel" relationship could exist even though "Of Counsel" activities were limited to consultation in a particular area of law. Several variant terms can be used to designate an "Of Counsel" relationship in which the lawyer has a special expertise. A consultant specializing in tax, patent and trademark, or antitrust could be designated as "tax counsel," "patent and trademark counsel," or "antitrust counsel" respectively, provided the consultant maintained a close and continuing relationship with the law firm or other lawyer. Formal Opinion 90-357 confirmed this view:

> Such terms, although in the Committee's view as permissible as other variants of the term "counsel," must like them be confined to relationships that in fact involved frequent and continuing contacts, and not merely an availability for occasional consultations.[30]

But the committee did not follow the position of several state bars that held that the designation should contain more descriptive language to indicate the limitations reflected by the variant terms.[31] The committee expressed its view that the variant term itself connotes the true nature of the relationship:

29. ABA Formal Op. 94-388, at 4, quoting (first sentence) Formal Op. 84-351, and citing Formal Op. 90-357 and Informal Op. 1315 (1975). *See infra* Chapter 7 (conflicts of interest) and Chapter 8 (imputed disqualification).

30. ABA Comm. on Ethics & Prof'l Responsibility, Formal Op. 90-357, at 4–5 (1990).

31. *E.g.*, Arizona State Bar Ethics Op. 87-24 (1987).

> There is, moreover, in the term designating a specialty, a clear representation that the of counsel lawyer in fact has a special expertise in the designated area; and, for the firm, that it also has, by reason of the of counsel relationship, that special expertise.[32]

Where Formal Opinion 330 seemed to limit the methods of compensation in "Of Counsel" relationships, Formal Opinion 90-357 wisely handled the issue by making it clear that compensation arrangements are not relevant to the determination of a permissible "Of Counsel" relationship:

> It is the Committee's view that, the other conditions just described having been met, it is not relevant to the permissibility of use of "of counsel" what the compensation arrangements are.[33]

The committee recognized that many "Of Counsel" attorneys are retired partners who have a pension or other retirement benefit or who share in the firm's profits. Under Formal Opinion 330, such persons could not be designated as "Of Counsel." Under 90-357, such considerations are simply inapplicable.

In dealing with various compensation arrangements, the ABA Committee on Ethics and Professional Responsibility and state and local bar associations have distinguished a wide variety of arrangements for the division of fees,[34] office sharing, and/or referrals of legal business from the typical compensation arrangements that characterize the "Of Counsel" relationship.

---

32. ABA Comm. on Ethics & Prof'l Responsibility, Formal Op. 90-357, at 5 (1990).

33. *Id.* at 4.

34. *Cf.* ABA Comm. on Ethics & Prof'l Responsibility, Formal Op. 93-374 (1993) (allowing the sharing of court-awarded fees between a lawyer and a nonprofit organization that sponsors pro bono litigation); Florida Ethical Op. 94-7, 1995 WL 815246 (Florida State Bar Association) (Of Counsel considered to be a member of the firm for purposes of the fee division rules only if practicing exclusively through that firm); Michigan Ethical Op. RI-216, 1994 WL 423011 (Michigan Prof'l & Judicial Ethics Comm.) (heirs and estate of deceased lawyer may make agreement with law firm wherein the valuation and payment for lawyer's interest could be based on pro rata portion of the future receipt by the firm of contingent fees to be paid by another law firm for referrals during decedent's life); Michigan Ethical Op. RI-133, 1992 WL 510804 (Michigan Prof'l & Judicial Ethics Comm.) (lawyer may rent office space from lawyer/landlord based on a calculation of gross income from the lawyer/tenant's law practice, so long as client confidences are not violated in determining the amount of rent due).

For example, where two lawyers acted more like forwarders and receivers of legal business, they could not properly hold themselves out as "Of Counsel":

> The "Of Counsel" lawyers maintained separate offices and appear to be the receivers of legal business forwarded by the firm. The method used to compensate the "Of Counsel" lawyers is more in the nature of paying an outside consultant rather than as *a sui generis* member of the firm. We are of the opinion that an "Of Counsel" relationship does not exist and that it is not proper for the firm to show the two lawyers as "Of Counsel" on their letterhead, exterior door listing or elsewhere.[35]

Any compensation between "Of Counsel" and a law firm or other lawyer must be arranged so that there is no implication that "Of Counsel" is a partner. An arrangement that involves a sharing in the firm's general profits or other indicia that might imply, or even make, one a partner would be inappropriate. If the drafter of an "Of Counsel" agreement wishes to use percentages of gross or net profits, for example, the percentage should be related to the services to be performed by "Of Counsel."

Issues of compensation are not limited to salary arrangements. More often than not, employee fringe benefits, such as medical insurance, life insurance, accident and disability insurance, eligibility in the firm's pension or profit-sharing plan, and coverage under the firm's professional liability plan, are equally important to a lawyer contemplating joining a firm as "Of Counsel."

In the past, it might not have been desirable for persons in the position of "Of Counsel" to participate in various benefit programs and other fringe benefits offered by the firm. The reasoning was twofold: First, Formal Opinion 330 precluded use of the term where the relationship resembled that of an associate or employee. Receipt of these benefits as part of a compensation package tended to make the relationship resemble that of an employer-employee, rather than independent contractor. Second, and perhaps more important, receipt of these benefits by an "Of Counsel" attorney could be

35. Illinois Advisory Op. 776, 1982 WL 198379 (Ill. St. Bar Ass'n).

an important indication of an employer-employee relationship in a malpractice claim against the firm.

Since Formal Opinion 90-357 expressed the committee's view that the compensation arrangement is irrelevant to the issue of using the designation, the "Of Counsel" attorney's receipt of these fringe benefits should not affect an ability to use the designation. But the committee did not address whether such arrangements expose the parties to vicarious liability for malpractice of another.[36]

Partner or Associate Status Is Not Permissible

The second aspect of the core characteristic described in Formal Opinion 90-357 is that the "Of Counsel" relationship must not resemble that of partner or associate. The ethical considerations that form the basis of this requirement are found in EC 2-13, which essentially provides that a lawyer should be scrupulous in representing an accurate professional status and should avoid any misrepresentations concerning it, and Model Rules of Professional Conduct, Rule 7.5(a), which provides in relevant part that a lawyer shall not use a professional designation that violates Rule 7.1 (which states in relevant part that lawyers shall not make a false or misleading communication about themselves or their services).

The headnote of Formal Opinion 330 precluded use of the "Of Counsel" designation where the relationship was like that of "partner, associate or outside consultant." Formal Opinion 330 concluded that the term "associates" describes those who are "lawyer-employees" of the firm who "are not partners and do not generally share in the responsibility and liability for the acts of the firm."[37] Changes in the practice of law since this opinion was issued made this definition obsolete.

Formal Opinion 90-357 cleared up much of this confusion. The committee precluded use of the "Of Counsel" designation where the relationship is like that of partner or associate, and it affirmatively defined "associate" as "a junior non-partner lawyer, regularly employed by the firm."[38] This

36. *See* Chapters 5 and 6.
37. *See* Chapter 2.
38. ABA Comm. on Ethics & Prof'l Responsibility, Formal Op. 90-357, at 3 (1990).

substantial improvement over the language used in Formal Opinion 330 made it possible for senior lawyers to be designated as "Of Counsel" without being characterized as associates.

Employee Status Is Permissible

One of the many problems of Formal Opinion 330 was its inconsistent use of the term "employee." A strict interpretation of the text of 330 precluded "Of Counsel" attorneys from being like an employee and precluded the "Of Counsel" arrangement from resembling an employer-employee relationship in any way. Thus, "Of Counsel" attorneys could not be compensated with a fixed salary and could not participate in any of the firm's benefit programs. This restriction precluded use of the term by lawyers brought into the firm laterally with the expectation of becoming partner within a relatively short time. It also limited use of the term to describe lawyers who were in a permanent status between partner and associate and senior lawyers whose compensation arrangements included some or all of the profits of their work product.

Formal Opinion 90-357 alleviated this problem by explicitly permitting the designation to be used in the two arrangements described above in which employee status was presumed:

> Insofar as Formal Opinion 330 may be read to conclude that either the probationary partner model or the permanent between-partner-and-associate model are not permissibly designated of counsel, that conclusion is disavowed.[39]

There may be other relationships that could be identified as "Of Counsel" relationships but for the fact that the parties assume an employer-employee arrangement. The committee did not express an opinion on the propriety of these arrangements. For the most part, Formal Opinion 90-357 dealt with independent-contractor situations. The retired partner, the part-time practitioner, and the lawyer entering a second career typically conform to this model.

39. *Id.* at 4.

By contrast, 90-357 based the "probationary partner-to-be" or the "permanent between-partner-and-associate model" on the employer-employee relationship. When drafting the "Of Counsel" agreement, the drafter should select one or the other—independent contractor or employer-employee relationship—for the bulk of the agreement, and make specific exceptions in those areas in which the alternate approach may be desired.[40]

Multiple Of Counsel Relationships

The committee's initial view was that a lawyer could not be "Of Counsel" to more than one law firm. This view was modified in Formal Opinion 330, which set a limit of two firms. Formal Opinion 90-357 removed any limitation on the number of firms with which a lawyer may have an "Of Counsel" relationship. The committee expressed its new position as follows:

> The proposition that it is not possible for a lawyer to have a "close, regular, personal relationship" with more than two lawyers or law firms is not a self-evident one. A lawyer can surely have a close, regular, personal relationship with more than two clients; and the Committee sees no reason why the same cannot be true with more than two law firms.[41]

The controlling criterion is "close, regular, personal" relationships. If the lawyer can maintain multiple close and regular relationships simultaneously, the designation is proper for each.[42] As a practical matter this may not be possible, since multiple "Of Counsel" relationships affect conflict-of-interest issues and attributions between the lawyer and firm or other lawyer. For purposes of conflicts of interest, "Of Counsel" firms and attorneys are "associated" with the firm.[43] For purposes of imputed disqualifications, if

40. *See* Chapter 11 for discussion of problems of drafting.
41. ABA Comm. on Ethics & Prof'l Responsibility, Formal Op. 90-357, at 5 (1990).
42. *See* Chapter 4.
43. *See* Chapter 7.

two or more firms share the same "Of Counsel" attorney, the two firms and the "Of Counsel" attorney all effectively become a single firm.[44]

Law Firms as Of Counsel

Prior views of the committee held that a law firm could not be held out as being "Of Counsel" to another firm or lawyer. Formal Opinion 90-357 reversed these views and expressed its new opinion as follows:

> [T]he Committee's prior opinions do not suggest, and the Committee does not now perceive, any reason of policy why a firm should not be "of counsel" to another firm.[45]

As with multiple "Of Counsel" relationships, the committee cautioned that relationships created between firms would "entail complete reciprocal attribution of the disqualifications of all lawyers in each firm."[46] Before entering into such relationships, a law firm would also have to consider very carefully the potential increase in liability for the errors and omissions of the other firm.

Of Counsel's Name in the Firm's Name

In Formal Opinion 90-357, the committee, for the first time, authorized use of an "Of Counsel" attorney's name in the firm's name but only if the lawyer was a retired name partner and "the firm is long-established and

44. *See* Chapter 8.

45. ABA Comm. on Ethics & Prof'l Responsibility, Formal Op. 90-357, at 6 (1990).

46. *See id.* and Chapter 4. In 1994, the ABA Committee on Ethics and Professional Responsibility stated that it was entirely proper for law firms to be "Of Counsel" to one another or to be associated or affiliated with one another. For purposes of conflicts of interest and imputed disqualification, a law firm must make a full disclosure of the resources that such an arrangement makes available to clients and of the precise relationship between the firms. ABA Comm. on Ethics & Prof'l Responsibility, Formal Op. 94-388 (1994), *reprinted in* Appendix I. *See* Chapters 7 and 8.

well-recognized."[47] If the "Of Counsel" attorney has recently joined the firm, his name cannot be included in the firm's name because it might give a misleading impression of the extent of this person's responsibility and potential liability. The committee stated:

> [We believe] that in the case of a new or recent firm affiliation there is no escaping an implication that a name in the new firm name implies that the lawyer is a partner in the firm, with fully shared responsibility for its work. On the other hand, the Committee also believes that there is not a similar misleading implication in the use of a retired partner's name in the firm name, while the same partner is of counsel, where the firm name is long-established and well-recognized.[48]

Even though the committee approved including an "Of Counsel" attorney's name in the firm's name in these limited situations, no view was expressed concerning the "Of Counsel" attorney's potential malpractice liability:

> The Committee does not express a view as to whether, when the retired partner's name remains included in the firm name, the retired partner may on that account be exposed to malpractice liability as if he or she were still a general partner.[49]

Summary

Many of the restrictions that the earlier Formal Opinion 330 placed upon parties entering into "Of Counsel" relationships were relaxed under Formal Opinion 90-357. This was a welcome change and has enhanced the ability of the parties to tailor the arrangement to suit their own needs. Under Formal Opinion 90-357, the designation can be used whether the parties

47. ABA Comm. on Ethics & Prof'l Responsibility, Formal Op. 90-357, at 6 (1990).
48. *Id.*
49. *Id.* n. 11, at 6.

anticipate the relationship to be temporary or permanent. A retired partner who will be available only for occasional consultation can still be listed as "Of Counsel" and such attorney's name may remain part of the firm's name. The term can also be used to describe the relationship between a part-time practitioner and a law firm. Lawyers can maintain multiple "Of Counsel" relationships. But perhaps the single most important change from the prior opinion was the ability of firms to list one another as "Of Counsel." The use of the term to describe relationships between foreign law firms and trans-continental law firms will undoubtedly become more common in the future.

CHAPTER 4

Particular Of Counsel Relationships

In Formal Opinion 90-357, the ABA's Standing Committee on Ethics and Professional Responsibility issued guidelines to follow when using the "Of Counsel" designation. While the committee was more liberal on this subject than in its prior Formal Opinion 330, it retained some restrictions on the use of the term and did not address a number of areas important to the practicing bar. The committee officially withdrew Formal Opinion 330 and the informal opinions that preceded it, but continued to cite these opinions, pointing out those instances where it disavowed what it had said in earlier opinions.

In Formal Opinion 330, the committee defined an "Of Counsel" relationship by focusing on the closeness and continuity of the relationship. The committee distinguished two common "Of Counsel" relationships: (1) where the lawyer practices or continues to practice in the offices of the lawyer or law firm and (2) where the lawyer does not practice in the office of the lawyer or firm but is in regular and frequent contact with the firm.

Although the committee made a number of significant changes regarding the details of the "Of Counsel" arrangement in 90-357, it retained the fundamental characteristic that the relationship must be *a close and continuing* one:

> That core characteristic properly denoted by the title "counsel" is, as stated in Formal Opinion 330, a "close, regular, personal" relationship. . . .[1]

The phrase "Of Counsel" has come to mean many different things. There are so many variant uses of the phrase that the only thing common to these relationships is that they do not fit neatly into one category. Both 90-357 and 330 considered some of these variants. This chapter considers these as well as other arrangements commonly designated as "Of Counsel" to determine whether they comport with the pronouncement of 90-357. We shall also consider how these arrangements are treated by various states.

Specifically Permitted Of Counsel Relationships

In Formal Opinion 90-357, the committee outlined four major instances wherein the "Of Counsel" designation could be properly used: part-time practitioners, retired partners, probationary partners, and senior attorneys. The part-time practitioner category was broken down into two subcategories: (1) lawyers who changed from a full-time to a part-time practice and (2) those who changed their careers.

Although the permitted categories may not conform precisely to the variety of situations confronting lawyers in practice, they provide a useful guide for those entering into "Of Counsel" contractual relationships. To the extent that the parties can draft an "Of Counsel" agreement that fits within one or more of these categories, they will be certain to satisfy the ethical standards of the profession.

The Retired Partner

In 1963, the ABA Committee on Professional Ethics issued its first opinion relating to the "Of Counsel" relationship. In that opinion, the committee

1. ABA Comm. on Ethics & Prof'1 Responsibility, Formal Op. 90-357, at 3 (1990), *reprinted in* Appendix G.

recognized that many "Of Counsel" attorneys are retired partners of a law firm. The committee stated:

> It is the impression of the members of this Committee that the term, "of counsel," . . . is customarily used to indicate a former partner who is on a retirement or semi-retirement basis, or one who has retired from another partnership or the general private practice or from some public position, who remains or becomes available to the firm for consultation and advice, either generally or in a particular field.[2] (Emphasis added.)

In 1972, when the committee first formally defined the "Of Counsel" relationship in Formal Opinion 330, it did not exempt retired partners from the "close, continuing, personal" requirement. But it did conclude that an "Of Counsel" attorney who is a retired partner of the firm will be deemed to have already developed *a close* association with the firm. Consequently, this lawyer would not be required to practice in the offices of the lawyer or firm to properly have "Of Counsel" status.[3] But for the association to be a "close, *continuing,* personal" one, the retired partner had to remain active in the practice of law, with frequent, "if not daily," contact with the firm.[4]

Such a reading imposed unnecessary limitations on the traditional "Of Counsel" arrangement.[5] A "close, continuing, personal" relationship was not found where the retired partner was available for occasional consultation only, resided in another city or state for all or part of the year, or merely maintained an office with the firm.[6] Even if the retired partner remained in

2. ABA Comm. on Prof'1 Ethics, Informal Op. 678 (1963).
3. ABA Comm. on Ethics & Prof'l Responsibility, Formal Op. 330 (1972).
4. ABA Formal Op. 330, at 69.
5. *See* ABA Informal Op. 678.
6. This interpretation was based on an earlier opinion rendered by the committee. In Informal Opinion 1189, the committee reaffirmed Informal Opinion 1173 and stated:

> It is our opinion that the continuing relationship necessary for the designation "Of Counsel" referred to in DR 2-102(A)(4) which we have defined as close daily in house association is susceptible to one exception which permits such classification to the designee if he had a previous continuing relationship with such other lawyer or law firm and during such relationship was physically present in the same office and/ or suite with such other lawyer or law firm but which association of many years has been interrupted by the designee's inability to

frequent contact with the office, there was no "close, continuing, personal" relationship if the "Of Counsel" attorney was not active in the practice of law, or if the retiree was not required to perform any duties for the firm. Merely going to the office because it was a place to stay away from home did not create an "Of Counsel" relationship.[7]

Thus, in *Mutual of Omaha Insurance Co. v. Chadwell*,[8] a federal district court, relying on the language of Formal Opinion 330, questioned whether an "Of Counsel" relationship existed where the retired partner merely maintained an office on the premises with no expectation that the retired partner would continue to render any legal services for the firm. The "Of Counsel" contract did not require the lawyer to fulfill a minimum number of work hours per week, nor was a physical presence in the office required for practicing law. But the contract did require the firm to provide the lawyer with office space, secretarial support, group insurance coverage, and a fixed annual compensation. The court, relying on Formal Opinion 330, doubted whether the relationship in question was in fact a "close" or "continuing" one.[9]

Today, many "Of Counsel" attorneys are retired partners who continue to serve the firm full-time as consultants on various matters. A retired partner may continue with the firm on an as "Of Counsel" basis, practicing law on a reduced basis. Or the retired partner may relocate to another area and become "Of Counsel" with a firm there, as well as with the former firm. In other arrangements, the retiring partner might maintain an office with the same or a different firm, while pursuing independent interests. Most observers saw the "close, continuing, personal relationship" required by

---

> come to the office or his removal from the city or geographical area of his prior practice providing he is not associated with or holding himself out as being associated with any other lawyer or law firm.

Thus, even though the committee acknowledged specific instances in which a lawyer would not be required to practice in the same office of the lawyer or law firm, those instances are so limited that they would not cover most present-day "Of Counsel" relationships.

7. Corinne Maskaleris, *"Of Counsel"—Defined* at 14 (compilation from transcript of *Of Counsel: Revisited*, a program presented by the Senior Lawyers Division of the American Bar Association at the Annual Meeting, Aug. 6, 1980) (available from Senior Lawyers Division, ABA).

8. 426 F. Supp. 550 (N.D. Ill. 1977).

9. *Id.* at 552.

Formal Opinion 330 as much too restrictive for many situations in which a retired partner desired to branch out and do other things independently of the law office at which he or she was once partner.

Formal Opinion 90-357 changed these rules, so that a retired partner now has many options. The new perspective in 90-357 was reflected in the following language of the committee:

> Formal Opinion 330 may be read as limiting the permissible use of the term "of counsel" by retired partners of a firm, because of possible implications from language in that opinion that an of counsel lawyer must be compensated for such legal work as the lawyer does, but only for that legal work which, if strictly read, would exclude both a retired partner whose sole income from the firm is the partner's pension or other retirement benefit and counsel who share in some degree in the firm's profits. *See also* Informal Opinion 710. It is the Committee's view that, other conditions just described having been met, it is not relevant to the permissibility of use of "of counsel" what the compensation arrangements are. Similarly, some retired partners might be deemed to be excluded by the suggestion in Formal Opinion 330 that an of counsel's relationship to the firm must be "so close that he is in regular and frequent, if not daily, contact with the office of the lawyer or firm" (citing Informal Opinion 1134). Again, insofar as Formal Opinion 330 carries any implication that the contact must be so frequent as to verge on daily, the Committee now disavows it.[10] (Footnotes omitted.)

Most states have followed the rules established by Formal Opinion 90-357 as they pertain to retired partners. For example, in Ohio, a retired lawyer may remain "Of Counsel" to a law firm so long as he or she remains an active member of the bar and provided the firm letterhead lists the lawyer as "retired."[11] In Arizona, a retired partner may be designated "Of Counsel"

---

10. ABA Comm. on Ethics & Prof'l Responsibility, Formal Op. 90-357, at 4 (1990).

11. Op. No. 91-18, Supreme Court of Ohio, Bd. of Commissioners on Grievances & Discipline (1991).

even if only an office is maintained on the premises of the former firm.[12] In Iowa, a retired partner need not be "active" in the practice of law to establish a proper "Of Counsel" relationship.[13]

Whatever the scope of the retired partner's activities, when that person becomes "Of Counsel," rights and duties vis-à-vis the firm should be spelled out in detail in writing and should include matters such as compensation and the extent of income from participation in a particular matter and/or activities of the firm.[14]

> [One] who practices law in association with a firm, but on a basis different from that of the mainstream lawyers in the firm. Such part-time practitioners are sometimes lawyers who have decided to change from a full-time practice, either with that firm or another, to a part-time one, or sometimes lawyers who have changed careers entirely, as for example former judges or government officials.[15]

In many situations, the category of the lawyer who changes from full-time to part-time practitioner will overlap with that of the retired partner. The committee made it clear that any lawyer may change from full-time to part-time practice and use the "Of Counsel" designation to describe that new status. The committee defined the part-time practitioner as one "who practices law in association with a firm, but on a basis different from that of mainstream lawyers in the firm."[16] Therefore, the "Of Counsel" designation is not reserved solely for lawyers who change from full-time practice to part-time practice with the same firm. The "Of Counsel" lawyer may

---

12. Arizona State Bar Ethics Op. 81-2 (1981).

13. Iowa State Bar Ethics Op. 80-27 (1980). But that state's ethics committee noted:

> Retired attorneys need not be active to be listed as "Of Counsel" on the firm stationery. Whether the retired lawyers "practice law" so as to require compliance with the rules governing the Client Security and Attorney Disciplinary Commission and/or the Commission on Continuing Legal Education, is a question each lawyer must determine for himself.

14. In Trittipo v. O'Brien, No. 1-88-2455 (Ill. App. 1990), it was held that law firms need not purchase the shares of partners upon their retirement from a professional service corporation or partnership. Because of this holding, a lawyer moving from partner to "Of Counsel" status should be certain to place everything in writing.

15. ABA Formal Op. 90-357, at 3.

16. *Id.*

join the firm on a part-time basis. Such a part-time practitioner is subject to all the rules governing lawyers generally with the limitations that arise because of the limited amount of time involved in practice.

The second subcategory described in 90-357 — the lawyer who changes careers — is quite a different species. Although Formal Opinion 90-357 mentioned only judges and government officials as lawyers who would fit into this category, corporate counsel and tenured professors are a couple of the other types of lawyers who may have to change careers because they are required to retire at a certain age. In this last category, the change may just as likely be to a full-time as to a part-time law practice.

The propriety of persons who have changed careers entirely to become "Of Counsel" centers around very different issues from those dealing with lawyers who have decided to change from a full-time practice to a part-time one. Typically, the arrangement between the lawyer and the firm has only recently been formed, so there is not a "close, regular, personal" relationship. Yet Formal Opinion 330 appeared to relax the requirement of a "close, continuing, personal" relationship at least when the lawyer was a retired public official. It required that, for there to be a "close and continuing" relationship, a retired public official need only be "regularly and locally available for consultation and advice." But this revision still implied that the retired public official's contact with the firm had to be frequent, "if not daily," as in the case of the retired partner.

The former official who becomes "Of Counsel" today will no doubt wonder whether the Formal Opinion 330 definition of a "close and continuing relationship" will apply under Formal Opinion 90-357 now that Formal Opinion 330 has been withdrawn. However, when we apply the 90-357 language dealing with the retired partner[17] to the situation of the public official, it would appear that the new rules have eliminated much of the earlier restrictions. Under 90-357, firms are discouraged from returning to the old practice of decorating the letterhead by using names of former public officials who have only a minimal relationship with the firm. Such an arrangement would not satisfy the requirement of a "close, regular, personal" relationship under Formal Opinion 330 or 90-357.

---

17. *See* the earlier discussion of the retired partner in this chapter.

The Probationary Partner

In Formal Opinion 90-357, the committee identified a third category of lawyers for specific mention as qualifying for the "Of Counsel" designation: the probationary partner-to-be. The committee described a "probationary partner-to-be" as "a lawyer brought into the firm laterally with the expectation of becoming partner after a relatively short period of time."[18]

In drafting agreements, lawyers and law firms both will welcome the committee's permission to use the "Of Counsel" designation for the probationary partner. Such an arrangement enables both the "Of Counsel" attorney and the law firm to try out one another. If the arrangement is a success, the probationary partner transitions to partnership status. If it should fail, the "Of Counsel" attorney can move on to another arrangement with relatively little complication or embarrassment either to himself or to the firm.

In one important respect, 90-357 adopted a new rule affecting both probationary partners and senior attorneys. Formal Opinion 330 implied that "Of Counsel" attorneys could not be employees of the firm. Formal Opinion 90-357 recognized that both of these categories "involve, as a technical matter, the status of an employee."[19] The committee stated:

> Insofar as Formal Opinion 330 may be read to conclude that either the probationary partner model or the permanent between-partner-and-associate model are not permissibly designated of counsel, that conclusion is disavowed.[20]

Obviously, the most important concern of probationary partners who are designated as "Of Counsel" will be their relationship with their new professional association. As with an antenuptial agreement, the terms of such a relationship should be reduced to writing. Since a probationary partner normally comes into the firm because of some special expertise or long experience, each agreement should be custom-tailored to the particular

18. ABA Formal Op. 90-357, at 3.
19. *Id.* at 4.
20. *Id.*

"Of Counsel" attorney and the firm to be joined. Matters of status, compensation, pension rights, and the like should be handled with great care.[21]

The Senior Attorney

Like the probationary partner, the senior attorney is technically an employee of the law firm. But unlike the probationary partner, the senior attorney is expressly denied the traditional goal of partner. As the committee noted, the senior attorney's status is a relatively new development:

> A fourth, relatively recent, use of the term ["Of Counsel"] is to designate a permanent status between those of partner and associate—akin to the category just described, but having the quality of tenure, or something close to it, and lacking that of an expectation of likely promotion to full partner status.[22]

An "Of Counsel" lawyer in this in-between status, the committee noted, is often referred to as a "senior attorney" or "principal attorney."

The growth of this particular category of the "Of Counsel" designation is not surprising in view of the changing needs of the lawyers and the law firms on opposite sides of the arrangement. Many lawyers welcome the security that such a position offers. Typically, the senior attorney receives a guaranteed income, without enjoying the possible profits or assuming any of the risks of loss that accompany the status of partner. The law firm will welcome the senior attorney's presence in that it will benefit from this person's expertise without having to involve the non-partner in the management of the firm or give him or her a share of the general profits. The arrangement may well be very desirable for all concerned.

In discussing the use of the term "Of Counsel" generally, the committee emphasized that many terms are used within the profession to describe the "Of Counsel" relationship:

---

21. *See* Chapter 11 and Appendices A through F.
22. ABA Formal Op. 90-357, at 3.

> [A]lthough "of counsel" appears to be the most frequently used among the various titles employing the term "counsel," it is by no means the only use of that term to indicate a relationship between a lawyer and a law firm. Other such titles include the single word "counsel," and the terms "special counsel," "tax [or other specialty] counsel," and "senior counsel." It is the Committee's view that, whatever the connotative differences evoked by these variants of the title "counsel," they all share the central, and defining, characteristic of the relationship that is denoted by the term "of counsel," and so should all be understood to be covered by the present opinion.[23]

Thus, 90-357 governs all forms of the "Of Counsel" designation, including such groups classified as "senior attorneys." Some firms seek to use different terminology for the various categories of their "Of Counsel" relationships. For example, the word "counsel" might be used to describe the senior attorney, so that the term "Of Counsel" could be reserved for retired partners.

Although the use of different terminology may be desirable for different contractual arrangements within a firm, we believe that the use of the "Of Counsel" designation on letterhead and other notices to the general public is the better practice. This is particularly true now that Formal Opinion 90-357 has officially recognized these many and varied relationships.

Specifically Prohibited Of Counsel Relationships

In Formal Opinion 90-357, the committee first provided four "safe harbors" for those entering "Of Counsel" relationships.[24] But it also identified four situations to avoid in the formation "Of Counsel" relationships:

> [I]t is not ethically permissible to use the term "of counsel" to designate the following professional relationships: a relationship involving only an individual case, *see* Informal Opinion 678, Formal Opinion 330;

23. *Id.*
24. *See* Chapter 3.

> a relationship of forwarder or receiver of legal business, see Formal Opinion 330; a relationship involving only occasional collaborative efforts among otherwise unrelated lawyers or firms, see *id.;* and the relationship of an outside consultant, *see id.*[25] (Footnote omitted.)

The common thread that runs through these four prohibited categories is their transitory nature.

The Lawyer Associated in a Single Case

In Informal Opinion 678, the committee noted that an "Of Counsel" relationship could not exist if it was based on consultation in only one particular case.[26] In proscribing the use of the "Of Counsel" designation in a single case, the committee was primarily concerned with the "Of Counsel" attorney's posture vis-à-vis the general public:

> The reference here is not to the appearance of a lawyer or firm on the court filings of a particular case, but rather to representation of an "of counsel" relationship on firm letterhead, professional cards, and the like on the basis of collaboration on a single case.[27]

Avoidance of the representation that a lawyer was "Of Counsel" where the association was only for a single case would prevent a potential misrepresentation of the lawyer's status to the general public. "Of Counsel" attorneys are free to use the designation in court filings, appellate briefs, and the like, which the general public, as distinct from the litigants, would normally never see.

The Forwarder-Receiver of Legal Business

The "Of Counsel" designation does not apply where the relationship consists of nothing more than the referral of prospective clients to the other lawyer or firm.[28] The designation requires a close, regular, and personal

25. ABA Formal Op. 90-357, *reprinted in* Appendix G.
26. *See* the later discussion of the law firm as "Of Counsel" in this chapter.
27. ABA Formal Op. 90-357, at 4 n.7.
28. ABA Comm. on Ethics & Prof'l Responsibility, Formal Op. 330 (1972); Alabama State

relationship with the other lawyer or law firm, qualities that are not ordinarily found in a typical forwarder-receiver relationship.

A relationship that is limited to the referral of prospective clients between lawyers will not satisfy the requirements of an "Of Counsel" relationship, regardless of the past relationship between the lawyers or their future anticipated relationship. Where the relationship is only that of forwarder-receiver, the designation is not proper, even if the lawyer is a former partner of the firm[29] or the lawyers anticipate a merger in the near future.[30] This is true even if the referral of clients is used as a means of handling a recurring problem of overflow work. The "Of Counsel" designation has also been held improper where a national law firm advertises and refers cases to the lawyer in return for a percentage of fees generated.[31]

The Occasional Collaborator

When a lawyer occasionally collaborates with otherwise unrelated lawyers or firms, the absence of a regular or continuing relationship again prompts a prohibition against the use of the "Of Counsel" designation. These collaborative efforts are isolated in-and-out situations in which the "Of Counsel" attorney does not continue to provide day-to-day professional advice to a law firm or lawyer.

The Outside Consultant

After retirement, partners frequently remain available to the firm as consultants, often to ensure continuity of cultivated business relationships. Likewise, a retired judge may become "Of Counsel" to be available to review briefs of the firm. A lawyer with expertise in a particular field of law may join a firm as "Of Counsel" to fill a need to compete against larger firms for clients.[32]

Ethics Op. 86-28 (1986); Arizona State Ethics Op. 81-1 (1981), *aff'd*, Op. 87-24 (1987); Illinois State Ethics Op. 87-12 (1988); Michigan Informal Ethics Op. CI-536 (1981); New Jersey State Ethics Op. 476 (1981); New York City Ethics Op. 81-109 (undated); Philadelphia State Ethics Op. 80-114 (undated).

29. Philadelphia State Ethics Op. 80-114 (undated).

30. ABA Comm. on Ethics & Prof'l Responsibility, Informal Op. 1378 (1976).

31. New Jersey State Ethics Op. 476 (1981); Illinois State Ethics Op. 840 (1981).

32. M. Altman & R. Weil, HOW TO MANAGE YOUR LAW OFFICE § 2.12 (Matthew Bender

In the earlier Formal Opinion 330, the committee recognized that attorneys designated as "Of Counsel" are often used as consultants:

> [The "Of Counsel"] relationship with the lawyer or law firm must be a close, regular, personal relationship like, for example, the relationship of a retired or semi-retired former partner who remains available to the firm for consultation and advice, or a retired public official who regularly and locally is available to the firm for consultation and advice.[33]

The committee stipulated that "Of Counsel" must be a "member or component part of the law office."[34] In the headnote, the committee concluded that the "Of Counsel" relationship must be "one that is not that of a partner, associate, or *outside consultant*"[35] (emphasis added). But the committee failed to define what it meant by the phrase "outside consultant." Formal Opinion 90-357 failed to throw any additional light on the meaning of "outside consultant." Through custom, the word "consultant" has come to refer to one who has particular expertise and who is used by a lawyer or law firm, either generally or on a case-by-case basis.[36] But there is no definition of "outside consultant" in the Model Code of Professional Responsibility or the Model Rules of Professional Conduct. And, since the committee failed to define when a consultant becomes an "outside consultant," its use of the phrase remains ambiguous.

This is particularly troublesome for "Of Counsel" attorneys whose primary role may be limited to that of consultation. If the lawyer's activities with the firm are limited to consultation, is the term "outside consultant" appropriate? If the lawyer has a close association with the firm but resides in another city or state, is that lawyer considered an "outside consultant"? Is the lawyer who has a separate office from that of the law firm or other lawyer an "outside consultant"? Or is the lawyer considered an "outside

---

1988) (quoting Flaherty, *The Many Roles for Of Counsel*, NAT'L L.J., Sept. 13, 1982).

33. ABA Comm. on Ethics & Prof'l Responsibility, Formal Op. 330 (1972).

34. *Id.*

35. *Id.*

36. *See* ABA Comm. on Prof'l Ethics, Informal Op. 1189 (1971).

consultant" only if he or she was not formerly associated with the lawyer or law firm as a partner or associate?

Some general guidelines can be gleaned from prior informal opinions. Informal Opinion 678[37] stated that an "Of Counsel" relationship cannot exist if the relationship is based on consultation in only one particular case. The facts that gave rise to the opinion were these: a firm proposed to designate an out-of-state lawyer "Of Counsel" for purposes of one case. The lawyer was in the office of the firm during the trial but was not admitted to practice in the state where the firm was located. He did not desire to become a member of the bar of that state, and intended to return to his home state at the end of the trial. The committee stated:

> [I]t seems to us it would be misleading if the relationship existed only as to one particular case even though it might be one of great importance which would require the very active participation of the outside counsel over an extended period of time, and even though a great deal of that time was actually spent in the office of the local firm.[38]

Informal Opinion 678 indicated that an "Of Counsel" relationship can exist between a lawyer and a law firm or another lawyer even though the first lawyer's activities are limited to consultation. But if the lawyer is not frequently available on an ongoing basis, the correct appellation would be "outside consultant," and the "Of Counsel" designation cannot be used. Given the 90-357 requirement of a "close, regular, personal" relationship, it appears that the same reasoning would apply today.

Several state bar panels addressing the question of when a consultant is an "outside consultant" appear to follow the reasoning of Informal Opinion 678. Indeed, in some states, the "Of Counsel" relationship requires something more than mere consultation, regardless of the frequency of contact between the lawyer and firm. In New York, an "Of Counsel" designation is appropriate where the lawyer is "available to the firm for consultation

37. ABA Comm. on Prof'l Ethics, Informal Op. 678 (1963).
38. *Id.*

and advice on a regular and continuing basis."[39] In Texas, an "Of Counsel" relationship does not exist if the lawyer is available only for consultation with firm members.[40]

Formal Opinion 90-357 appears to continue the basic philosophy of prior ABA informal and formal opinions. The "outside consultant" is precluded from using the "Of Counsel" designation because that person does not have the sufficient continuing relationship with the law firm or lawyer to satisfy the committee's concept of the "Of Counsel" designation.

Since the emphasis in Formal Opinion 90-357 was on the closeness and regularity of the relationship, consultation limited to a particular area of law will not preclude the existence of an "Of Counsel" relationship.[41] Prior ABA informal opinions and several state bar opinions have expressed the view that a consultant specializing in tax law or in patent, trademark, and copyright law may be designated "Of Counsel," provided the consultant maintains a close and continuing relationship with the other lawyer or firm.[42] Arizona has held that a lawyer available for consultation in a particular field of law can be designated "Of Counsel," but that "more descriptive language should be included to explain the true nature of the relationship."[43] The "Of Counsel" designation is also permitted where the consultant does not practice law but, in his employment as a government official or university professor, has acquired expertise in a certain area of law.[44]

---

39. New York State Bar Association, Committee on Professional Ethics, Op. 793 (2006).

40. Texas State Bar Ethics Op. 402 (1982).

41. ABA Formal Op. 90-357, reprinted in Appendix G.

42. ABA Comm. on Prof'l Ethics, Informal Ops. 1132 (1970) and 901 (1965); Arizona Ethics Op. 87-24 (1987); Philadelphia Ethics Op. 86-143 (1986) (holding that the lawyer may even be designated "tax counsel"); South Carolina Ethics Op. 81-2 (1981) (patent, trademark, and copyright law). After Formal Opinion 330 was issued, questions remained concerning whether the firm could list the particular lawyer's specialty in legal lists or on the firm's letterhead. ABA Informal Opinion 901 prohibited the lawyer from being designated "Tax Counsel" on the firm's letterhead, even though the lawyer would handle all tax matters for the firm. A better designation, the committee wrote, would be that the lawyer is "Of Counsel or Counsel" for the firm. Formal Opinion 90-357 resolves this question by allowing "Of Counsel" to list their areas of specialty on the letterhead.

43. Arizona State Ethics Op. 87-24 (1987).

44. Iowa State Ethics Op. 87-12 (1987).

Other of Counsel Relationships

Having specifically approved four categories of "Of Counsel" relationships and prohibited four others, the committee in Formal Opinion 90-357 provided some guidance for several situations that it did not directly address but that may, nonetheless, satisfy the requirements necessary for using the "Of Counsel" designation. In reaching our conclusions whether the designation is or is not appropriate, we shall also consider the informal opinions and the state bar ethics decisions.

The Public Official

In 90-357, the committee's discussion of the use of the "Of Counsel" designation by former judges and public officials was in connection with second careers, that is, where the lawyer gave up a public position and title in order to practice law. As a practical matter, many lawyers want to maintain or develop a professional working arrangement with a law firm or individual lawyer while still in public office.

The more complicated case, and one not specifically addressed by 330 or 90-357, occurs where the lawyer wants to maintain an "Of Counsel" relationship with a firm or other lawyer while *currently* holding a public office. The questions raised by this scenario are twofold: first, do a public official's duties interfere with an ability to develop and maintain a continuing relationship with a firm or other lawyer to the extent required by 90-357? Second, would the person's current status as a public official create an unjustified expectation in third persons that an undue influence might be exerted to achieve a desired result?

The ABA informal opinions do not prohibit a public official from entering into an "Of Counsel" relationship; instead, permissive use of the term appears to turn on whether the lawyer has established a close, personal, and continuing relationship with the lawyer or law firm. ABA Informal Opinion 1134[45] addressed the question of whether the term could be used to describe a relationship between a firm and a United States senator. The senator wished to become affiliated with the firm as "Of Counsel." Because

45. ABA Comm. on Prof'l Ethics, Informal Op. 1134 (1969).

of his senatorial duties, his practice of law was limited. However, he did practice law whenever his duties permitted. Although he had an established continuing relationship with the firm, he had never been a member of the firm. The committee allowed the senator to be designated "Of Counsel," so long as he engaged in the practice of law, practiced in the offices of the firm, and rendered legal advice to the firm's clients.[46] By this view, in the case of the *current* office-holder, a continuing relationship exists and the "Of Counsel" designation is proper where his official duties allow sufficient time to engage in the practice of law with that firm.

Some states followed the requirements set out in the ABA Informal Opinion. Michigan prohibits current political officeholders from using the "Of Counsel" designation if the officeholder does not "actively and regularly engage in the practice of law with that firm."[47] Mississippi similarly prohibits public officeholders from using the "Of Counsel" designation to describe their relationship with law firms, unless they actively practice law in the firm or render legal advice to the clients of the firm.[48] The officeholder's past relationship with the firm even if he or she is a former partner with an established close relationship is irrelevant. If the former partner would not now be active in the practice of the firm, the designation is inappropriate, and the former partner can no longer be listed on the firm's letterhead.[49] Similarly, Maryland does not permit the name of a lawyer holding a public office to be used in the firm name, or in communications on its behalf, during the period in which the lawyer is not actively and regularly practicing with the firm.[50]

Other states have adopted a different standard. For example, in Illinois it is permissible for current officeholders to be designated as "Of Counsel" to a firm even if they do not actively and regularly practice law if their relationship with the law firm is sufficient to satisfy traditional notions of what constitutes "Of Counsel," such as for retired lawyers.[51]

46. *Id.*
47. Michigan State Bar Ethics Op. CI-886 (1983).
48. Mississippi State Bar Ethics Op. 66 (1981).
49. *Id.*
50. Maryland Rules of Professional Conduct R. 7.5(c).
51. Illinois State Bar Ethics Op. 817 (1982).

The Law Professor

Closely related to the situation of the public official is that of the full-time law professor who practices with a law firm on a part-time basis. As long as there is a close, continuing, and personal relationship between the firm and the law professor, there is no objection to the professor's being considered "Of Counsel" to the firm. A law school may restrict the extent of activity of a member of its full-time faculty; but more often than not, the law firm and the law school will find that the designation of a faculty member as "Of Counsel" to the firm will be to the advantage of both.

The Out-of-State Of Counsel

Several ABA informal opinions have held that it is not per se improper for a lawyer in one state to be "Of Counsel" to a lawyer or law firm in another state.[52] The primary questions addressed by these informal opinions is whether "Of Counsel" must be licensed to practice in the state where he or she is listed as "Of Counsel," and if not, whether the lawyer must list such jurisdictional limitations on the letterhead of the firm.[53]

The states have developed diverse and conflicting rules regarding out-of-state "Of Counsel." A number of states allow the term "Of Counsel" to be used to refer to out-of-state lawyers who have a close continuing relationship with a firm, so long as identification of such lawyers in an office of the firm indicate the jurisdictional limitations on those not licensed to practice in the jurisdiction where the office is located.[54] Other states favor a requirement that "Of Counsel" be admitted to practice in the state where the affiliated lawyer or firm is located. For example in North Carolina, an out-of-state lawyer may maintain an "Of Counsel" relationship with a firm located in North Carolina only if the lawyer is licensed to practice in North

52. ABA Comm. on Prof'l Ethics, Informal Ops. 83-1499 (1983), 1315 (1975), and 1173 (1971).

53. See Chapter 9.

54. *E.g.*, Alaska Rules of Prof'l Conduct R. 7.5(b) and (e); Michigan State Ethics Op. CI-1018 (1984); and Alabama Rules of Prof'l Conduct R. 7.5(b), which provides in part that "[a] firm with any lawyers not licensed to practice in Alabama must, if such lawyer's name appears on the firm's letterhead, state that the lawyer is not licensed to practice in Alabama."

Carolina.[55] The state of Washington requires "Of Counsel" to be an active member of the state bar association.[56]

In California, where law firms may be listed as "Of Counsel" to other lawyers or firms, a lawyer or law firm may list an out-of-state firm as "Of Counsel" even if none of the out-of-state firm's lawyers are licensed to practice in California, so long as the lawyer or law firm contemplating listing an out-of-state law firm as "Of Counsel" in California negates any impression that the firm is a California firm, that the firm employs lawyers licensed to practice in California (unless true), or that the firm is available for employment in California when it is not.[57] Language designed to clarify the status of the "Of Counsel" law firm (such as "A New York Law Firm") has been deemed to be sufficient to make clear to the public that the "Of Counsel" firm is not a California firm, and thus avoid confusing, deceiving, or misleading the public.[58]

Similarly, in New York and South Carolina, a lawyer may be designated "Of Counsel" to an in-state firm even though the lawyer is not admitted to practice in that state, provided that jurisdictional limitations are listed on the firm letterhead.[59]

Expense-Sharing Arrangements

Lawyers often enter into loose arrangements with other lawyers. Some of these arrangements may be for long-term sharing of over-head expenses. Or one lawyer may associate with another lawyer on a temporary basis,[60] particularly where the lawyer experiences a short-term increase in work. An older lawyer may, instead of fully retiring, enlarge his or her office to provide reduced rental space for a younger lawyer in return for that lawyer's promise to devote a fixed number of hours per week to the older lawyer's practice.

55. North Carolina Ethics Op. 34 (1988).

56. Washington State Bar Ethics Op. 178 (1984).

57. California Bus. & Prof. Code 6126; California State Bar Formal Op. 1986-88 (undated); *see also* Chapter 3 for a discussion of using the term to describe a relationship between law firms.

58. *Id.*

59. *See* New York Rules of Prof'l Conduct R. 7.5 (a) and (d); *see also* South Carolina Rules of Prof'l Conduct R. 7.5(b).

60. A. Wolfson, *State High Court Approves Temporary Lawyers With Restrictions*, Courier J. (Louisville, Ky.), Nov. 19, 1989, at B1.

Two or more solo practitioners, while otherwise maintaining complete autonomy, may agree to share office space and the expenses incurred in the practice of law. In all of these arrangements, the associated lawyers may share office space and expenses.

Can these office-sharing arrangements ever create an "Of Counsel" relationship? In general, the answer is no. The mere sharing of office space and expenses is insufficient to establish an "Of Counsel" relationship.[61] To be closely related for purposes of satisfying the first aspect of the core characteristic of the "Of Counsel" relationship, most states require that lawyers currently "practice together."[62] In Kansas, lawyers who once practiced together, but who now only share office space, may not designate each other as "Of Counsel" unless they intend to continue to work closely together.[63]

Liberalized Rules Governing Of Counsel Relationships

Although much of Formal Opinion 90-357 was devoted to a discussion of varying fact situations that may, or may not, give rise to an "Of Counsel" relationship, the opinion articulated a number of rules affecting all "Of Counsel" relationships. For the most part, these rules are less restrictive than those reflected in Formal Opinion 330 or the informal opinions of the ABA's ethics committee.

The Law Firm as Of Counsel

A good example of such liberalization is the change that now allows a law firm, as distinct from an individual lawyer, to be "Of Counsel" to another lawyer or law firm. In Informal Opinion 1173,[64] the committee relied on the literal language of DR 2-102(A)(4) of the Model Code and, in part, on a rule pertaining to law lists and legal directories found in DR 2-102(A) (6) (which

61. ABA Comm. on Ethics & Prof'l Responsibility, Informal Op. 84-1506 (1984); *see also* Washington State Rules of Prof'l Conduct R. 7.5(d) and Comment 2.

62. Kansas Rules of Prof'l Conduct R. 7.5(d) and Comment 2; Maine Rules of Prof'l Conduct R. 7.5(d) and Comment 2.

63. Kansas Rules of Prof'l Conduct R. 7.5(d) and Comment 2.

64. ABA Comm. on Prof'l Ethics, Informal Op. 1173 (1971), *aff'd*, ABA Comm. on Ethics & Prof'l Responsibility, Formal Op. 330 (1972).

was later deleted from the Model Code) in finding that a law firm located in one city could not be designated "Of Counsel" to a lawyer in another city. DR 2-102(A)(4) provides:

> A lawyer may be designated "Of Counsel" on a letterhead if he has a continuing relationship with a lawyer or law firm other than as a partner or associate.

The committee held that "the very omission of the words 'law firm' precludes a law firm from using the "Of Counsel" designation." The committee further held that, because "the practice of law is personal in nature and a law firm as such is never admitted to practice in any state," the phrase should not encompass law firms.[65]

The holding of Informal Opinion 1173 was later affirmed in Formal Opinion 330, but was subsequently overruled in part in Formal Opinion 84-351. Formal Opinion 84-351, which was written after several United States Supreme Court decisions expanded First Amendment protections for lawyer advertising,[66] acknowledged that there can be no per se bar against one firm being "Of Counsel" to another.[67] But the opinion stopped short of allowing the phrase "Of Counsel" to describe a continuing relationship between law firms. Instead, the committee authorized the terms "associated" or "affiliated" to describe such a relationship.[68] An "affiliated" or "associated" law firm, the committee wrote, must be available to the other firm and its clients for consultation and advice, much as the individual "Of Counsel" is.[69] The committee, in fact, stated:

---

65. ABA Informal Op. 1173.

66. *In re* R.M.J., 455 U.S. 191 (1982); Bates v. Arizona State Bar Ass'n, 433 U.S. 350 (1977). After these decisions, Model Code provisions DR 2-101 through DR 2-105 were substantially revised. DR 2-102(A)(4) was retained, but DR 2-102(A)(6) was deleted. The Model Rules, adopted after R.M.J., prohibit any "false or misleading communication about the lawyer or the lawyer's services." *See* Model Rules of Prof'l Conduct, R. 7.1 and 7.5.

67. ABA Comm. on Prof'l Ethics, Formal Op. 84-351 (1984).

68. *Id.*

69. *Id.*

> The type of relationship that is implied by designating another firm as "affiliated" or "associated" is analogous to the ongoing relationship that is required by Model Code DR 2-102(A)(4) when using the designation "Of Counsel" as amplified by the guidelines in Formal Opinion 330 and Informal Opinion 1315.[70]

Some states still adhere to the traditional rule and do not recognize the use of the "Of Counsel" designation to describe a law firm's relationship with another law firm.[71] But other states have adopted rules or issued opinions similar to the view set forth in ABA Formal Opinion 90-357.[72]

California and New York are among the states that allow law firms to use the phrase "Of Counsel" to describe their relationship.[73] Massachusetts has allowed a professional corporation of lawyers to be "Of Counsel" to another firm or lawyer.[74] Michigan allows law firms to be designated as "Of Counsel" to other lawyers or law firms whether located in Michigan or out-of-state.[75]

Other states recognize that a continuing relationship can exist between law firms, but nonetheless do not allow the phrase "Of Counsel" to describe that relationship. The District of Columbia prohibits the use of the "Of Counsel" designation to describe a relationship between law firms.[76] Such states permit firms to use only the terms "associated" or "affiliated" for this purpose.

Formal Opinion 90-357 overruled all prior ABA opinions that prevented a law firm from being "Of Counsel" to another law firm or lawyer. In the committee's words:

---

70. *Id.*

71. Iowa Rules of Prof'l Conduct R. 32:7.5(a)(4).

72. New York Rules of Prof'l Conduct R. 7.5(a)(4); Wisconsin Ethics Opinion E-93-1; Arizona Rules of Prof'l Conduct ER 7.5 Comment 3; California Rules of Prof'l Conduct R. 1-400 Standard 8; Kentucky Ethics Op. 311 (1986); Massachusetts State Bar Ethics Op. 82-10 (1982); Op. No. RI-102, State Bar of Michigan, Standing Comm. on Prof'l & Judicial Ethics (1991).

73. California State Bar Formal Op. 1986-88 (undated); New York City Ethics Op. 1995-8 (1995).

74. Massachusetts State Ethics Op. 82-10 (1982).

75. Op. No. RI-102, State Bar of Michigan, Standing Comm. on Prof'l & Judicial Ethics (1991).

76. District of Columbia Ethics Ops. 192 (1988) and 197 (1989).

> The Committee has also previously held that *a firm* cannot be of counsel to another lawyer or law firm, *see* Informal Opinion 1173, Formal Opinion 330. The reasoning here was that the term connotes an individual rather than a firm. This may be still so as a matter of current usage, but semantics aside, the Committee's prior opinions do not suggest, and the Committee does not now perceive, any reason of [sic] policy why a firm should not be of counsel to another firm. Moreover, the Committee held in Formal Opinion 84-351 (1984) that two law firms could ethically present themselves as "affiliated" or "associated" with each other, and in Informal Opinion 1315 (1975), the Committee gave its approval to arrangements whereby two firms effectively became "of counsel" to each other, by each designating a partner of the other firm as "of counsel" to itself. As with multiple of counsel relationships of a single lawyer, the relationships between firms addressed in Formal Opinion 84-351 and Informal Opinion 1315 would of course entail complete reciprocal attribution of the disqualifications of all lawyers in each firm.[77]

Allowing law firms to serve as "Of Counsel" to one another was a welcome change that caused some state bar ethics committees to reconsider their positions. For states that have not yet taken a position on this point, 90-357 represents the sounder view from a policy standpoint, as long as law firms are aware of the attribution and disqualification rules inherent in these arrangements.[78]

Multiple Of Counsel Relationships

Another example of the liberalization of the "Of Counsel" rules in Formal Opinion 90-357 is the change with respect to a lawyer (or law firm) serving as "Of Counsel" to multiple firms or lawyers. Formal Opinion 330 held that it was improper for a lawyer to be "Of Counsel" to more than two law firms. This view was first expressed in ABA Informal Opinion 1173,[79]

77. ABA Formal Op. 90-357, at 5–6.
78. *See* Chapters 7 and 8.
79. ABA Informal Op. 1173 (1971).

in which the committee stated:

> [I]t is not proper, in our opinion, for any lawyer or law firm to be designated "Of Counsel" to more than one lawyer or law firm . . . especially because the continuing relationship . . . connotes a close, daily, in-house association, free and clear of problems of conflict.

Informal Opinion 1189 affirmed the view that a lawyer cannot be "Of Counsel" to more than one lawyer or law firm.[80] These opinions were modified in the text of ABA Formal Opinion 330, which stated:

> While it would be highly unusual for a lawyer to be able to maintain simultaneously with two law firms the close, personal relationship indicated by the term "Of Counsel," it may not be impossible for such a situation to exist. It is obviously impossible, however, for one to maintain such a relationship with more than two law firms.[81]

The headnote of Formal Opinion 330 concluded that a lawyer could not be "Of Counsel" to more than two law firms. Although the headnote did not precisely comport with the view that the committee expressed in the text, many states held that a lawyer may be "Of Counsel" to no more than two firms.[82] At least one state set a limit of one.[83]

Although at some point the number of "Of Counsel" relationships may be too great to maintain the close relationship necessary for use of the designation, the arbitrary limit set by the committee that issued 330 was not warranted. In allowing a lawyer or law firm to be "Of Counsel" to multiple lawyers or law firms, the committee that wrote 90-357 recognized that it was quite possible to maintain a continuing relationship with multiple law firms. In adopting this more liberal approach, the committee stated:

---

80. ABA Informal Op. 1189 (1971).

81. ABA Comm. on Ethics & Prof'l Responsibility, Formal Op. 330 (1972).

82. Connecticut State Ethics Op. 88-13 (1988) (a lawyer who is designated "Of Counsel" at two different law firms may use his name and designation on the letterhead of each firm); Texas State Ethics Op. 402 (1982).

83. Iowa State Ethics Op. 87-9 (1987) (lawyers may not hold themselves out as "Of Counsel" to more than one firm located in different towns in the state).

> [T]he Committee's initial view, expressed in Informal Opinion 1173, was that a lawyer could not be of counsel to more than a single firm; and this was modified in Formal Opinion 330 to set a limit of two firms. On further consideration, the Committee finds the conclusion it reached on this subject in Formal Opinion 330 to be a doubtful one. The proposition that it is not possible for a lawyer to have a "close, regular, personal relationship" with more than two lawyers or law firms is not a self-evident one. A lawyer can surely have a close, regular, personal relationship with more than two clients; and the Committee sees no reason why the same cannot be true with more than two law firms. There is, to be sure, some point at which the number of relationships would be too great for any of them to have the necessary qualities of closeness and regularity, and that number may not be much beyond two, but the controlling criterion is "close and regular" relationships, not a particular number.[84]

Formal Opinion 90-357 caused some state ethics committees to reconsider their prior positions with respect to multiple "Of Counsel" relationships. In Ohio, for example, a retired lawyer may serve as "Of Counsel" to different law firms formed by the retired lawyer's former partners.[85] The Board of Commissioners on Grievances and Discipline of the Supreme Court of Ohio ruled:

> The ABA view is that an attorney may be "of counsel" to more than one firm. In Formal Opinion 90-357 (1990) the ABA committee stated that "[a] lawyer can surely have a close, regular, personal relationship with more than two clients; and the Committee sees no reason why the same cannot be true with more than two law firms." That advice is a departure from its earlier views in Formal Op. 330 (1972) that an attorney may be "of counsel" to only two firms and in Formal

84. ABA Formal Op. 90-357, at 5.

85. Op. No. 97-2, Supreme Court of Ohio, Bd. of Commissioners on Grievances & Discipline (Apr. 11, 1997).

Op. 1173 (1971) that an attorney may not be "of counsel" to more than a single firm.

In Michigan, a lawyer may be designated "Of Counsel" to one or more lawyers or law firms whether in Michigan or out of state.[86]

Of Counsel's Name in the Firm's Name

Among the states, opinions diverge as to whether the "Of Counsel" attorney's name can be included in the firm's name. Part of the desire to use an "Of Counsel" attorney's name in the firm's name may be attributed to the goodwill value associated with the "Of Counsel" attorney's name. But when the "Of Counsel" attorney's name is included in the firm's name, there is a likelihood that third persons will misconstrue the true nature of the "Of Counsel" attorney's relationship and the accompanying responsibilities among the lawyers.

Against this backdrop, many states have developed specific guidelines concerning firm names and "Of Counsel" attorneys, in many cases adopting Model Rule 7.5 (Firm Names And Letterheads) or a variation thereof.[87]

Some states allow the firm to include the "Of Counsel" attorney's name in the firm's name, at least where the "Of Counsel" attorney is a former name partner.[88] The Vermont Ethics Committee justified the use of the former partner's name in the firm's name, reasoning that as long as the departing lawyer maintains a close relationship with the firm, the public is not misled about the identity of the firm or the responsibilities of its principals.[89] But one state even allows the firm to include in the firm name the name of a newly associated "Of Counsel" attorney, at least where the law firm is composed of one full-time lawyer and one "Of Counsel" attorney who is available for consultation on a regular basis, and there is a mutual sharing of responsibility.[90]

---

86. Op. No. RI-102, State Bar of Michigan, Standing Comm. on Prof'l & Judicial Ethics (Oct. 1, 1991).

87. See Appendix J, Model Rule 7.5 and the state-by-state variations.

88. Vermont State Ethics Op. 83-7 (undated).

89. Vermont State Ethics Op. 83-7 (undated).

90. Maine State Ethics Op. 86 (1988).

Other states do not allow the firm name to include the "Of Counsel" attorney's name, even though the "Of Counsel" attorney may have at one time been a partner in the firm, unless there remains a close and continuing relationship between the lawyer and the firm.[91] The Philadelphia Ethics Committee has determined that including the "Of Counsel" attorney's name in the firm's name would be misleading, since it would connote partnership, with all the accompanying rights and responsibilities.[92]

Formal Opinion 330 did not address whether the "Of Counsel" attorney's name could ethically be included in the firm's name. Formal Opinion 90-357 allows the "Of Counsel" attorney's name to be included in the firm's name in limited circumstances.[93] Under 90-357, two different results occur when the firm to which the lawyer is "Of Counsel" wants to include his or her name in the firm's name. The committee distinguished the familiar situation that occurs when a name partner of the firm retires from active practice and thereafter assumes an "Of Counsel" position with the same firm. The second situation occurs when the parties have only recently become affiliated, but the firm or individual lawyer wants to include the "Of Counsel" attorney's name in the firm's name. The committee noted that both of these situations raise the same issue: whether including the "Of Counsel" attorney's name in the firm's name entails implicit misrepresentations of the sort that would mislead the public. In the case of a new or recent affiliation, "there is no escaping an implication that a name in the new firm name implies that the lawyer is a partner in the firm, with fully shared responsibility for its work."[94] But there is no similar misrepresentation in the use of a retired partner's name in the firm name "while the same partner is "Of Counsel," where the firm name is long-established and well-recognized."[95]

Aside from the ethical mandates imposed by the states and the ABA committee, "Of Counsel" attorneys should exercise careful consideration before allowing his or her name to be included in the firm's name. Inclusion in the firm's name may connote partnership status, with vicarious liability to the

91. Michigan Ethics Op. CI-1001(1984).
92. Philadelphia Ethics Op. 88-31 (1988).
93. *See* Chapter 3.
94. ABA Comm. on Ethics & Prof'l Responsibility, Formal Op. 90-357, at 6 (1990).
95. *Id.*

"Of Counsel" attorney for torts committed by other members of the firm.[96] Although 90-357 allows the "Of Counsel" attorney's name to be included in the firm's name in limited circumstances, in footnote 11 of the opinion the committee refused to express a view concerning any possible exposure to general partnership liability for malpractice when the name of the "Of Counsel" attorney is included in the firm's name.

Summary

"Of Counsel" arrangements take a variety of forms. Formal Opinion 90-357 discarded the approach of Formal Opinion 330, which distinguished two forms of "Of Counsel" arrangements: (1) where the lawyer practices in the same office as the other lawyer or firm and (2) where the lawyer does not practice in the same office but is in regular and frequent contact with the other lawyer or firm. Although a close, personal, and continuing relationship is still essential, 90-357 is far less restrictive than 330. Under 90-357, four categories of "Of Counsel" relationships are specifically recognized: the part-time practitioner, the retired partner, the probationary partner, and the senior attorney. Four other categories are specifically prohibited: the lawyer on a single case, the forwarder or receiver of legal business, the occasional collaborator, and the outside consultant. Between these two groups lie countless other situations more or less comparable to one or the other of the two extremes.

Under 330, if the "Of Counsel" attorney was a retired partner, he or she was deemed to have a close association with the lawyer or firm. This lawyer did not need to practice *in the offices* of the lawyer or firm. But, to satisfy the notion of a "continuing" relationship, there was an implied requirement to remain active in the practice of law and to remain in *daily contact* with the lawyer or firm. While 90-357 removed any requirement of daily contact with the law firm or lawyer, it retained a requirement of a continuing relationship.

---

96. *See generally* Chapter 9.

Formal Opinion 90-357 permits the "Of Counsel" designation to be used by current political officeholders and other public officials, provided they actively practice law in the same offices as the lawyer or firm, regardless of their prior affiliation with the firm. Some states follow the view of the ABA opinions; others do not. In the latter jurisdictions, the "Of Counsel" attorney need not actively engage in the practice of law with the firm, provided the parties' past relationship satisfies the requirement of a continuing relationship.

Some arrangements contemplate that "Of Counsel" attorneys will not practice law in the same office as the lawyer or firm. An out-of-state lawyer, a lawyer who acts as a consultant to one firm while maintaining a full-time position with a corporation or other law firm, or a lawyer who engages in multiple "Of Counsel" relationships cannot be physically present on a full-time basis in the office of the lawyer or firm with which he or she is affiliated as "Of Counsel." Despite this, 90-357 would seem to allow these relationships, where they might have been prohibited under 330. "Of Counsel" attorneys must be available to the lawyer or firm on a frequent, ongoing, and continual basis. Consultation on a single case is insufficient to establish an "Of Counsel" relationship, even where the consultant is a former partner of the firm. Some state bars follow the mandates established by the ABA; others are more liberal.

Some arrangements can never be designated "Of Counsel" relationships. The sharing of office space and expenses is insufficient to satisfy the requirement of a continuing relationship. The lawyer who merely refers or forwards clients to another lawyer or firm cannot be considered "Of Counsel" to that lawyer or firm.

Formal Opinion 90-357 permits law firms to use the "Of Counsel" designation. It also permits a lawyer to be "Of Counsel" to more than two law firms. Probationary partners and senior attorneys who normally have an employee relationship with the firm are now recognized as appropriate candidates for the "Of Counsel" designation.

Checklists for Issue Spotting

Retired Partners

(1) To what extent does the retired partner maintain a continuing relationship with the other lawyer or law firm?

   a. Is the retired partner active in the practice of law, or is the retiree merely maintaining an office with the firm to have a place to go? Does the retired partner maintain an independent client base? Does the "Of Counsel" agreement require the retired partner to perform certain duties for the firm or its clients? Is the retired partner available to the firm or its clients for consultation and advice on an ongoing basis?

(2) Does the retired partner's name appear in the firm's name? Is the firm's name "long-established and well-recognized"?

Former Public Officials

(1) Is the former public official available for consultation and advice?

(2) Does the firm specify the "Of Counsel" attorney's former status on its letterhead? If so, does the state in which the firm is located allow the former status to be listed on business communications? If the state does allow it, does it require that the public official's retired status be included on the communication?

Public Officials

(1) Is the public official currently engaged in the "practice of law"? Does the official render legal advice to clients of the other lawyer or firm? If not, is he or she a former partner of the firm?

(2) Does the public official practice in the offices of the firm or other lawyer?

The Of Counsel as Consultant

(1) Is the "Of Counsel" attorney or firm available only for consultation? If so, is the "Of Counsel" attorney or firm a member or component part of the law office?

(2) Is the "Of Counsel" attorney or firm frequently available for consultation on an ongoing basis? Is the relationship between the "Of Counsel" attorney or firm and the firm limited to one particular case?

Out-of-State Of Counsel

(1) Is the "Of Counsel" attorney or firm admitted to practice in the state in which the other lawyer or law firm is located? Does that state require that out-of-state "Of Counsel" be admitted to practice there before being listed on the firm's or other lawyer's business communications?

(2) If the state allows out-of-state "Of Counsel" to be listed on business communications, does the state require that "Of Counsel" attorney's jurisdictional limitations be listed?

Expense-Sharing Arrangements

Is the relationship between the lawyers limited to the sharing of an office and expenses? Do the lawyers "practice law" together?

Law Firms as Of Counsel

Does the state, or states, in which the law firm is located allow firms to be listed as "Of Counsel" to each other? If not, does it allow firms to be listed as "associated" or "affiliated" with each other?

Forwarder-Receiver of Legal Business

(1) Is the relationship between the lawyer and the law firm or other lawyer limited to the referral of prospective clients?

(2) Alternatively, is the relationship between the parties such that the lawyer involved is performing professional service for the law firm or other lawyer, rather than for the client?

Multiple Of Counsel Relationships

(1) Does the state in which the "Of Counsel" attorney or firm practices law allow multiple "Of Counsel" relationships? If so, are there any geographical limitations?

(2) If the state permits multiple "Of Counsel" attorney or firm relationships, is it wise for the "Of Counsel" attorney or firm and the other

law firm or other lawyer to enter into a particular relationship in light of potential conflicts and vicarious liability?

Of Counsel's Name in the Firm's Name

(1) Is the "Of Counsel" attorney's name included in the firm's name?

(2) If so, does the state in which the firm is located allow the name of the "Of Counsel" attorney to be included in the firm's name? Does the state allow the firm's name to include the "Of Counsel" attorney's name only if the "Of Counsel" attorney was formerly a partner of the firm?

CHAPTER 5

LEGAL RELATIONSHIPS

Many firms now identify some lawyers by terms such as "special counsel," "senior counsel," "resident counsel," or simply "counsel." These terms counter the prevailing notion that the "Of Counsel" attorney is a retired partner.[1] This change in language also indicates that many "Of Counsel" attorneys and firms serve in functions other than the traditional ones of consultation and advice. They may resemble an employee of the firm, performing specialized tasks such as coordinating the firm's in-house training program or carrying a workload similar to that of an associate in the firm.[2] Or, if they are treated as a probationary partner-to-be, they may resemble a partner and be on the firm's "partnership track."

Under the prior Formal Opinion 330, an "Of Counsel" attorney could not be used to describe an employee of the firm. While Formal Opinion 90-357 made it clear that "Of Counsel" can never be used to describe a partner or associate, the ABA Committee on Ethics and Professional Responsibility recognized that some "Of Counsel" relationships, such as probationary partners-to-be and senior attorneys, involve an employer-employee relationship. In these limited situations, an "Of Counsel" attorney may have employee status without interfering with his or her ability to use the designation.

---

1. Faust, *The New "Of-Counsel": Increasing Flexibility in Law Firm Careers*, Docket Call, Winter 2008.
2. *Id.*

Formal Opinion 90-357 also recognized that the "Of Counsel" designation is appropriately used for various kinds of specialty counsel:

> [a]lthough "of counsel" appears to be most frequently used among the various titles employing the term "counsel," it is by no means the only use of that term to indicate a relationship between a lawyer and a law firm. Other such titles include the single word "counsel," and the terms "special counsel," "tax [or other specialty] counsel," and "senior counsel." It is the Committee's view that, whatever the connotative differences evoked by these variants of the title "counsel," they all share the central, and defining, characteristic of the relationship that is denoted by the term "of counsel," and so should all be understood to be covered by the present opinion.[3] (Footnotes omitted.)

Although the committee withdrew Formal Opinion 330 when it issued Formal Opinion 90-357, it continued to rely on it for purposes of defining the "core characteristic" of the "Of Counsel" relationship:

That core characteristic properly denoted by the title "counsel" is, as stated in Formal Opinion 330, a "close, regular, personal relationship"; but a relationship which is neither that of a partner (or its equivalent, a principal of a professional corporation), with the shared liability and/ or managerial responsibility implied by that term; nor, on the other hand, the status ordinarily conveyed by the term "associate," which is to say a junior non-partner lawyer, regularly employed by the firm.[4] (Footnotes omitted.)

The fact that the Of Counsel relationship may be analogous to an employee, partner, or outside-consultant relationship raises significant issues. Especially important is the area of vicarious liability for malpractice in which third parties try to hold "Of Counsel" liable for the unlawful acts of the firm, or the firm for the unlawful acts of "Of Counsel." Also, classification of their relationship may determine whether "Of Counsel" can be included as an employee of the firm in the firm's health insurance coverage.

---

3. ABA Comm. on Ethics & Prof'l Responsibility, Formal Op. 90-357, at 3 (1990).
4. *Id.* at 4–5.

To determine whether a lawyer can be designated as "Of Counsel," the relationship must be contrasted with these other legal relationships. This task may prove difficult, since all of these varying relationships may, and often do, contain common and overlapping characteristics, and one might reach different conclusions with respect to the appropriate classification for different purposes. Yet each relationship contains essential elements or core criteria that distinguish it from other legal relationships.

In establishing an "Of Counsel" relationship, the firm must identify and contrast the essential elements of these various relationships. This chapter examines the basic core criteria necessary to the relationships of partner, associate, and outside consultant, and contrasts these with the requirements needed to establish a permissible "Of Counsel" relationship.

Of Counsel Contrasted with Partner

Under Formal Opinion 90-357, the "Of Counsel" relationship is not that of a partnership.[5] This requirement stems from one clause found in the Model Code of Professional Responsibility, which states:

> A lawyer may be designated "of counsel" on a letterhead if he has a continuing relationship with a lawyer or law firm, other than as partner or associate.[6]

This Model Code provision addressed the concern that some professional arrangements might be misleading to the public. Lawyers should not explicitly or implicitly hold themselves out as being partners if they are not in fact partners.[7] Explicit misrepresentation occurs when a lawyer expressly states that he or she is a partner in the firm if in fact he or she is not. Implicit misrepresentation arises when and "Of Counsel" attorney's status is not

5. *Id.*

6. ABA MODEL CODE OF PROF'L RESPONSIBILITY [hereinafter MODEL CODE] DR 2-102(A)(4) (1983). There is no counterpart to DR 2-102(A) in the Model Rules.

7. MODEL CODE EC 2-13 (1983); *see also* MODEL RULES OF PROF'L CONDUCT, Rules 7.1 and 7.5.

properly indicated in professional listings, letterheads, or professional cards, or where the "Of Counsel" attorney's name is included in the firm name. Misrepresentation also arises where the relationship itself contains traits common to a partnership, such as the "Of Counsel" attorney's assumption of management responsibilities or sharing in firm profits. As to the latter concern, the earlier Formal Opinion 330 stated:

> It would be misleading to refer to a lawyer who shares in the profits and losses and general responsibility of a firm as being "Of Counsel."[8]

The "Of Counsel" designation is improper where the parties' outward acts manifest or imply that a partnership relationship exists,[9] or where the relationship itself contains characteristics essential to a partnership.[10] For example, one of the essential elements of a partnership is the partner's right to share in the profits of the business. When there is a sharing of profits coupled with other elements essential to a partnership, most courts would conclude that a true partnership relation exists, regardless of the words chosen by the parties to describe it. Thus, an "Of Counsel" attorney who shares in the profits of the firm clearly risks vicarious liability as a partner.

Even if the relationship does not contain any of the common elements of a partnership, caution must be taken so that an implied partnership does not arise. There are many ways in which a non-partner might be held out as a partner. The non-partner, or other persons in the business with the consent of the non-partner, might be referred to as a partner. The non-partner's name might be included in the firm's name, letterheads, signs, and other advertisements, or in pleadings, motions, and appearances.

---

8. ABA Comm. on Ethics & Prof'l Responsibility, Formal Op. 330 (1972); *see also* Arizona State Bar Ethics Op. 81-1 (1981); California State Bar Ethics Op. 1986-88 (1987); Michigan State Bar Ethics Op. CI-617 (1981); Washington State Bar Ethics Op. 178 (1984).

9. The elements of an implied partnership are (1) representations, either public or private, that tend to imply the existence of a partnership; and (2) reasonable reliance on the representation by the person seeking enforcement.

10. These elements include (1) the intention to form a partnership; (2) an agreement to carry out a business for profit; (3) a sharing of profits and losses; (4) co-ownership of the business; and (5) general responsibility through joint management and control of the business. Unif. Partnership Act § 202 (1997), enacted into law by thirty-seven states.

The "Of Counsel" relationship need not be created through a written agreement, but reducing the arrangement to writing is strongly recommended. A good written agreement will define the rights and duties of the parties and raise a rebuttable presumption of their intention to create an "Of Counsel" relationship, rather than a partnership. It should be possible for the drafters to create an agreement that will satisfy both the "Of Counsel" attorney and the law firm without causing the "Of Counsel" attorney to be treated as a partner.

The drafters should eliminate any of the identifying traits of partnership. For example, the "Of Counsel" attorney or firm should not share in the profits of the firm. Nor should the agreement give the "Of Counsel" attorney or firm any of the duties and responsibilities of a partner, such as the authority to manage or control the business. Such responsibilities could cause the "Of Counsel" to be personally liable for the torts of the firm. In one such sample agreement, for example, the "Of Counsel" attorney appears to assume the duties of a partner:

> [Of Counsel] shall perform legal services on behalf of the Firm and, except as otherwise provided herein, shall, with respect to the rendering of legal services, have all of the duties and responsibilities *as if he were a partner of the Firm* as provided in [the Firm Partnership Agreement]. (Emphasis added.)

That same sample agreement contains other indicia of a partnership, instead of an "Of Counsel" relationship between the parties:

> In consideration of the services performed by [Of Counsel], the Firm shall pay to [Of Counsel] an amount equal to the amount to which [Of Counsel] would be entitled, pursuant to provisions of [the Firm Partnership Agreement], if he were a partner of the Firm. . . .

Even though the agreement states an intent to establish the lawyer's status as "Of Counsel," the specific terms of the agreement could be used as evidence that a partnership relationship actually existed between the parties.

Instead, the agreement should clearly negate any elements of a partnership relationship. The following provision is commonly used to achieve this result:

> As [Of Counsel], Lawyer is not required to contribute capital to the Firm, nor will he have any formal voting rights at any Partnership meetings. Otherwise, he will be welcome to participate in discussions and meetings of the Firm and of the Partnership, except as to Partnership meetings or portions of meetings where only Equity Partners may participate. . . . Lawyer will not share in or be liable for any profits or losses of the Firm, including any malpractice liability not arising from his acts.[11]

To avoid liability as an implied partner, the "Of Counsel" attorney or firm should not present to the public as a partner of that firm. The name of an "Of Counsel" attorney who is not a former partner should not be included in the firm's name,[12] and the "Of Counsel" status should be clearly communicated in the firm letterhead,[13] professional announcement cards, shingles, and directories or law lists such as the Martindale-Hubbell directory.[14] The agreement should contain provisions stating the parties' intention to list the lawyer as "Of Counsel." A common provision would state:

> During the term of this agreement, the Corporation shall, at its sole expense, cause [Of Counsel's] name to be listed as "Of Counsel" on the Corporation's stationery, in the Martindale-Hubbell Directory,

---

11. Appendix A § 6.

12. ABA Comm. on Ethics & Prof'l Responsibility, Formal Op. 90-357, at 7 (1990).

13. *Id.* For ethical rules and opinions relating to the "Of Counsel" designation in letterheads and other advertising, *see* Model Rules of Prof'l Conduct, R. 7.1 and 7.5, and Model Code of Prof'l Responsibility DR 2-102(A)(4), which states in part:

> A letterhead of a law firm may also give the names of members and associates, and names and dates relating to deceased and retired members. A lawyer may be designated "Of Counsel" on a letterhead if he has a continuing relationship with a lawyer or law firm, other than as a partner or associate.

See also ABA Comm. on Ethics & Prof'l Responsibility, Formal Op. 90-357, at 6 (1990), and ABA Comm. on Ethics & Prof'l Responsibility, Formal Op. 84-351 (1984) (holding that letterhead designation of "affiliated" or "associated" law firms is not prohibited).

14. Missan v. Schoenfeld, 465 N.Y.S.2d 706, 95 A.D.2d 198 (1983).

> [state and county] Bar directories, telephone directories and in other listings or directories, in which the Corporation may from time to time list its name and the names of its members and associates of the Corporation.[15]

In addition, the "Of Counsel" status should be clearly set out in pleadings, memoranda, opinion letters, and court appearances, although the designation as used in those contexts does not have the same significance as when the designation is used on the firm's letterhead.[16]

Of Counsel Contrasted with Associate

Formal Opinion 90-357 made it clear that the "Of Counsel" designation indicates a continuing relationship with a lawyer or law firm that is neither that of a partner nor that of an associate. An associate is usually described as a regular full-time non-partner lawyer employee of the firm.[17] The term "associate" has acquired a special significance within law firms, as distinct from the firm's other lawyer-employees. Indeed, 90-357 states, "[T]he status ordinarily conveyed by the term 'associate,'. . . is to say a junior non-partner lawyer, regularly employed by the firm."[18]

A generation ago, law firms classified lawyers within the firm as partners or associates. Associates were lawyers who aspired to become partners of the firm. But with the many changes that have affected the law practice in the last three decades, law firms today often have different classes of partners. Two tiers of partners are sometimes established for management and control. Different arrangements for lawyer-employees have also been created, depending upon the objectives of the lawyer and the firm. Some lawyers are hired or promoted into a permanent non-partner position and

15. Appendix C § 12.

16. ABA Formal Op. 90-357, at 5.

17. *In re* Sussman, 241 Or. 246, 405 P.2d 355 (1965). *Webster's New Collegiate Dictionary* (1981) defines "associate" as "a fellow worker, partner, colleague." As an adjective, it is defined as: "1: closely connected with another, 2: closely related esp. in the mind, 3: having secondary or subordinate status." ABA Formal Op. 84-351, at 4, n.6 (1984).

18. ABA Formal Op. 90-357, at 5.

given such titles as "resident counsel," "senior attorney," "special counsel," or just "counsel." The relatively simple structure of a law firm with just two classes of lawyers partners and associates — is now confined to the smaller firms. Thus, although associates are employees, not all employees of a law firm are "associates."

Formal Opinion 90-357 permits an employer-employee relationship in two specific types of "Of Counsel" arrangements: (1) where the lawyer is a probationary partner-to-be; and (2) where the term designates a permanent status between those of partner and associate. Whether the committee permits elements of the employer-employee relationship to exist in other "Of Counsel" relationships is not clear from the wording of the opinion. However, the appropriateness of the "Of Counsel" designation is not determined by the method of compensation or whether the "Of Counsel" is characterized as an employee versus independent contractor.

Of Counsel as Employee or Independent Contractor

Many persons find that their legal relationships with others are enhanced if they are considered to be "independent contractors" rather than "employees." The law of agency developed primarily in the nineteenth century in response to the demands of the industrial revolution. Before that time, the laborer (artisan) supplied the necessary tools, worked independently, trained apprentices, and so forth. Then the law affecting the status of independent contractors was overshadowed by the development of the concept of the corporate entity, the doctrine of *respondeat superior*, the doctrine of apparent authority, and many other legal concepts that responded to the problems created by the growth of a capitalist society.

Today there are many advantages in being treated as an employee. Many firms provide their lawyer-employees with such fringe benefits as individual liability coverage, hospital and major medical insurance, and pension benefits. The firm also shares the responsibility of paying an employee's Social Security taxes.[19] But there are also distinct disadvantages. As an

19. See the discussion of income taxation later in this chapter.

employer, the firm can exercise considerable control and supervision over the "Of Counsel" attorney's services. The firm may require the "Of Counsel" attorney to perform a minimum number of hours per week or month. Or it may prohibit the "Of Counsel" attorney from performing legal services outside the firm.

Likewise, there are advantages and disadvantages in being treated as an independent contractor rather than an employee. For example, an independent contractor retains a greater amount of freedom. A lawyer in such an arrangement can devote any number of hours to the firm and use the balance to work independently. Although the independent contractor pays the full amount of Social Security taxes, there are tax advantages in this arrangement.[20] By reporting income on Schedule C of Form 1040, an independent contractor has the advantage of deducting all business expenses before calculating adjusted gross income and therefore avoids the two percent floor for deductions that might otherwise have to be itemized as miscellaneous deductions. The disadvantages of being treated as an independent contractor include the exclusion from the firm's employee benefits, such as medical and disability insurance and pension and profit-sharing plans.[21]

The factors that determine whether a particular relationship constitutes an employer-employee (that is, master-servant) or independent-contractor relationship are discussed on the Internal Revenue Service website to help employers determined whether they are required to characterize a worker as an employee and withhold income taxes, withhold and pay Social Security and Medicare taxes, and pay unemployment tax on wages (employers do not generally have to withhold or pay any taxes on payments to independent contractors). The IRS provides the following guidelines:

> In determining whether the person providing service is an employee or an independent contractor, all information that provides evidence of the degree of control and independence must be considered.
>
> **Common Law Rules**

20. See the discussion of income taxation later in this chapter.

21. For more complete discussion of the problem of the independent contractor, *see* Chapter 10.

Facts that provide evidence of the degree of control and independence fall into three categories:

> **Behavioral:** Does the company control or have the right to control what the worker does and how the worker does his or her job?
> **Financial:** Are the business aspects of the worker's job controlled by the payer? (these include things like how worker is paid, whether expenses are reimbursed, who provides tools/supplies, etc.)
> **Type of Relationship:** Are there written contracts or employee type benefits (i.e. pension plan, insurance, vacation pay, etc.)? Will the relationship continue and is the work performed a key aspect of the business?

> Businesses must weigh all these factors when determining whether a worker is an employee or independent contractor. Some factors may indicate that the worker is an employee, while other factors indicate that the worker is an independent contractor. There is no "magic" or set number of factors that "makes" the worker an employee or an independent contractor, and no one factor stands alone in making this determination. Also, factors which are relevant in one situation may not be relevant in another.
>
> The keys are to look at the entire relationship, consider the degree or extent of the right to direct and control, and finally, to document each of the factors used in coming up with the determination. [22]

When drafting a particular agreement with respect to the employer-employee or the independent-contractor relationship, the drafter should characterize the relationship by using as many of these factors as possible that point in the desired direction. If enough factors indicate an employer-employee or

22. www.irs.gov/Businesses/Small-Businesses-&-Self-Employed/Independent-Contractor-%28Self-Employed%29-or-Employee%3F (last visited Nov. 17, 2012).

independent-contractor relationship, it is immaterial how the parties designate it. In *Mutual of Omaha Insurance Co. v. Chadwell*,[23] the estate of a deceased "Of Counsel" lawyer claimed benefits under the firm's accident insurance policy by attempting to characterize the "Of Counsel" attorney as an employee of the firm.[24] Upon his retirement from the partnership, the lawyer had agreed to continue with the firm on an "Of Counsel" basis. In return, the firm agreed to compensate him for past services. In addition, it provided him with office space and group insurance.[25] But the "Of Counsel" agreement specified no duties expected of the lawyer in return. This indicated a lack of control over the lawyer. The court found that the lawyer was not an employee, and the lawyer's estate could not claim any benefits under the accident policy.[26]

The "Of Counsel" relationship does not fit perfectly into the conventional categories of principal and agent or master and servant. Nor would it be desirable that it do so. On the contrary, one of the blessings of the "Of Counsel" relationship is that it can be whatever the contracting parties want it to be within the limits of Formal Opinion 90-357. Therefore, when drafting an "Of Counsel" agreement, the parties must be constantly aware of the pros and cons of the independent contractor versus the employee status and the factors that would dictate how the "Of Counsel" attorney may legally be characterized.

In three areas — contracts, torts, and taxation — the parties may find that they would prefer the relationship between the "Of Counsel" attorney and the contracting firm to be more closely related to the law of independent contractor than to the law of agency.

---

23. 426 F. Supp. 550 (N.D. Ill. 1977).

24. The insurance policy limited eligibility to "[a]ll lawyers associated with the Policyholder [law firm] as a partner or employee." *Chadwell*, 426 F. Supp. at 551.

25. *Id.* at 552.

26. *Id.*; *see also* Rev. Rul. 68-324, 1968-1 C.B. 433 (law firm exerted sufficient control over lawyer to establish employer-employee relationship when it furnished lawyer with a place to work and required him to work certain hours) and Technical Advice Memorandum 8013016 (Dec. 27, 1969) (lawyers were employees of law partnership, not independent contractors, even though they were not required to work a specified number of hours; because firm retained right to control lawyers' work, lawyers were not permitted to engage in practice of law in their spare time, and lawyers worked under direct supervision of law partner).

Of Counsel and Contractual Liability

In the area of contracts, much of the traditional doctrine of agency law centers around such doctrines as apparent authority, authority by estoppel, implied authority, and the like. The independent contractor will want to negate these relationships. A law firm might wish to be held responsible for the acts of an "Of Counsel" attorney only to the extent that the "Of Counsel" attorney's actions were specifically authorized by the firm. So long as third parties have adequate notice of the precise terms of the relationship between the firm and the "Of Counsel" attorney, there is no reason why the parties could not operate in this fashion. Similarly, by providing third parties with adequate notice of the extent of the "Of Counsel" attorney's authority — whether acting as an independent contractor or as an employee — "Of Counsel" attorneys may avoid potential liability for the firm's acts and omissions. The contractual relationship of the parties must be carefully spelled out in an agreement designed to protect both the "Of Counsel" attorney and the firm.

Of Counsel and Tort Liability

Whether "Of Counsel" is an employee or an independent contractor (instead of being a partner), he or she would normally not be responsible for the torts of partners or associates of the firm. In footnote 6 of Formal Opinion 90-357, the ethics committee avoided making any comment on an "Of Counsel" attorney's potential malpractice liability were his or her compensation tied to firm profits:

> The Committee expresses no view, however, on whether an arrangement under which the of counsel lawyer shares in the profits of the firm may expose the lawyer to malpractice liability as a partner.[27]

"Of Counsel" attorneys and firms must seek protection against the potential of malpractice liability through proper malpractice insurance. "Of Counsel" attorneys will expect the law firm to pay for this insurance and many "Of Counsel" agreements provide that the firm will be responsible for this

27. ABA Comm. on Ethics & Prof'l Responsibility, Formal Op. 90-357, n.6 (1990).

cost. Such an arrangement is appropriate whether the "Of Counsel" attorney is an independent contractor or an employee. A law firm would have a more difficult time limiting the scope of its liability for the tortious acts (for example, malpractice) of its "Of Counsel" and will want to ensure their coverage includes them.

Of Counsel and Income Taxation

Many lawyers have found that retaining independent contractor status is especially important in the tax area. The tax status of such a person is different from that of an employee. The independent contractor normally reports business income on Schedule C to Form 1040, Profit or Loss from Business (Sole Proprietorship). The use of this form, in contrast with treating the "Of Counsel" as an employee, presents some major tax advantages. Another option may be for the "Of Counsel" attorney to practice through his or her own professional corporation, or other form of entity, just as some partners in law firms do. The reasons cited for the use of an entity vary, but usually involve tax planning, such as the desire to avoid a lengthy Schedule C as part of the attorney's personal tax return based on statistics showing that corporations, LLCs, and partnerships are less likely to be audited.[28]

All of the independent contractor's business expenses may be taken "above the line" — that is, deducted in determining the taxpayer's adjusted gross income. By contrast, an employee determines adjusted gross income by deducting only those business deductions that are specifically listed in Section 62 of the Internal Revenue Code.

A lawyer filing Schedule C reports only the net profit (or loss) from the business, and all business deductions are taken on Schedule C. The lawyer can still choose to itemize deductions or take the standard deduction after the net profit from business has been included in adjusted gross income.

Since all business deductions are taken on Schedule C, the lawyer who reports income taxes in this fashion need not be concerned with the floor

28. Bonnie Lee, "Five Audit-Proofing Tips for the Self Employed," FOXBusiness, May 12, 2011, http://smallbusiness.foxbusiness.com/finance-accounting/2011/05/12/audit-proofing-tips-self-employed/.

of two percent of adjusted gross income that applies to the miscellaneous business deductions of an employee.

Self-Employment and FICA Taxes

Independent contractors pay federal tax on their net annual income from self-employment, if that income exceeds $400.[29] A special tax form, Form SE, is used to compute the amount of self-employment tax. The Social Security tax rate for 2012 is 13.3 percent on self-employment income up to $110,100, and if your net earnings exceed $110,100, you continue to pay only the Medicare portion of the Social Security tax, which is 2.9 percent, on the rest of your earnings.[30] Half of the self-employment tax can be deducted as a business expense for federal income tax purposes.

Employees, in contrast, share this tax burden with their employer under the Federal Insurance Contributions Act (FICA). In 2012, an employer and employee each pay Social Security tax of 6.20 percent on the first $110,100 of the employee's wages and Medicare tax of 1.45 percent on all wages.[31] For employees, Social Security taxes are not deductible for federal income tax purposes.

What constitutes wages of the employee is important in determining the amount of FICA taxes owed.[32] "Wages" means the gross amount of pay an employee received for employment covered by FICA unless the pay is specifically excluded by law. Pay that is not for covered employment is not wages for FICA purposes, even though the amounts are included for purposes of determining the annual earnings. Wages include payments by the employer, whether the payment is made in cash, or by check, promissory note, or in noncash forms such as goods or clothing. Food and lodging are included unless they are furnished by or on behalf of the employer. The first

---

29. 4 RIA Federal Tax Coordinator 2D ¶ A-6034 (Research Institute of America, 2004); *see also* http://www.irs.gov/Businesses/Small-Businesses-&-Self-Employed/Self-Employment-Tax-%28Social-Security-and-Medicare-Taxes%29#2 (last visited May 14, 2013).

30. SSA Publication No. 05-10022, Mar. 2012, ICN 454900.

31. *OASDI and SSI Program Rates & Limits 2012*, http://www.ssa.gov/policy/docs/quickfacts/prog_highlights/RatesLimits2012.pdf (last visited Nov. 17, 2012).

32. *See* 42 U.S.C.A. § 409 and 20 C.F.R. §§ 404.1041–60; *see also* 20 C.F.R. § 404.429 for definition of "earnings."

six months of sick pay or accident disability pay are considered wages.[33] Amounts received under certain deferred-compensation plans are treated as wages for FICA purposes [34] as is the cost of employer-provided group term life insurance if such insurance is includable in gross income for federal income tax purposes.[35] Certain *de minimis* and noncash remunerations are excluded from wages.[36]

Right to Discharge, Right to Terminate

The associates in a law firm know that under the employment at-will doctrine of the common law, the employer has the right to discharge them and terminate the relationship at any time. This traditional doctrine is now disappearing with the growth of the tort of wrongful discharge, where an employee's termination is based on discrimination, retaliation, the employee's refusal to commit an illegal act, or where the employer fails to observe its own termination procedures. Formal Opinion 90-357 recognized the permanent status of the senior attorney "in between those of partner and associate — akin to the last category just described [in other words, associate], but having the quality of tenure, or something close to it, and lacking that of an expectation of likely promotion to full partner status."[37]

By contrast, termination of an independent contractor with a written agreement is governed by the contract specifications. If the law firm or lawyer with which the independent contractor has contracted terminates the contract other than in accordance with the termination provisions in the agreement, the independent contractor will have a remedy for any damages suffered under breach of contract.

---

33. *See* 42 U.S.C.A. § 409(b) and 20 C.F.R. § 404.1051.

34. 26 U.S.C.A. §§ 403, 457, 3121, 3201, 3316; 29 U.S.C.A. § 1002; § 209 of the Social Security Act, as amended, 42 U.S.C.A. § 409.

35. *See* § 9003 of the Omnibus Budget Reconciliation Act of 1987, Pub. L. No. 100-203, amending clause 3 of § 209(b) of the Social Security Act, as amended, and subparagraph (C) of § 3121(a)(2) of the Internal Revenue Code; *see also* Technical and Miscellaneous Revenue Act § 8013 (1988).

36. Internal Revenue Service Publication 15-B, *Employer's Tax Guide to Fringe Benefits.*

37. ABA Comm. on Ethics & Prof'l Responsibility, Formal Op. 90-357, at 4 (1990).

Of Counsel Contrasted with Outside Consultant

Unlike the terms "partner" and "associate," the phrase "outside consultant" has not acquired a precise meaning, and the committee did not attempt to define it. The requirement that an "Of Counsel" attorney or firm *not* be like an outside consultant restates in negative terms the requirement that lawyers and firms who are "Of Counsel" *must* have frequent and continuing contacts with the law office.

Although the committee in Formal Opinion 90-357 did not further elucidate the meaning of "outside consultant," the determination of whether "Of Counsel" is a member or component part of a law office should depend on whether there is a "close, continuing, personal" relationship with the lawyer or law firm.[38] Whether a relationship limited to consultation and advice satisfies the requirements of a "close, continuing, personal" relationship has important legal consequences, particularly in the areas of imputed disqualification and fee splitting. Being treated as a member of the firm may expose the "Of Counsel" attorney or firm to conflicts of interest. Furthermore, treating the "Of Counsel" attorney as a member of the firm influences the forms of compensation allowable.

Conflicts of Interest

"Of Counsel" attorneys must withdraw from the law firm or the law firm must withdraw from its current representation of a client if that representation conflicts with the interests of other current or former clients of the "Of Counsel" attorney or firm.[39]

Compensation

In Formal Opinion 90-357, the committee specifically stated that "it is not relevant to the permissibility of use of the 'of counsel' designation what the compensation arrangements are."[40] Although this gives both the law firm and the "Of Counsel" attorney or firm the freedom to contract for whatever

38. *See* Chapter 4.

39. Michigan State Bar Ethics Op. CI-1071 (undated); New Jersey State Bar Ethics Op. 541 (1984); Texas State Bar Ethics Op. 445 (1987). *See generally* Chapters 7 and 8, *infra.*

40. ABA Formal Op. 90-357, at 4.

arrangement they deem appropriate, the lessons of Formal Opinion 330 should not be overlooked. In the earlier opinion, the committee said:

> [T]he lawyer who is "Of Counsel" may be compensated either on a basis of division of fees in particular cases or on a basis of consultation fees. He is compensated as a sui *generis* member of that law office, however, and not as an outside consultant.[41]

In other words, Formal Opinion 330 implied that "Of Counsel" attorneys could split fees with the firm, but only for cases in which he or she rendered services. Lawyers in an "Of Counsel" relationship were treated as *members* of the law office. Outside consultants, on the other hand, were not members of the law office, and their compensation had to be directly related to the work performed for each client.

Under 90-357, the liberalization of the rules regarding compensation arrangements for "Of Counsel" have similarly liberalized the rules governing outside consultants. The relationship of the firm with outside consultants and the "Of Counsel" attorney or firm is entirely contractual, with the result that drafters can negate either one of these designations depending upon their goals.

Currently, many states allow "Of Counsel" attorneys to split fees with the firm without regard to the amount of services performed on the grounds that the "Of Counsel" attorney is part of the firm.[42] Other states prohibit an "Of Counsel" attorney from splitting fees with the firm or other lawyer. In these states, the "Of Counsel" attorney must be compensated in accordance

41. ABA Comm. on Ethics & Prof'l Responsibility, Formal Op. 330 (1972).

42. Alabama State Bar Ethics Op. 81-536 (undated) (A law firm may share legal fees with a lawyer who is "Of Counsel" to the firm pursuant to a contract or agreement providing for such division. The Model Code provision prohibiting fee division with another lawyer who is not a partner or associate without the client's consent after full disclosure is inapplicable.); New Jersey Ethics Op. 689 (2000); Texas State Bar Ethics Op. 450 (1987) (The Model Code provision governing division of legal fees is not applicable to a law firm that intends to share a fee with a lawyer who is publicly represented to be "Of Counsel" to the firm. The "Of Counsel" lawyer is considered to be a member of the firm for purposes of this Model Code provision.); Virginia State Bar Ethics Ops. 1735 (1999) and 442 (1983) (A lawyer who does part-time legal work for a law firm may be designated "Of Counsel" on the firm's stationery and may divide legal fees with the firm.).

with the rules regulating division of fees between lawyers who are not in the same firm, or as outside consultants.[43]

Normally, outside consultants are not allowed to split fees unless the firm and the outside consultant comply with the Rules of Professional Conduct applicable in their state.[44] The Model Rules prohibit a lawyer from splitting fees with another lawyer who is not a member of the law firm, unless the fee-sharing arrangement is fully explained to the client, the client consents in writing, the fee is divided in proportion to the services rendered, and the total amount of the fee is reasonable.[45]

Summary

Formal Opinion 90-357 is an improvement over Formal Opinion 330. The later opinion (90-357) focuses on what the "Of Counsel" relationship can, rather than what it cannot, be. It articulates a number of relationships (the part-time practitioner, the former judge or governmental official, the retired partner, the probationary partner, and the senior attorney) as appropriate for the "Of Counsel" designation. It specifically excludes others: the relationship involving only an individual case, the forwarder or receiver of legal business, the lawyer who occasionally collaborates, and the outside consultant.

---

43. Arizona State Bar Ethics Op. 86-3 (1986) (a law firm and a lawyer who is "Of Counsel" to the law firm may share fees only on the basis of the amount of work done by each on behalf of the other's clients); *see* California State Bar Ethics Op. 1986-88 (undated); District of Columbia Ethics Op. 151 (1985) (the Model Code provisions prohibiting fee splitting apply to the "Of Counsel" relationship, unless the lawyer's relationship with the firm or other lawyer is "akin to that of a partner or associate").

44. *See also* Illinois State Bar Ethics Op. 776 (1982) (law firm may pay outside legal consultants and keep portion of fee billed to the client for the consultant's time, provided the client has consented in writing to the employment of the outside lawyer after written disclosure of facts relating to the referral and the firm discloses that it will receive a referral fee).

45. Model Rules, Rule 1.5(e):

> (e) A division of a fee between lawyers who are not in the same firm may be made only if:
>
> (1) the division is in proportion to the services performed by each lawyer or each lawyer assumes joint responsibility for the representation;
>
> (2) the client agrees to the arrangement, including the share each lawyer will receive, and the agreement is confirmed in writing; and
>
> (3) the total fee is reasonable.

Yet, apart from its positive, flexible approach to defining the "Of Counsel" relationship, Formal Opinion 90-357 relies on one negative aspect contained in Formal Opinion 330. It mandates that the relationship must not be like that of a partner or associate. If the relationship has facets commonly found in one of these other relationships, use of the "Of Counsel" designation is improper. When the relationship more nearly resembles that of partner or associate, the "Of Counsel" attorney is exposed to other problems, particularly in the area of vicarious liability. Thus, an "Of Counsel" attorney should never share in the firm's general profits, or assume management and control of the business. Likewise, an "Of Counsel" attorney should be careful to avoid the *appearance* of a partnership. An implied partnership could exist when the parties represented to the public that a partnership existed, and there was reasonable reliance upon that representation by the person seeking to establish the partnership. If an implied partnership is found, an "Of Counsel" attorney will be liable to an injured third party for torts committed by the firm.

Formal Opinion 90-357 makes it clear that the "Of Counsel" relationship is a special contractual relationship. The drafter of an "Of Counsel" agreement must be sensitive to the "Of Counsel" attorney's need for freedom of action, and draft an agreement that will satisfy the needs of all parties.

Checklists for Issue Spotting

Does the Relationship Resemble a Partnership?

(1) Does the "Of Counsel" relationship contain characteristics essential to a true partnership? Does the "Of Counsel" share in the profits and losses of the partnership? Does the "Of Counsel" have general responsibility in the management of the firm? Is the "Of Counsel" a member of the firm's executive committee? Does the "Of Counsel" possess joint management and control in other areas of the firm?

(2) Is there an implied partnership between the "Of Counsel" and the firm? Do the parties publicly or privately hold themselves out as partners? Is the "Of Counsel" attorney's name included in the firm's name? Is the "Of Counsel" status clearly represented on the firm's letterheads,

advertisements, law listings, professional announcement cards, firm directory, court appearances, legal briefs, and other documents filed with the court?

Is Of Counsel More Like an Associate?

(1) Does the "Of Counsel" attorney's relationship to the firm contain indicia common to the employer-employee relationship? Does the firm have the right to exercise control over the "Of Counsel" attorney?

  a. Does the firm require the "Of Counsel" attorney to work in the firm's offices?
  b. Does the firm supply the "Of Counsel" attorney with materials and supplies (including telephone, desk, computer services, law library) or support staff (secretaries, paralegals, and so forth)?
  c. Does the firm bill clients for services performed by the "Of Counsel" attorney?
  d. Is the "Of Counsel" attorney required to work full-time or a specified number of hours exclusively for the firm?
  e. Is the "Of Counsel" attorney compensated with a fixed salary?
  f. Does the firm pay for the "Of Counsel" attorney's business or travel expenses?
  g. Does the firm have the right to discharge the "Of Counsel" attorney at any time?
  h. Does the "Of Counsel" attorney work under the direction or supervision of another lawyer in the firm?
  i. Does the "Of Counsel" attorney automatically have certain benefits, such as life, health, or malpractice insurance?

(2) Is there any expectation that the "Of Counsel" attorney will attain partnership status within the near future? Is the "Of Counsel" designation being used to describe a probationary position?

Is Of Counsel More Like an "Outside Consultant"?

(1) Is the "Of Counsel" relationship limited to one particular case?

(2) Is the "Of Counsel" attorney or firm compensated in the same way as an outside consultant?

(3) Does the state in which the "Of Counsel" attorney or firm practices permit "Of Counsel" attorneys to split fees with the firm without regard to work performed? If so, do the parties desire a fee-sharing arrangement?

CHAPTER 6

Legal Malpractice

Introduction

Since the publication of the first edition of this book, the law with respect to both the "Of Counsel" designation and legal malpractice has seen substantial development. In the first edition, we stated that there was little or no case authority with reference to the liability of an "Of Counsel" attorney for legal malpractice. Nor was there any authority regarding the extent of liability of a law firm or lawyer by reason of an "Of Counsel" attorney's wrong-doing. Even now, in preparing this fourth edition, it remains difficult to find judicial authority addressing the issue of malpractice liability of an "Of Counsel" attorney or the law firm to which he or she is attached. However, a number of cases dealing with "Of Counsel" or associated counsel point in the general direction of familiar legal principals, particularly with respect to vicarious liability. In this chapter, we consider some of these illustrations of the application of familiar principles of common law to similar fact patterns. In passing, we note some of the more obvious trends in the law:

- In tort, the law firm or lawyer will be responsible for the tortious conduct of the "Of Counsel" attorney either because of *respondeat superior* or because it was negligent in the selection or control of the "Of Counsel" attorney. Liability in contract will depend upon the specific contractual arrangements between the firm and the "Of Counsel" attorney or firm. While the "Of Counsel" attorney will normally seek to be an independent contractor, the law firm may still be vicariously liable where it has clothed the "Of Counsel" attorney with actual or apparent authority.

- The "Of Counsel" attorney will normally not be liable for the errors or omissions of partners, associates, or employees of the firm. But factual patterns may negate the usual independent contractor status. Characterization of the relationship between the "Of Counsel" attorney and the firm as partnership by estoppel, joint venture, or employer-employee can enter into a particular situation to vary the result.
- Legal malpractice may be based on breach of fiduciary duty, negligence, or breach of contract. The application of any one or all of these doctrines in typical fact situations appears to be on the increase. In some cases, in the absence of an attorney-client relationship, it may not be possible to prove liability in negligence or breach of contract, but the same facts may be the basis for a suit for breach of fiduciary relationship.[1]
- Privity of contract is required for a law firm or lawyer to be held liable for negligence or breach of fiduciary obligation, but this doctrine is being eroded where lawyers have reason to believe that third parties will be relying on their work.
- The rules with respect to conflicts and imputed disqualification continue to play an important role in all litigation involving legal malpractice.[2]

Vicarious Liability in Tort

Law firms and lawyers are responsible for the torts committed by their employed lawyers and office staff. If the "Of Counsel" attorney is characterized as an employee, rather than an independent contractor, the liability of the law firm is premised on the doctrine of *respondeat superior*. The tort must have been committed by the employee while acting within the scope of

---

1. *See, e.g.*, Cacciola v. Nelhaus, 733 N.E.2d 133 (Mass. App. Ct. 2000) (law partner could not state claim for legal malpractice absent express attorney-client relationship, but same allegations stated claim for breach of fiduciary duty).

2. We defer the discussion of these matters until later. *See infra* Chapters 7 and 8.

employment.[3] Apart from liability under *respondeat superior*, the firm may also be liable for its failure to control or supervise the employee adequately. In various cases, the firm or employer has been held liable for the acts and omissions of another lawyer employed by them.[4] In contrast to vicarious liability, proof of negligent supervision usually requires expert testimony.[5]

Liability Based on Contractual Arrangements

Where liability is based on breach of contract or breach of fiduciary relationship, the act of the agent in the ordinary course of the principal's business or within the scope of the actual or apparent authority is binding upon the principal. The ordinary course of a law firm's business includes the practice of law and other activities normally related to it. Thus, liability can be imposed for various actions by a law firm's agents, including legal malpractice, incurring indebtedness for services or supplies, misapplication of funds in the firm's custody, and torts other than malpractice.[6] Apparent authority exists when the agent's acts or omissions are ordinarily perceived to be within the agent's scope of authority. For example, a lawyer can be held liable for the negligence of his or her secretary in filing a client's papers.[7]

But acts not within the practice of law, such as a lawyer's entry into an unrelated business partnership that is not part of the firm's practice and related activities, are not included.[8] And apparent authority does not exist if the acts or omissions are not ordinarily within the scope of the agent's duties. A former member of a law firm was not acting within the scope of his apparent authority when he misappropriated funds borrowed from the

3. McGarity v. Craighill, Rendleman, Ingle & Blythe, 83 N.C. Ct. App. 106, 349 S.E.2d 311(1986).

4. Young v. Bridwell, 20 Utah 2d 332, 437 P.2d 686 (1968); Mahoney v. Middlesex County Comm'rs, 144 Mass. 459, 11 N.E. 689 (1887).

5. *See* R. Mallen & J. Smith, Legal Malpractice § 5.8, at 522 & n.6 (5th ed. 2000).

6. Restatement (Third) of the Law Governing Lawyers § 58 cmt. (d).

7. DeVaux v. American Home Assurance Co., 387 Mass. 814, 444 N.E.2d 355 (1983).

8. Restatement (Third) of the Law Governing Lawyers § 58 cmt. (d); Sheinkopf v. Stone, 927 F.2d 1259 (1st Cir. 1991).

law firm's clients. There was no evidence that the law firm was in the business of investing, or that it had benefited from the former member's acts.[9]

Independent Contractors

The individual lawyer or law firm may not be vicariously liable for the torts committed by an "independent contractor" hired by the lawyer or firm. In *Bockian v. Esanu, Katsky Korins & Siger*,[10] the court ruled that a law firm and its partners were not vicariously liable for the acts of a process server in his attempt to effect personal process, since he was an "independent contractor" of the firm. The Restatement (Third) of the Law, The Law Governing Lawyers (2000) 439–440, Section 58, indicates that a law firm has no vicarious liability unless at least one principal or employee of the firm is liable. Entitled "Vicarious Liability," it provides:

> (1) A law firm is subject to civil liability for injury legally caused to a person by any wrongful act or omission of any *principal or employee* of the firm who was acting in the ordinary course of the firm's business or with actual or apparent authority. (Emphasis added.)

Despite this general rule, vicarious liability may still be imputed to a lawyer or law firm for the acts of its independent contractor where the lawyer or firm expressly directs the independent contractor to commit the wrongs or where the lawyer or firm knew that the independent contractor was untrustworthy or the independent contractor is performing a non-delegable duty on behalf of the firm.[11]

---

9. *McGarity*, 83 N.C. Ct. App. 106, 349 S.E.2d at 313.

10. 124 Misc. 2d 607, 476 N.Y.S.2d 1009 (N.Y. Sup. Ct. 1984) ("attorney does not generally retain a sufficient degree of control over an independent process server's performance of his duties as would be necessary to render the process server an agent or employee of the attorney" citing *Restatement (Second) of Agency*, Sec. 2(3)); *see also* Kirschenbaum v. Rehfield, 539 So. 2d 12 (Fla. Dist. Ct. App. 1989) (law firm not vicariously liable for criminal attack by former investigator employee; attack was outside any apparent agency relationship and in no way furthered the interests of the firm).

11. Kleeman v. Rheingold, 598 N.Y.S.2d 149, 81 N.Y.2d 270 (N.Y. 1993) (firm liable for negligence of process server, because firms' duty of care to client in serving process is

The Of Counsel Relationship

A 1993 case from Maryland illustrates the liability of both the "Of Counsel" attorney and the law firm for misrepresentation and breach of fiduciary duty. In *Homa v. Friendly Mobile Manor, Inc.*,[12] Leonard S. Homa, a member of the Maryland Bar, contracted with the law firm of Levan, Schimel, Richman and Belman, P.A. (LSRB) to perform services "as counsel/manufactured housing consultant . . . on behalf of Friendly . . . in connection with the sale of [mobile parks]."[13]

Friendly Mobile Manor, Inc. (Friendly) owned two mobile home parks. John S. Weiner, a real estate lawyer, and Kenneth Rossignol, a real estate broker, owned all of its stock. Weiner and Rossignol sold one of the two parks without the aid of Homa. Homa then offered to buy the second mobile home park.

In October 1986, Homa and Friendly entered into a contract whereby Homa was to purchase[14] the second mobile park, with a provision that, at closing, the buyer would assume responsibility for the payment of installment loans on specified financed mobile homes. Homa prepared the written contract on the law firm stationery of LSRB, on which his name appeared as "Of Counsel."

William T. Poole, a stockholder of Pascal Turner, Ltd. II (P/T), a corporation to be formed, agreed to take an assignment of Homa's contract to buy the second mobile home park, provided the assignment excluded any "contracts or agreements affecting the park for any matter for which the Purchaser will be required to assume or will become obligated."[15]

On December 3, 1986, the parties (Poole, Homa, Rossignol, and Weiner) met to settle the transaction. When a dispute arose concerning the

---

nondelegable); Noble v. Sears Roebuck & Co., 33 Cal. App. 3d 654, 109 Cal. Rptr. 269 (Cal. Ct. App. 1973) (corporation and house counsel liable for negligent choice of investigator).

12. 93 Md. App. 337, 612 A.2d 322 (Md. 1992).

13. *Homa*, 93 Md. App. 337, 612 A.2d at 325 (ellipsis in the original).

14. Homa presumably intended to resell the property, since the parties had a handwritten agreement that provided "Homa was entitled to a commission whether he bought the park or whether an assignee purchased it, in which case the commission was to be paid by the assignee." 93 Md. App. 337, 612 A.2d at 325.

15. *Id.*

assumption of the loans, Poole left the room, and Homa told Rossignol and Weiner that "he didn't think it really made any difference whether Mr. Poole signed the bill of sale with that assumption language in it . . . that Mr. Poole had taken the assignment of the contract, and that . . . P/T was responsible under the contract of sale to assume the loans."[16] The parties then deleted the language about assuming the installment loans from the bill of sale.

Prior to the settlement, Poole and Homa discussed the possibility of Homa becoming an investor in P/T. At the time of the settlement, Homa's son was employed by Poole. On December 2, 1986, the day before the settlement, Homa attended a meeting of the investors. P/T was incorporated in January 1987, and Homa began to do consulting work for it. In February, he became a shareholder.

In a declaratory judgment action by P/T against Friendly, the court ruled that P/T was not obligated to assume the installment loans.[17] Friendly then sued Homa and LSRB for breach of the October 1986 purchase contract, and for fraud.

Sitting without a jury, the trial court first bifurcated the two actions, and found Homa liable for fraud and breach of his legal services contract. The court awarded Friendly a judgment of $159,948.16 in compensatory damages, plus $31,440.00 in punitive damages.

In sustaining the lower court, the Maryland Court of Special Appeals concluded that Homa was guilty of fraud by virtue of the common law of misrepresentation:

- Friendly had proven a case of fraud as against Homa by showing:
    1. that Homa had made a false representation of a material fact;
    2. that Homa either knew of the falsity, or acted with reckless disregard of the truth;
    3. that Homa intended that Friendly would rely on the false representation;
    4. that Friendly did in fact rely upon it;
    5. that Friendly's reliance was justified; and

16. *Id.*
17. P/T Ltd. II v. Friendly Mobile Manor, 79 Md. App. 227, 556 A.2d 694 (1989).

6. that Friendly had suffered damages in reliance on the representation.[18]

The court then dealt with the fiduciary responsibility of a lawyer:

- The fiduciary relationship between lawyer and client placed upon Homa an affirmative duty to disclose all known facts material to their relationship. Failure to disclose constitutes fraud.[19]

Homa sought a reversal of the trial court's holding with respect to legal malpractice, because of Friendly's failure to produce any expert testimony with respect to Homa's alleged breach of fiduciary duty. The appellate court recognized that expert testimony may be required in some legal malpractice cases to establish the standard of care for negligence, but not where legal malpractice is based upon breach of fiduciary duty:

> Homa's failure to inform Friendly of his impending financial interest in P/T was a clear violation of his fiduciary duty as Friendly's attorney, was easily recognizable as such by a lay person, and most certainly was recognizable by a judge acting in the capacity of factfinder.[20]

Homa also contended that he was not liable on his contract with Friendly because a novation had occurred wherein P/T had been substituted for Homa on his contract with Friendly. The court responded:

> Even though the assumption language in the bill of sale was deleted, Weiner, based on Homa's counsel, believed P/T was responsible nonetheless to assume the loans. Because Friendly believed P/T was obligated to assume the loans, it is clear that Friendly did not agree to excuse the performance of this duty and did not agree to substitute the new agreement with P/T for its agreement with Homa. There was

18. *Homa*, 612 A.2d at 326 (paraphrase).
19. *Id.* at 327 (paraphrase).
20. *Id.* at 329.

> not a novation because the evidence does not establish a clear and definite intent to substitute one contract for another.[21]

As noted earlier, the appellate court bifurcated the case, treating Homa's appeal as to his liability to Friendly separate from Friendly's appeal regarding the liability of LSRB. On the latter aspect of the case, the trial court ruled that Friendly had failed to prove that Homa acted with the authority of LSRB.

In affirming this result, the Maryland court first discussed the common law of agency. Agency is a fiduciary relationship wherein the agent acts under the control and with the actual or apparent authority of the principal. The three elements integral to the relationship are

(1) the agent is subject to the principal's right of control;
(2) the agent acts primarily for the benefit of the principal; and
(3) the agent has the power to alter the legal relations of a principal.

Homa had no actual authority to act on behalf of LSRB:

> Although the agreement was on LSRB letterhead, the express contents of the [engagement] letter, and the testimony of Weiner and Rossignol, leave no doubt that the agreement was made with and for the services of Homa personally and exclusively and not with or for the services of LSRB or any employee thereof. . . . [The letter] also lists the services that "Consultant" will perform personally and provides that Friendly will pay to "Consultant" directly the fee for services rendered. . . . There is no indication in the agreement that LSRB would in any manner manage, supervise, or otherwise control Homa's performance under the agreement. The agreement was signed by Homa individually, and without reference to the title of his position with LSRB.[22]

---

21. *Id.* at 330. The appellate court also ruled that an award for punitive damages was appropriate, and that Homa's egregious conduct constituted gross fraud. *Id.* at 332.
22. *Id.* at 334.

Homa was not engaged in this transaction for LSRB's benefit; nor was LSRB to receive any benefit for Homa's services. Until he received the engagement letter, Rossignol was unaware of Homa's relationship with LSRB; the relationship, however, helped him "sell the idea" of using Homa's services to Weiner. But Weiner would have hired Homa regardless of his association with LSRB. From all this evidence, the appellate court concluded that the trial court properly held that Homa was acting for himself, and not for LSRB.

The trial court was equally correct in determining that Homa had no apparent authority, since there was no evidence that LSRB knew or should have known about this particular transaction.

Homa was the first decision to discuss the liability of a law firm for legal malpractice based on an agreement between the firm and an "Of Counsel" attorney. The case is useful in delineating the area where a law firm would *not* be subject to liability because of contractual arrangements that the "Of Counsel" attorney or firm might make with clients. It is of less help as a precedent for the typical "Of Counsel" situations outlined in ABA Formal Opinion 90-357.[23]

The first part of *Homa* provides an analysis of the liability of the lawyer to the client for malpractice:

- Homa was guilty of intentional misrepresentation by virtue of his representation to Friendly that P/T had agreed to assume the installment loans.
- Homa breached his fiduciary relationship with his client by his failure to disclose a conflict of interest because of his relationship with Poole and P/T. This nondisclosure of a material fact constituted fraud.
- Expert testimony was not required to prove the standard of care "where the common knowledge of laymen is extensive enough to recognize or infer negligence [or an intentional violation] from the facts."[24]

Punitive damages were recoverable by the client against the lawyer "where the wrong involved some violation of duty springing from a relationship

23. *See supra*, Chapter 4.
24. *Homa*, 93 Md. App. 337, 612 A.2d at 328.

of trust or confidence, or where the fraud is gross, or the case presents extraordinary or exceptional circumstances clearly indicating malice and wilfulness."[25]

The second part of the *Homa* decision, by negative inference, is helpful in establishing the extent of liability of a law firm for an "Of Counsel" attorney's wrongdoing. There is little in the opinion of the court to indicate the extent of the relationship between Homa and LSRB. The contract between them indicated that the reason for the "Of Counsel" arrangement was to affect the sale of the mobile home parks to the best advantage for Friendly. This was not the "close, continuing, and personal relationship" required of an appropriate "Of Counsel" designation under Formal Opinion 90-357. In finding an absence of apparent authority, the court commented:

> Friendly presented no evidence of any contact with or reliance upon any conduct by LSRB that would establish that LSRB authorized Homa to act on its behalf in this transaction or that LSRB stood to benefit in any way from the agreement between Friendly and Homa. Even though there is one piece of correspondence on LSRB letterhead, and as Friendly notes Homa shared office space with LSRB, there is no evidence LSRB knew or should have known about this particular transaction. No fees were to be paid to LSRB; moreover, fees were to be paid to Homa only if he personally procured a bona fide qualified purchaser for Friendly Manor (the agreement did not provide a separate fee for his legal services). In addition, . . . the evidence is sufficient to support the finding that Homa was not hired by Rossignol and Weiner because of his association with LSRB and would have been hired even if not associated with LSRB.[26]

From all appearances, the relationship between Friendly and Homa was for a single transaction, and not the "close, continuing, and personal relationship" required by Formal Opinion 90-357; but the case delineates the

25. *Id.* at 331, quoting Loyola Fed. Sav. & Loan Assn v. Trenchcraft, Inc., 17 Md. App. 646, 663, 303 A.2d 432 (1973).

26. *Homa*, 93 Md. App. 337, 312 A.2d at 335.

scope of liability for legal malpractice of both the "Of Counsel" attorney and the law firm.

Although *Homa* was concerned with a single transaction, rather than the "close, continuing, and personal relationship" required by 90-357, the same principles apply where a lawyer is properly designated as "Of Counsel." In *Staron v. Weinstein*,[27] a New Jersey appellate court reversed a summary judgment for defendant, holding that the related firm (or lawyer) was liable if the plaintiff could show that an "Of Counsel" attorney acted negligently with the firm's apparent authority.

Plaintiff Mariuz Staron was injured in an automobile accident. A friend referred him to Sheldon G. Weinstein, a lawyer practicing in Summit, New Jersey. Weinstein missed a two-year statute of limitations, thereby causing plaintiff to lose a substantial amount of potential damages covered by liability insurance.

On November 7, 1985, plaintiffs Mariuz and Elzbieta Staron, husband and wife,[28] entered into a retainer agreement with Weinstein, on the second page of which a law firm was listed as "Robert C. Thelander, Esq." above Weinstein's signature. On the day after the execution of the agreement, Weinstein wrote the insurer, on Thelander stationery, that "we represent" Mariuz Staron, and requested personal injury protection benefits. On the same day, also on Thelander stationery, Weinstein made a claim based on the driver's negligence. On the top right corner of the Thelander stationery, Weinstein was listed as "Of Counsel." Weinstein sent copies of both letters to the plaintiffs.

On August 15, 1986, Thelander advised Weinstein that he was terminating their "Of Counsel" relationship. He also advised those of Weinstein's clients of whom he had knowledge of the termination, giving them Weinstein's home address. Thelander never knew of the relationship between the Starons and Weinstein until a summons and complaint was filed against him.

27. 305 N.J. Super. 236, 701 A.2d 1325 (1997), *cert. denied*, 153 N.J. 214, 708 A.2d 65 (1998).

28. Elzbieta Staron was not involved in the automobile accident, but apparently joined with her husband for any potential damages, such as loss of services, to which she might be entitled by virtue of her marital status.

The lower court granted Thelander's motion for summary judgment, finding that there was no apparent authority by which Weinstein could bind Thelander or his firm. In reversing, the appellate court said:

> Proper resolution of the issues in this case requires a detailed evaluation of the facts including whether plaintiffs intended to retain only Weinstein to represent them as their attorney; whether his relationship with Thelander became relevant to their decision to sign the retainer agreement; whether Thelander was to be involved in the handling of Weinstein's trials and in whose name the pleadings were to be filed; what fees, if any, Thelander was to receive upon recovery; whether plaintiffs knew of the dissolution of the Thelander relationship before the malpractice occurred and continued to have Weinstein represent them, and why Thelander failed to notify plaintiffs of the dissolution.[29]

That the use of the "Of Counsel" designation on Thelander's letterhead was significant is indicated by the following comment of the court:

> In the context of a motion for summary judgment, plaintiffs made a sufficient showing that Thelander's firm became counsel for plaintiffs by virtue of both the retainer agreement and the fact that defendant [Weinstein] had at least apparent authority to enter into such agreements on behalf of the firm.[30]

Similarly, *Hirsch v. Weisman*[31] was a single-transaction situation, wherein personal injury plaintiffs sought recovery against lawyer Weisman for his failure to bring their personal injury suit in a timely manner. Weisman had contracted with the law firm of Zuller & Bondy, and one of its partners, Thomas Bondy, to serve as trial counsel. In January 1988, Bondy negotiated a favorable settlement in the amount of $80,000, on behalf of Weisman,

---

29. 701 A.2d 1325, 1327, 305 N.J. Super. 236, 240 (A.D. 1997).
30. 701 A.2d 1325, 1327, 305 N.J. Super. 236, 241 (A.D. 1997).
31. 189 A.D.2d 643, 592 N.Y.S.2d 337 (1st Dept.), *appeal dismissed*, 81 N.Y.2d 1067, 619 N.E.2d 662 (1993).

under the mistaken belief that the policy limits of the defendants' liability insurance policy was $100,000.

When the plaintiffs learned that the limit was actually $500,000, they sought leave of court to amend their pleadings and to serve the amended pleadings on the Bondy defendants. The trial court granted leave to amend, and held that the action was governed by the six-year statute of limitations for contracts, rather than the three-year malpractice statute, which would have barred the action.

The appellate court reversed, stating that the only damages recoverable in an action beyond the three-year period, but within the six-year period, would be those attributable to a breach of contract. It added:

> [A] plaintiff had better be able to point with specificity to some contractual agreement, express or implied, that has been breached in order to avail himself of the additional time in which to bring an action for damages.
>
> Here, there was no contractual relationship between plaintiffs and the Bondy defendants. Plaintiffs were in privity only with Weisman, their retained counsel. At best, the Bondy defendants had an "of counsel" relationship with plaintiffs. Historically, such a relationship has been held not to provide a basis for recovery by the retained trial counsel directly from the client, . . . even where the client may ultimately have benefited from the services performed. . . . The lack of privity runs both ways, and without showing knowledge of the contractual agreement between Weisman and the Bondy firm, plaintiffs cannot be considered third-party beneficiaries of that arrangement.[32]

32. *Hirsch*, 592 N.Y.S.2d at 338. In New York, "Of Counsel" must be in privity with the client to recover directly from him. Kiser v. Bailey, 92 Misc. 2d 435, 400 N.Y.S.2d 312 (1977) ("Of Counsel" retained to assist in litigation could not recover from client's estate); *see also In re* Muscillo's Estate, 159 N.Y.S.2d 253 (Sur. 1957); Levy v. Jacobs, 3 Misc. 2d 994, 148 N.Y.S.2d 507 (1955); *In re* Loomis, 273 N.Y. 76, 6 N.E.2d 103 (1937); Grennan v. Well Built Sales of Richmond County, Inc., 35 Misc. 2d 905, 231 N.Y.S.2d 625 (1962) (lawyers retained as trial counsel are entitled to withdraw because they never had a contractual relationship with the client).

Associated Counsel

When a law firm or lawyer associates outside counsel for a particular matter, with the client's knowledge and consent, the first lawyer is ordinarily not vicariously liable for the second lawyer, provided the latter's negligence was an independent act. In the agreement between the firm and outside counsel, the parties should specify their respective duties to avoid any misunderstanding and protect each other from possible joint liability.[33]

The courts are reluctant to impose liability on the delegating lawyer for the errors and omissions of outside counsel. The outside lawyer is usually an independent agent of the client, especially if he or she represents the client in another jurisdiction in which the delegating lawyer is not licensed.[34] But if the associated lawyers are practicing together, sharing equal responsibility and authority, or sharing in the profits of the matter, there is a strong rationale for imposing vicarious liability on the lawyers for the torts of each other.[35] Liability may be premised on a theory that the parties were engaged in a joint venture.[36] At the other end of the scale, if the outside lawyer acts in a limited and passive role, such as co-counsel for one aspect of a case[37] or a *pro hac vice* lawyer hired to advise on matters of local law,[38] courts

33. ABA Division of Education, Professional Responsibility: A Guide for Attorneys 311, 315 (1978). *See* Chapter 11.

34. Restatement (Third) of the Law Governing Lawyers § 58 cmt. (e).

35. *Id.;* Ortiz v. Barrett, 222 Va. 118, 278 S.E.2d 833 (1981); *see also* C. Wolfram, Modern Legal Ethics § 5.6, at 237–38 (West 1986).

36. Fitzgibbon v. Carey, 70 Or. App. 127, 688 P.2d 1367 (1984), *review denied,* 298 Or. 553, 695 P.2d 49 (1985); *see also* discussion of *Duggins, infra.*

37. Some courts have held that co-counsel are liable for each other's acts. *See* Floro v. Lawton, 187 Cal. App. 2d 657, 10 Cal. Rptr. 98 (2d Dist. 1960). Specific arrangements may vary the recovery attributable to outside counsel. *See, e.g.,* Boskoff v. Yano, 57 F. Supp. 2d 994 (D. Haw. 1998); McKernan v. DuPont, 192 Ariz. 550, 968 P.2d 623 (Ariz. Ct. App. 1998), *overruled in part,* Panzino v. City of Phoenix, 196 Ariz. 442, 999 P.2d 198 (Ariz. Ct. App. 2000); Lapkin v. Garland Bloodworth, Inc., 2001 Okla. Civ. App. 29, 23 P.3d 958 (Okla. Civ. App. 2001). *But see* Armor v. Lantz, 207 W. Va. 672, 535 S.E.2d 737 (W. Va. 2000) (associated local counsel failed to advise principal counsel that West Virginia was inappropriate forum in which to bring automobile accident litigation.).

38. *See* Misner, *Local Associated Counsel in the Federal Courts: A Call for Change,* 67 Cornell L. Rev. 345 (1982).

are reluctant to impose vicarious liability on outside counsel for the errors and omissions of the delegating firm or lawyer.[39]

In *Duggins v. Guardianship of Washington*,[40] for example, the mother and guardian of a five-year-old boy sought to recover damages in a medical malpractice action for the inadequate treatment of a traumatic injury to her son's eye. She executed a contingent-fee contract with a lawyer, Duggins, providing that he could employ additional counsel at no additional expense to the guardianship. Duggins employed Barfield, a specialist in medical malpractice litigation.

While pretending to file suit, Barfield settled the case with the insurer without informing it of his co-counsel relationship with Duggins. He then misappropriated $53,089 of the insurance proceeds from the guardianship, and ultimately went to prison for the commission of a felony. The guardian sought to recover from Duggins this amount, plus prejudgment interest, to reconstruct the guardianship.

The Supreme Court of Mississippi treated the relationship between Duggins and Barfield as one of joint venture, and held Duggins liable for the restoration of the guardianship. But the court noted that even in the absence of partnership liability, Duggins would be accountable because he had procured Barfield's involvement in the litigation.

Tormo v. Yormark[41] presented a fact pattern similar to that of *Duggins.* A New York lawyer associated a New Jersey negligence specialist in a personal injury case. Unbeknownst to the first lawyer, the specialist obtained a settlement from the insurer, who delivered two checks to him. He forged the client's endorsement on one of the checks and applied the proceeds to

39. *See* Wolfram, *supra* note 38, at 238.

40. 632 So. 2d 420, 35 ALR5th 909 (Miss. 1993); *see also* Doe v. Salvation Army, 835 So. 2d 76 (Miss. 2001) (punitive damages not recoverable from principal whose employee sexually assaulted minors at camp); Pittman v. Weber Energy Corp., 790 So. 2d 823 (Miss. 2001) (parol evidence used to establish the absence of a joint venture, despite language to the contrary). *But see* note 43 *infra* for cases involving law partnerships.

41. 398 F. Supp. 1159 (D.N.J. 1975); *see also* Streit v. Covington & Crowe, 82 Cal. App. 4th 441, 98 Cal. Rptr. 2d 193 (Cal. Ct. App. 2000) (attorney appearing specially for litigant, instead of litigant's attorney of record, owes duty of care to litigant); Rallis v. Cassady, 84 Cal. App. 4th 285, 100 Cal. Rptr. 2d 763 (Cal. Ct. App. 2000), *opinion withdrawn, review denied,* 2001 Cal. LEXIS 32 (Cal. 2001); Roderick v. Ricks, 54 P.3d 1119, 2202 UT 84 (Utah 2002) (no breach of fiduciary duty by attorney for representing another party); Norman v. Arnold, 57 P.3d 997, 2002 Ut. 81 (Utah 2002).

his own use. Whether the New York lawyer was guilty of negligence by virtue of the specialist's misappropriation of the client's funds was a fact question for the jury. The New York lawyer's only inquiry was to look into a lawyers' directory to make sure that the New Jersey lawyer was licensed in New Jersey.

Similarly, in *Cohen v. Lipsig*,[42] where a lawyer retained outside trial counsel to pursue the client's cause, the Appellate Division reversed the granting of defendant's motion for summary judgment, holding that there were several fact questions for the jury:

- Was the outside counsel negligent?
- Did the lawyer obtain the informed consent of the plaintiff about the choice of trial counsel?
- Did the lawyer use reasonable care in the selection of trial counsel?
- Should the lawyer be estopped from denying the derivative liability for the alleged negligence of his chosen trial counsel?

All members of a law partnership are jointly and severally liable for the torts committed by other members of the partnership or its agents within the scope of their authority.[43] Partnership assets may be reached to satisfy the judgment, as may the personal assets of each individual partner, if the partnership assets are insufficient. But individual partners must be named as parties, or they will not personally be liable for a judgment.[44] If an "Of Counsel" attorney is guilty of legal malpractice, there is a likelihood that

42. 92 A.D.2d 536, 459 N.Y.S.2d 98 (2nd Dept. 1983).

43. *See, e.g.*, Williams v. Burns, 463 F. Supp. 1278 (D. Colo. 1979); Peterson v. Harville, 445 F. Supp. 16 (D. Or. 1977); *aff'd*, 623 F.2d 611 (9th Cir. 1980); Blackmon v. Hale, 1 Cal. 3d 548, 463 P.2d 418, 83 Cal. Rptr. 194 (1970) (former member of partnership held liable for law partner's misappropriation of funds, since law partner was acting within scope of apparent authority); Moore v. State Bar, 62 Cal. 2d 74, 396 P.2d 577, 41 Cal. Rptr. 161 (1964); Husted v. Gwin, 446 N.E. 2d 1361 (Ind. Ct. App. 1983) (law partnership liable and estate of deceased partner liable for other partner's misrepresentation of settlement and misappropriation of funds). *But see* Jackson v. Jackson, 20 N.C. App. 406, 201 S.E.2d 722 (1974) (malicious prosecution outside scope of partnership business); Musser v. Provencher, 28 Cal. 4th 274, 48 P.3d 408 (Cal. 2002) (legal malpractice insurers may be subrogated to the attorney's indemnity claims against concurrent counsel or co-counsel). *See* MALLEN & SMITH, LEGAL MALPRACTICE § 5.3, at 461 & n. 11 (5th ed. 2000).

44. *See* MALLEN & SMITH, LEGAL MALPRACTICE § 5.3, at 463 & n.22.

the law firm or lawyer to whom he or she is attached will also be held liable. The reverse of this situation, that is, whether the "Of Counsel" attorney will be liable for the wrongdoing of the partners or associates of the firm, is much less likely. But the contractual arrangements among the parties should make it clear that the "Of Counsel" attorney acts completely independently of the firm or lawyer.

A legal malpractice action raises the issue of whether a partner or agent acted within the scope of his authority. Because lawyers practice law in a variety of business arrangements, there is always the recurrent issue of whether an actual partnership existed. Although a partnership in fact may not have existed among the lawyers, an ostensible or apparent partnership may exist for purposes of liability to third persons.[45] If a partnership is established, the "Of Counsel" attorney may be just as liable for the wrongdoing of the partners and associates of the firm, as the firm would be liable for the "Of Counsel" attorney's torts.[46]

---

45. Section 16 of the Uniform Partnership Act states:

> (1) When a person, by words spoken or written or by conduct, represents himself, or consents to another representing him to anyone, as a partner in an existing relationship or with one or more persons not actual partners, he is liable to any such person to whom such representation has been made, who has, on the faith of such representation, given credit to the actual or apparent partnership, and if he has made such representation or consented to its being made in a public manner he is liable to such person, whether the representation has or has not been made or communicated to such person so giving the credit by or with the knowledge of the apparent partner making the representation or consenting to its being made.
>
> (a) When a partnership liability results, he is liable as though he were an actual member of the partnership.
>
> (b) When no partnership liability results, he is liable jointly with the other persons, if any, so consenting to the contract or representation as to incur liability, otherwise separately.
>
> (2) When a person has been thus represented to be a partner in an existing partnership, or with one or more persons not actual partners, he is an agent of the persons consenting to such representation to bind them to the same extent and in the same manner as though he were a partner in fact, with respect to persons who rely upon the representation. Where all the members of the existing partnership consent to the representation, a partnership act or obligation results; but in all other cases it is the joint act or obligation of the person acting and the per-sons consenting to the representation.

46. It should be noted, moreover, that a law partnership differs from the typical business partnership in that a law partnership and its members owe fiduciary obligations to their clients. MALLEN & SMITH, LEGAL MALPRACTICE, *supra* note 4, § 5.3, at 460 & n. 4

Under more limited circumstances, the partnership by estoppel doctrine operates to prevent lawyers from denying that a partnership existed, with the result that liability will attach. To prevail under this doctrine, a plaintiff must prove: (1) that the lawyer has been held out as a partner; (2) that such holding out was done directly by the lawyer, or with the lawyer's knowledge and consent; and (3) that the plaintiff relied on the apparent partnership to his detriment.

Ordinarily, the sharing of office space and profits, or the use of a joint name on a letterhead alone, will not create a "holding out," or partnership by estoppel. In *Brown v. Gerstein*,[47] for example, the court found the evidence insufficient to apply the doctrine. There, the plaintiff sued a lawyer for malpractice and deceit in a foreclosure action, and attempted to hold a second lawyer derivatively liable because he had practiced law with the first lawyer. The two lawyers had practiced in the same offices and had used each other's name on office stationery. But there was no evidence that the uninvolved lawyer had consented to, or had knowledge of, the transactions that gave rise to the dispute. The court said:

> [T]he use of a person's name in business, even with that person's knowledge, is too slender a thread to warrant a favorable finding on the consent element.[48]

Despite this holding, there is a risk in the use of a joint name on office doors and letterheads, particularly where other acts foster the impression of a partnership.[49] In *Bonavire v. Wampler*,[50] the court found that a lawyer's acts in defrauding prospective investors were attributable to a law firm from which the pieces of evidence, taken together, supported the conclusion that a "holding out" had occurred. Throughout the course of a fraudulent investment scheme, the plaintiffs had met with the lawyer at the

---

47. 17 Mass. App. 558, 460 N.E.2d 1043, *review denied*, 391 Mass. 1105, 464 N.E.2d 73 (1984). The common law doctrine of partnership by estoppel, reflected in this case, has been codified in most jurisdictions. *See* Uniform Partnership Act § 16, *supra* note 45.

48. 17 Mass. App. 558, 460 N.E.2d 1043, 1053.

49. Hart v. Comerica Bank, 957 F. Supp. 958 (E.D. Mich. 1997); MALLEN & SMITH, LEGAL MALPRACTICE, *supra* note 4, § 5.3, at 475.

50. 779 F.2d 1011 (4th Cir. 1985).

law firm's offices, the names of the lawyer and the law firm appeared, the lawyer's name was included on the law firm's letterhead, and an agreement with the client was prepared on the law firm's stationery.[51] In addition, the lawyers had advertised in the yellow pages together as a "full service law firm," and the defrauding lawyer had introduced the other lawyer to the client as his partner.[52]

On these facts, the court concluded that the law firm had not dispelled the notion of a partnership and had, in fact, ratified the lawyer's acts, thereby making itself liable for compensatory and punitive damages.[53]

Partnership by Estoppel

In *Myers v. Aragona*[54] the court relied on the doctrine of partnership by estoppel to hold a lawyer liable under the Uniform Partnership Act to the plaintiff for funds misappropriated by another lawyer working for him. The nonparticipating lawyer was estopped to deny the existence of a partnership in which the two lawyers had listed themselves on their letterhead and had openly referred to themselves as "partners." Since the lawyers had displayed themselves as though they were partners in fact, and the third person had relied on such representations, the nonparticipating lawyer was jointly and severally liable for the torts of the misappropriating lawyer.[55]

Even though the mere use of a joint name and the sharing of office space will not in itself create liability under the estoppel theory, a prudent lawyer should specify on all communications the precise nature of his or

51. *Id.* at 1016.
52. *Id.*
53. *Id.* at 1011.
54. 21 Md. App. 45, 318 A.2d 263 (1974).
55. *See* Johnson v. Shaines & McEachern, 835 F. Supp. 685 (D.N.H. 1993) (motion for summary judgment denied because material issues of fact existed as to whether two affiliated law firms were an actual partnership or partnership by estoppel); Cottman v. Cottman, 56 Md. App. 413, 468 A.2d 131 (1983) (concept of partnership by estoppel not basis for liability where outward representations of partnership were not made until after occurrence of acts that gave rise to litigation); *see also* Duggins v. Guardianship of Washington, 632 So. 2d 420, 35 ALR5th 909 (Miss. 1993) (partnership by estoppel applied where two lawyers held to have entered into a joint venture).

her relationship with the firm or associated lawyers. The same rules apply whether an "Of Counsel" attorney is practicing primarily as a solo practitioner, with a firm, or with another lawyer. The "Of Counsel" attorney should detail the nature of his or her relationship with the firm or other lawyer in all communications, including letterheads, pleadings, shingles, law lists, legal directories, firm brochures, and professional announcement cards.[56] It is also advisable for the "Of Counsel" attorney to follow his or her signature on all business communications with the words "Of Counsel."[57] Use of terms such as "in association with" or "special tax counsel" may be misleading in that the lawyer's relationship with the firm is not clearly stated.[58]

Prudence dictates that the "Of Counsel" attorney's name be dropped from the firm's name upon withdrawing from the partnership. Although ethically permissible in some jurisdictions,[59] the retention or inclusion of the "Of Counsel" attorney's name in the firm name may signify to the public that the "Of Counsel" attorney shares mutual responsibility for legal services rendered.[60]

The retainer agreement with the client should describe the nature of the "Of Counsel" attorney's relationship with the firm or other lawyer. It should also delineate the extent of the lawyer's services and the services of other lawyers, if such services are needed.

---

56. It is good practice to apply these same principles to modern electronic communications, such as web sites and e-mail, as well as to telephonic communications, such as outgoing voice mail messages.

57. *But see* New York County Lawyers' Association Op. 662 (1984) (holding it is unnecessary for "Of Counsel" to follow name with the words "Of Counsel").

58. *See* California Ethics Op. 1986-90 (undated) (criticizing the description "a legal association" as being vague and misleading); Michigan State Ethics Op. CI-657 (1981) (criticizing the designation "special tax counsel" as misleading, since Michigan does not recognize specialties in the area of tax law, and the designation does not clearly state the lawyer's relationship with the firm). By contrast, the use of the term "Of Counsel" has a word-of-art meaning, spelled out in ABA Comm. on Ethics & Prof'l Responsibility, Formal Op. 90-357, and also conveys the nature of the relationship between the lawyer and the firm.

59. Maine Ethics Op. 86 (1988); Vermont State Ethics Op. 83-7 (undated).

60. *See* Michigan Ethics Op. CI-1001 (1984); Philadelphia Ethics Op. 88-31 (1988). If the "Of Counsel" attorney is a former member of the firm who has retired, it is proper to leave that name in the firm name. *See* discussion in Chapter 3.But if the "Of Counsel" attorney becomes an active practitioner in another firm upon retirement, his or her name should be removed from the former firm's name.

Since there is a risk that the partnership by estoppel doctrine can exist after the lawyer's withdrawal or dissolution of the partnership,[61] the "Of Counsel" attorney should promptly announce a separation from the former firm or any new status within the same firm. The "Of Counsel" attorney's name should be removed from the former firm's letterhead, office doors, and windows, as well as from the firm's checking and other accounts.

For purposes of vicarious liability, a 1997 case illustrates the distinction between partnership and partnership by estoppel. Monon Corporation retained Henry J. Price to pursue a claim of patent infringement against Wabash. Despite Monon's specific instructions not to release Wabash from any agreement that the parties might reach, Price did so. As a result, Monon brought suit against Price for legal malpractice.

At the time Price was retained, he was a partner of Barnes & Thornburg. He then joined Townsend, Yosha, Cline & Price, where he completed the work for Monon, and drafted the release. Monon also joined the individual lawyers in the firm (the "attorneys") as defendants. One of the lawyers was the sole shareholder of a professional corporation, Louis Buddy Yosha Professional Corporation. The Attorneys contended that they were employees of the corporation. The trial court granted their motion for summary judgment, but the appellate court reversed:

> Although the Attorneys indicate that the evidence shows that they worked within the framework of the professional corporation, the evidence supports the view that they carried on as co-owners of a business for profit. We conclude a genuine issue of fact exists about whether the firm really was a partnership for the purposes of vicarious liability.[62]

---

61. Royal Bank & Trust Co. v. Weintraub, Gold & Alper, 68 N.Y.2d 124, 506 N.Y.S.2d 151, 497 N.E.2d 289 (1986) (partnership remained liable for money misappropriated by former partner where partners continued to maintain all outward appearances of the partnership entity for purposes of winding up). *But see* Ventro v. Darlson, 468 So. 2d 463 (Fla. Dist. Ct. App. 1985) (failure of lawyer to remove old firm's name from window of office he continued to occupy with his new firm was insufficient to create liability under estoppel doctrine where transactions were initiated well after the lawyer left the firm, and plaintiff knew that he had done so).

62. Monon Corporation v. Townsend, Yosha, Cline & Price, 678 N.E.2d 807 (Ind. Ct. App. 1997), discussed in Chapter 1.

The court rejected the concept that the firm was a partnership by estoppel:

> . . . Monon hired Price before he joined the firm of Townsend, Yosha, Cline & Price. Although it certainly kept Price as its lawyer despite his move to the new firm with new attorneys, Monon has not demonstrated that it acted upon any representations that the firm was a partnership such that it was "influenced thereby to do some act" in reliance on the representations. . . . Monon has identified sufficient evidence to support the conclusion that the firm in question was, in fact, a partnership but has not established that it is entitled to insist upon an estoppel.[63]

Summary

Tort liability often reaches beyond the lawyer who actually committed the wrong to make other nonparticipating lawyers vicariously liable. Since "Of Counsel" relationships commonly contain characteristics of partnerships and other legal relationships, there is the risk that third parties might attempt to hold the "Of Counsel" attorney vicariously liable for the torts of other members of the firm. Much can be done to avoid this liability by careful drafting of an agreement between the "Of Counsel" attorney and the firm and advising prospective clients of the nature of this arrangement.

Because of the doctrines of *respondeat superior,* apparent authority, and partnership by estoppel, the law firm may find it more difficult to avoid vicarious liability for the wrongdoing of an "Of Counsel" attorney.

The "Of Counsel" attorney should take precautions to avoid potential liability by negating any inference to third parties that a partnership relationship exists between the parties. This necessarily means that the "Of Counsel" attorney's name should not be included in the firm's name. The "Of Counsel" attorney's status should be clearly designated on all firm communications. Finally, the "Of Counsel" attorney should never practice

63. *Id.*, discussed at 11.

law without adequate coverage under a legal malpractice policy. Coverage under such a policy, and who is responsible for the payment of the premium, should be one of the terms negotiated and included in the "Of Counsel" agreement.

Checklists for Issue Spotting

Of Counsel's Acts as Employee

(1) Is the firm vicariously liable for the "Of Counsel" attorney's acts as an employee?

(2) Was the tort committed within the scope of the "Of Counsel" attorney's actual authority?

(3) Was the tort committed while the "Of Counsel" attorney was acting within the scope of employment?

(4) Can liability attach because of the firm's failure to adequately supervise the "Of Counsel" attorney?

(5) Were the acts committed within the "Of Counsel" attorney's apparent authority? Was the third party reasonable in believing that the "Of Counsel" attorney performed the tortious acts within the scope of employment?

(6) Was the transaction one that the firm routinely provided for its clients?

Of Counsel's Acts as Independent Contractor

(1) Is the firm liable for acts of the "Of Counsel" attorney as an independent contractor? Did the firm cloak the "Of Counsel" attorney with such actual or apparent authority that he or she could bind the firm?

(2) Did the firm expressly direct the "Of Counsel" attorney to commit certain acts?

(3) Did the firm know or should it have known that the "Of Counsel" attorney was untrustworthy?

Partnership

(1) May the agreement be construed as making the "Of Counsel" attorney a partner?

(2) Is the conduct of the parties such as to give the appearance of the existence of a partnership?

(3) Was the "Of Counsel" attorney held out as a partner? Did the "Of Counsel" attorney have knowledge of the holding out? Did the "Of Counsel" attorney consent to it?

(4) Did the plaintiff reasonably rely on the implied partnership to his or her detriment?

(5) Did the parties use a joint name on office doors, letterheads, and other business communications?

(6) Where the "Of Counsel" attorney is a retired partner, has the separation from the firm as a partner been clearly announced?

CHAPTER 7

Conflicts of Interest

A lawyer who becomes "Of Counsel" may find that the interests of a new client are adverse to the interests of a client the firm currently represents or may have previously represented. Conversely, the firm may have a conflict with one or more of the "Of Counsel" attorney's current or former clients. If a lawyer maintains multiple "Of Counsel" relationships, the potential for such conflicts increases exponentially.

This chapter explores what the "Of Counsel" attorney or law firm should do when it discovers such a conflict. The ABA Model Rules of Professional Conduct[1] provide the necessary guidelines to determine the existence of a conflict. If the "Of Counsel" attorney or law firm finds a conflict, he, she, or it must decline or withdraw from representing the client, just as the firm or attorney they are associated with may not represent a client where the representation would adversely affect its relationship with another client.

It is often difficult to determine whether an "Of Counsel" attorney's conflict should be imputed to the firm or the firm's conflict imputed to the "Of Counsel" attorney. A proper analysis of this "imputed disqualification" requires two steps: (1) Does the "Of Counsel" attorney or the law firm have

1. The Model Rules, promulgated by the American Bar Association (ABA) in 1983, and amended through 2002, are the basis for the ethics rules in forty-nine states. The Model Rules replaced the earlier Model Code of Prof'l Responsibility (the Model Code), adopted in 1969, and amended through 1980. State and local bar associations have also published their own bar rules, which may or may not be consistent with the Model Rules or the Model Code. A lawyer or law firm must refer to all of these sources to determine a potential conflict.

a conflict when either is asked to represent a client because of a present or past representation? (2) If the answer is yes, is the conflict imputed to the other party such that it could cause a disqualification? We examine the first of these issues in this chapter, and defer the issue of imputed disqualification to the next chapter.

The Duties of the Lawyer

Loyalty and confidentiality are essential elements in a lawyer's representation of a client. But fulfillment of these duties may be threatened when an "Of Counsel" attorney represents two or more clients with adverse interests, or represents a client with interests adverse to a former client. These duties are also threatened when the "Of Counsel" attorney's obligations to the client conflict with his or her own personal or financial interests, or when the "Of Counsel" attorney is asked to appear as a witness at a trial where the "Of Counsel" attorney or the firm he or she is associated with represents one of the parties.

If a lawyer has reason to believe that his or her representation will be directly adverse to another client, the lawyer should decline the representation, or withdraw if the agreement has already been made to represent the client.[2] The lawyer should also decline or withdraw from representation if there is a "significant risk" the representation will be "materially limited" by responsibilities to another client, former client, or third party, or the lawyer's personal interests.[3] However, it has been recognized that the withdrawal of an attorney may work undue hardship on the client.[4] Therefore, the Model Rules permit the lawyer to represent the client if (1) "the lawyer reasonably believes that the lawyer will be able to provide competent and diligent representation to each affected client," (2) "the representation is

2. Note, *Developments in the Law: Conflicts of Interest in the Legal Profession*, 94 HARV. L. REV. 1243, 1284 (1981).

3. MODEL RULE, R. 1.7(a).

4. *See, e.g.*, Nemet v. Nemet, 112 A.D.2d 359, 491 N.Y.S.2d 810 (2d Dept. 1985), *appeal dismissed*, 66 N.Y.2d 602 (1986) (Of Counsel and law firm disqualified from representing wife in a divorce action, despite her alleged hardship).

not prohibited by law, (3) "the representation does not involve the assertion of a claim by one client against another,," and (4) each client gives "informed consent, confirmed in writing."[5] Informed consent requires the lawyer to make a full disclosure of the ramifications of the representation that might make it adverse.[6]

In addition to possible adverse client situations, the lawyer must not represent a client if the representation might be "materially limited" by his or her own interests or by "responsibilities to another client or third person."[7] Again, the lawyer may still represent the client if the conditions of Rule 1.7(b) are met. As part of the consultation for informed consent, the lawyer must explain "the material risks of and reasonably available alternatives to the proposed course of conduct."[8]

The issue of positional conflicts is addressed in detail in ABA Formal Opinion 93-377 reprinted in its entirety in Appendix H. Formal Opinion 93-377 provides useful guidance for the attorney, or firm, faced with the proposition of advocating opposing positions on a single substantive issue in which such lawyer or firm has more than one interested client, namely:

---

5. Model Rules R. 1.7 provides:

> (a) Except as provided in paragraph (b), a lawyer shall not represent a client if the representation involves a concurrent conflict of interest. A concurrent conflict of interest exists if:
>
> (1) the representation of one client will be directly adverse to another client; or
>
> (2) there is a significant risk that the representation of one or more clients will be materially limited by the lawyer's responsibilities to another client, a former client or a third person or by a personal interest of the lawyer.
>
> (b) Notwithstanding the existence of a concurrent conflict of interest under paragraph (a), a lawyer may represent a client if:
>
> (1) the lawyer reasonably believes that the lawyer will be able to provide competent and diligent representation to each affected client;
>
> (2) the representation is not prohibited by law;
>
> (3) the representation does not involve the assertion of a claim by one client against another client represented by the lawyer in the same litigation or other proceeding before a tribunal; and
>
> (4) each affected client gives informed consent, confirmed in writing.

6. The terminology section of the Model Rules, Rule 1.0, provides that "Informed consent" denotes the agreement by a person to a proposed course of conduct after the lawyer has communicated adequate information and explanation about the material risks of and reasonably available alternatives to the proposed course of conduct.

7. *See* Model Rules R. 1.7 *supra*.

8. *See note 5 supra*.

> When a lawyer is asked to advocate a position with respect to a substantive legal issue that is directly contrary to the position being urged by the lawyer (or the lawyer's firm) on behalf of another client in a different and unrelated pending matter which is being litigated in the same jurisdiction, the lawyer, in the absence of consent by both clients after full disclosure, should refuse to accept the second representation if there is a substantial risk that the lawyer's advocacy on behalf of one client will create a legal precedent which is likely to materially undercut the legal position being urged on behalf of the other client. If the two matters are not being litigated in the same jurisdiction and there is no substantial risk that either representation will be adversely affect by the other, the lawyer may proceed with both representations.

Common Conflict Problems under the Model Rules

Conflict problems may arise at any time after a client seeks a lawyer for help. Even if the client elects not to retain the lawyer, the duty of confidentiality remains.[9] For conflicts purposes, the prospective client would become a "former client."[10] The lawyer may not act as an advocate against a person represented in another matter, even if it is unrelated. But the lawyer is free to represent persons or entities whose interests are only generally adverse, such as competing businesses.[11]

The lawyer may not represent a client where the interests of another client or third person, or the lawyer's own interests, might "materially limit" the lawyer's representation.[12] For example, a lawyer may not undertake work

---

9. *See* ABA Comm. on Ethics & Prof'l Responsibility, Formal Ethics Op. 90-358 (1990), holding that if a prospective client consults a lawyer to obtain legal representation or advice, the duty of confidentiality continues even though no lawyer-client relationship is ultimately agreed upon. A lawyer or firm may not reveal information learned from a prospective client to an existing client.

10. *See* Chapter 8 for discussion of the difference between current and former clients in the conflicts setting.

11. Model Rules R. 1.7.

12. Model Rules R. 1.7(a).

for a client that he or she cannot handle competently and at a reasonable fee simply to gain income. Or the lawyer may not refer a client to a business in which he or she has an undisclosed interest.[13]

Rule 1.7(b) prohibits representation of opposing parties in litigation. Such conflicts are readily discernible. Difficulties may arise where the parties are on the same side, as coplaintiffs or codefendants. There may be substantial differences in the parties' testimony, incompatibility in their positions with reference to an opposing party, or different possibilities with regard to settlement of the overall dispute.[14]

Such conflicts are not uncommon in estate planning and estate administration. A lawyer may be called upon to represent several family members whose interests may prove to be adverse. Some jurisdictions take the position that a lawyer represents the fiduciary; others hold that the client is the estate or trust, including the beneficiaries. In either event, the lawyer should make clear his or her relationship to each of the parties.[15] If there is a conflict between the beneficiaries and the fiduciary, or among the beneficiaries, the lawyer should advise them to retain appropriate counsel.

May a lawyer represent another lawyer in a legal malpractice action, where the two lawyers are adversaries in another litigation? The representation of the colleague might materially limit the representation of the client in the other litigation. In determining whether to withdraw from representing the adversary, the lawyer should consider:

- The relative importance of the matter to the represented lawyer;
- The relative size of the fee expected by the representing lawyer;
- The relative importance to each lawyer and to his or her client of the matter involving the third-party clients;
- The sensitivity of the matter;
- The substantial similarity between the subject matter or issues of the two representations; and

13. Model Rules R. 1.7 cmt. [10].

14. Model Rules R. 1.7 cmt. [23]. In criminal cases, the potential for conflict among criminal defendants is "so grave that ordinarily a lawyer should decline to represent more than one codefendant." *Id.*

15. Model Rules R. 1.7 cmt. [27].

- The nature of the relationship of one lawyer to the other and of each lawyer to his or her third-party client[16]

The potential for conflict in this situation is apparent: One or both of the lawyers may fail to provide their respective clients zealous representation; or the demands of their regular clients may jeopardize their own lawyer-client relationship. The "preferable approach is to examine each of the various types of lawyer-lawyer relationships that might be involved and assess questions of conflict based on a consideration of all relevant factors, including the nature of the representations and the relationship between the lawyers."[17]

Where a lawyer represents multiple clients on the same side, conflicts often arise because of discrepancies in the parties' testimony, incompatible positions as to the opposing party, or different possibilities for settlement. For the lawyer to continue to represent these parties, he or she must explain the ramifications and intricacies of all persons and entities involved in the litigation, and obtain their consents. Sometimes the lawyer may act as a third-party neutral to assist parties in resolving their differences, such as through arbitration or mediation; but in doing so, the lawyer must ensure such parties understand there is no attorney-client relationship between them.[18] In the event one of the parties later seeks to retain the lawyer in connection with a matter in which the lawyer participated as a neutral, the

16. ABA Comm. on Ethics & Prof'l Responsibility, Formal Ethics Op. 97-406 (ABA 1997); Rhode Island Supreme Court Ethics Advisory Panel Op. 96-23 (1996) (semble); Comm. on Prof'l Ethics of the Association of the Bar of the City of New York, No. 1996-3 (1996), quoting the former "First Brother" Billy Carter as saying "Sometimes even lawyers need lawyers," citing A DICTIONARY OF LEGAL QUOTATIONS, 88.13 at 103 (S. James & C. Stebbings eds. 1987); Alabama State Bar Op. RO-96-06 (1996).

17. RESTATEMENT (THIRD) OF THE LAW GOVERNING LAWYERS § 124 cmt. [d] (1998).

18. MODEL RULES R. 2.4, Lawyer Serving as Third-Party Neutral, provides as follows:

> (a) A lawyer serves as a third-party neutral when the lawyer assists two or more persons who are not clients of the lawyer to reach a resolution of a dispute or other matter that has arisen between them. Service as a third-party neutral may include service as an arbitrator, a mediator or in such other capacity as will enable the lawyer to assist the parties to resolve the matter.
>
> (b) A lawyer serving as a third-party neutral shall inform unrepresented parties that the lawyer is not representing them. When the lawyer knows or reasonably should know that a party does not understand the lawyer's role in the matter, the lawyer shall explain the difference between the lawyer's role as a third-party neutral and a lawyer's role as one who represents a client.

lawyer must obtain the informed consent of all parties to the proceeding, confirmed in writing.[19]

Effect of Formal Opinion 90-357 on Conflict Problems

A conflict-of-interest problem may arise in several ways, but most conflict problems are caused by the lawyer's simultaneous or successive representation of clients with adverse interests. After Formal Opinion 90-357, conflict problems are also likely to arise from a lawyer's ability to maintain "Of Counsel" relationships with more than two law firms at the same time.

Although Formal Opinion 90-357 eliminated the prohibitions against lawyers entering into multiple "Of Counsel" relationships, it emphasized that one must guard against too many "Of Counsel" relationships because of the rules governing disqualification:

> As a practical matter, nonetheless, there is a consideration that is likely to put a relatively low limit on the number of "of counsel" relationships that can be undertaken by a particular lawyer: this is the fact that . . . the relationship clearly means that the lawyer is "associated" with each firm with which the lawyer is of counsel. In consequence there is attribution to the lawyer who is of counsel of all the disqualifications of each firm, and, correspondingly, attribution from the of counsel lawyer to each firm, of each of those disqualifications. See Model Rule 1.10(a). In consequence, the effect of two or more firms sharing an of counsel lawyer is to make them all effectively a single firm, for purposes of attribution of disqualifications.[20]

Additional conflict problems will likely result from law firms being able to enter into "Of Counsel" relationships with other law firms.[21] Under these

---

19. Model Rules R. 1.12.

20. *See* Appendix G.

21. *See* Mustang Enterprises, Inc. v. Plug-In Storage Systems, Inc., 874 F. Supp. 881 (N.D. Ill. 1995) (law firms that state on their letterheads that they are "associated" become one for conflicts purposes.) Regarding relationships among law firms in general, *see* ABA Comm. on

circumstances, lawyers and law firms should be very careful about entering into multiple "Of Counsel" relationships. The potential for conflicts and imputed disqualification will deter lawyers from entering into certain "Of Counsel" relationships as well as from too many "Of Counsel" relationships.

Conflicts in Simultaneous Representation

Both the Model Code and the Model Rules prohibit the lawyer from simultaneously representing multiple clients with interests that are directly adverse to one another. Model Code DR 5-105(A) provided that a lawyer must decline to represent a client if, in the lawyer's independent professional judgment, the client could be adversely affected by the lawyer's acceptance of the proffered employment, or if such representation might involve the lawyer in representing differing interests. Model Rule 1.7(a) bars representation of a client if that representation will be "directly adverse" to another client, even if that representation is wholly unrelated.[22] Model Rule 1.7(a) further prohibits multiple representation if the lawyer's ability to represent one client will be "materially limited by the lawyer's responsibilities to another client or to a third person, or by the lawyer's own interests."[23] However, Rule 1.7(b) provides for a waiver of these rules if the following conditions are met:

> (1) the lawyer reasonably believes that the lawyer will be able to provide competent and diligent representation to each affected client;
> (2) the representation is not prohibited by law;
> (3) the representation does not involve the assertion of a claim by one client against another client represented by the lawyer in the same litigation or other proceeding before a tribunal; and
> (4) each affected client gives informed consent, confirmed in writing.

Therefore, if handled properly, lawyers can responsibly undertake representation of potentially conflicting interests — for example, when giving advice

---

Ethics & Prof'l Responsibility, Formal Ethics Op. 94-388 (1994), *reprinted in* Appendix I.
22. Model Rules R. 1.7(a).
23. *Id.*

to both the buyer and seller in drafting a contract, or to both the husband and wife in a divorce proceeding. Sometimes the clients so trust the lawyer that they are willing to overlook their minor differences, and thereby reduce lawyer fees, by permitting the lawyer to serve as an intermediary and seek to establish or adjust a relationship between them on an amicable and mutually advantageous basis.[24] But a lawyer should proceed cautiously in representing both sides of a transaction; if hostility between the parties should arise, there will also arise an inability to represent either party.[25]

A law firm may ask, for example, whether its "Of Counsel" relationship with a lawyer who represents the majority ownership interests of a seller in a particular transaction precludes it from undertaking representation to document the sale. In one such situation raised before the State Bar of Michigan, a law firm had for several years represented two different clients, each engaged in the construction business. One client was a corporation involved in commercial construction. The other was a partnership involved in multifamily residential construction composed of two corporations. The majority shareowner of each partnership corporation was deceased, and the estate's personal representative and fiduciary was a retired partner of the law firm, who remained with the firm in an "Of Counsel" capacity. The law firm had appeared in probate court on behalf of the estate fiduciary.

Beneficiaries of the estate and the personal representative sought to sell certain partnership assets to the corporation client. The economic terms of the transaction had been negotiated between the partnership and the corporation with the "Of Counsel" lawyer's participation. The parties then sought counsel to document the terms of the transaction.

The law firm asked whether it may represent the purchaser corporation in documenting the transaction under the following circumstances:

---

24. *See* Model Rules R. 1.7, cmt. [28]; and Model Code of Prof'l ResponsibilityDR 5-105(C).

25. *See* Model Rules R. 1.7. and Nemet v. Nemet, 112 A.D.2d 359, 491 N.Y.S.2d 810, 811 (2d Dept. 1985), *appeal dismissed,* 66 N.Y.S.2d 602 (1986) (Of Counsel and law firm disqualified from representing wife where "Of Counsel" had been formerly employed by husband's law firm; "appearance of impropriety" evident in the "Of Counsel" arrangement).

(1) Separate counsel would be retained to represent the interests of the partnership, the two partnership corporations, and the estate beneficiaries;
(2) The purchasing corporation would retain separate counsel to advise it on the issue of conflict waiver;
(3) All parties to the transaction would consent to the law firm's representation of the purchasing corporation in the matter after consultation with separate counsel; and
(4) The terms of the transaction would be presented to the probate court for approval, and the consent of all estate beneficiaries would be obtained.

Relying on Model Rule 1.7, the Michigan Standing Committee on Professional and Judicial Ethics[26] concluded that the fiduciary duties of the "Of Counsel" lawyer materially limited his ability to undertake representation to document the sale for the seller and purchaser.

> Having already represented the interests of the seller in determining the terms of the transaction, even though this "representation" was in a fiduciary capacity and not as counsel for the estate, the "of counsel" lawyer could not now switch sides and purport to impartially document the transaction for both parties. The conflict is not vitiated by the involvement of the probate court, since the estate fiduciary is responsible for recommending the matter to the court and is not impartial.[27]

Because the "Of Counsel" attorney's fiduciary duties would adversely affect his ability to document the sale, client consent would not vitiate the conflict. The committee went further, holding that the law firm was precluded from representing the selling partnership and the estate fiduciary in the sale transaction.

26. State Bar of Michigan, Standing Comm. on Prof'l & Judicial Ethics, Op. No. RI-237 (1995).
27. *Id.*

> Even if the proposed representation is seen as merely documenting the arrangements already agreed upon, a direct conflict is presented under the terms of MRPC 1.7(a). . . . Although the selling partnership and the estate fiduciary may be in agreement concerning the sale of assets to the purchasing corporation, the fact that both the selling partnership and the estate fiduciary are current clients of the law firm exacerbates the law firm's conflict in documenting the transaction impartially and independently for all parties.[28]

However, the committee found that, unlike the Of Counsel lawyer, the law firm might be able to undertake the documentation representation if no member of the law firm had been involved in the transaction on behalf of the seller if it obtained informed con-sent of the partnership and the purchasing corporation.

Conflict problems are often obvious from the moment the lawyer undertakes the representation.[29] Differing interests between clients can arise in many, often subtle, ways. For this reason, identifying a conflict problem often requires a careful and ongoing analysis of the facts, as well as the interests and expectations of the parties.

Conflicts in Successive Representation

Successive representation raises questions regarding the lawyer's dual duties of loyalty and confidentiality. A breach of these duties is generally confined to matters that are "substantially related."[30] Although the Model Code did not specifically address this problem, case law developed the doctrine of the "substantial relationship" test, a two-part inquiry: First, are the former and present representations adverse in a material way? Second, are the matters

28. *Id.*

29. For example, a law firm was disqualified from representing a debtor-in-possession where an attorney who was "Of Counsel" to the law firm was the son of a partner of the debtor. *In re* ZB Surfside Co., 1994 Bankr. LEXIS 1852 (Bankr. S.D.N.Y. 1994).

30. Model Rules R. 1.9(a). The text of Rule 1.9(a) is as follows:

> A lawyer who has formerly represented a client in a matter shall not thereafter represent another person in the same or a substantially related matter in which that person's interests are materially adverse to the interests of the former client unless the former client gives informed consent, confirmed in writing.

substantially related? If the answer to both these questions is in the affirmative, the lawyer is prohibited from continuing in the matter, unless the former client consents in writing after consultation.[31]

When there is a substantial relationship between the former and current representations, two basic presumptions arise: First, if there is a lawyer-client relationship, it is presumed the lawyer has access to and receives privileged information from the client.[32] Second, when the matters are related, it is presumed that the lawyer will divulge former client confidences. The need for these presumptions stems from the view that the former client should not be forced to prove that confidential information was in fact given.[33]

Sometimes it is a close question as to whether a particular client is a current or former client. A current client can bar the lawyer from representing another client whose interests are "directly adverse." If the client is a former one, the substantial relationship test must be satisfied to disqualify a present representation.

In *Heathcoat v. Santa Fe International Corp.* for example, a law firm prepared a client's will.[34] Later, it represented someone else who was adverse to its former client. During this adverse representation, it sent a form letter to the former client, inviting her to call the firm for advice in view of recent changes in the tax law. Despite this letter, the court characterized the client as a former client, and refused to disqualify the law firm.[35] However, court decisions are very fact specific on this subject and will vary by jurisdiction.

For example, in a similar case in Washington, a law firm was disqualified from representing a party with interests adverse to former client in a substantially related matter, even though the partner who had represented the former client was no longer with law firm, where the attorney remaining with the law firm was significantly involved in the former client's suit and several other firm employees who had worked on suit were unaccounted for.[36]

31. *Id.*

32. *Supra* note 2, at 1328–29.

33. *Id.*

34. 532 F. Supp. 961 (E.D. Ark. 1982).

35. *Id.* at 963-64.

36. Oxford Systems, Inc. v. Cellpro, Inc., 45 F. Supp. 2d 1055 (W. D. Wash. 1999); Mindscape, Inc. v. Media Depot, Inc., 973 F. Supp. 1130 (N.D. Cal. 1997) (defense counsel had

In still another case, a law firm represented a company and its president individually over a period of years. It eventually billed the company $785 for its last work, but never sought to collect the bill. Meanwhile, it sent out firm newsletters addressed to "clients and friends." It also retained the company's corporate minute books and the president's will. One of the firm's lawyers casually referred to the company and its president as his "clients." The court ruled that the mailings of the newsletters were "routine ministerial actions" and that the lawyer's comments about the company and its president still being clients were "ice-breaking" comments that could not be given "significant weight." It concluded:

> It is unreasonable to continue to demand an attorney's undivided loyalty for an indefinite period of time when the attorney's last bill is both disputed and unpaid, and when each of several opportunities to use the attorney's services is directed to another firm.[37]

Lawyers Moving between Firms

As explained above, Model Rule 1.9(a) provides a strict rule of disqualification in the case of a lawyer's representation of a current client adverse to that lawyer's former client. This rule is not always appropriate when the lawyer has moved to a new firm and the representation of the former client took place at his or her former firm. Although the client previously represented by the former firm has a strong interest against compromise of the principle of loyalty, there are competing considerations: The new client should have reasonable choice of counsel, and the ethics rules should

---

ongoing relationship with plaintiff and was disqualified from representing defendant where counsel had yet to correct mistake on patent filed for plaintiff; plaintiff had granted power of attorney for patent to counsel and counsel had never advised plaintiff that counsel considered its representation terminated); and Research Corp. Technologies v. Hewlett-Packard Co., 936 F. Supp. 697 (D. Ariz. 1996) (plaintiff law firm's recent contact with defendant made defendant a current client of law firm).

37. Artromick Int'l, Inc. v. Drustar, Inc., 134 F.R.D. 226, 231 (S.D. Ohio 1991); *see also* McCook Metals L.L.C. v. Alcoa, 2001 U.S. Dist. LEXIS 497, 2001 WL 58959 (N.D. Ill. Jan. 18, 2001) (in case involving patent counsel, current relationship did not exist where law firm had one discrete project and other communications between parties were merely "business development").

not unreasonably restrict lawyer mobility. These competing interests are recognized in the comments to Rule 1.9 and the relevant considerations are described as follows:

> When lawyers have been associated within a firm but then end their association, the question of whether a lawyer should undertake representation is more complicated. There are several competing considerations. First, the client previously represented by the former firm must be reasonably assured that the principle of loyalty to the client is not compromised. Second, the rule should not be so broadly cast as to preclude other persons from having reasonable choice of legal counsel. Third, the rule should not unreasonably hamper lawyers from forming new associations and taking on new clients after having left a previous association. In this connection, it should be recognized that today many lawyers practice in firms, that many lawyers to some degree limit their practice to one field or another, and that many move from one association to another several times in their careers. If the concept of imputation were applied with unqualified rigor, the result would be radical curtailment of the opportunity of lawyers to move from one practice setting to another and of the opportunity of clients to change counsel.[38]

For these reasons, Rule 1.9(b)[39] operates to disqualify the lawyer only if he or she has actual knowledge or information concerning the client that is protected by Rules 1.6[40] and 1.9(c). Therefore, if the lawyer during his or

---

38. *See* Model Rules R. 1.9 cmt. [4].

39. The text of Model Rule 1.9(b) is as follows:

> (b) A lawyer shall not knowingly represent a person in the same or a substantially related matter in which a firm with which the lawyer formerly was associated had previously represented a client,
>
> (1) whose interests are materially adverse to that person; and
>
> (2) about whom the lawyer has acquired information protected by Rule 1.6 and 1.9(c) that is material to the matter; unless the former client gives informed consent, confirmed in writing.

40. Model Rule 1.6(a) provides that "[a] lawyer shall not reveal information relating to the representation of a client unless the client gives informed consent, the disclosure is impliedly authorized in order to carry out the representation or the disclosure is permitted by paragraph (b)." Model Rule 1.6(b) permits disclosure "to the extent the lawyer reasonably

her association with the former firm acquired no knowledge or information concerning a particular client of that firm, and the lawyer joins a new firm, neither the lawyer nor the new firm is disqualified from representing a current client in the same or a related matter even though the two clients have conflicting interests.

The Peripheral-Representation Exception

Thus, even if a substantial relationship is found between the former and current representations, the "Of Counsel" attorney who has moved to a new firm may avoid disqualification if he or share is able to demonstrate they were only "peripherally involved" in the former representation at his or her former firm.[41] If disqualification of the lawyer is sought because of matters that the firm handled, and not because of his or her own personal involvement, the court, in essence, allows the irrebuttable presumption to be rebutted.[42] Thus, an actively and heavily involved lawyer must be distinguished from one who "enter[ed] briefly on the periphery for a limited and specific purpose relating solely to legal questions."[43] In the latter case,

---

believes necessary":

(1) to prevent reasonably certain death or substantial bodily harm;
(2) to prevent the client from committing a crime or fraud that is reasonably certain to result in substantial injury to the financial interests or property of another and in furtherance of which the client has used or is using the lawyer's services;
(3) to prevent, mitigate or rectify substantial injury to the financial interests or property of another that is reasonably certain to result or has resulted from the client's commission of a crime or fraud in furtherance of which the client has used the lawyer's services;
(4) to secure legal advice about the lawyer's compliance with these Rules;
(5) to establish a claim or defense on behalf of the lawyer in a controversy between the lawyer and the client, to establish a defense to a criminal charge or civil claim against the lawyer based upon conduct in which the client was involved, or to respond to allegations in any proceeding concerning the lawyer's representation of the client;
(6) to comply with other law or a court order; or
(7) to detect and resolve conflicts of interest arising from the lawyer's change of employment or from changes in the composition or ownership of a firm, but only if the revealed information would not compromise the attorney-client privilege or otherwise prejudice the client.

41. Atasi Corp. v. Seagate Technology, 847 F.2d 826, 829 (Fed. Cir. 1988).

42. *See* Trone v. Smith, 621 F.2d 994, 998 n.3 (9th Cir. 1980); Silver Chrysler Plymouth, Inc. v. Chrysler Motors Corp., 518 F.2d 751 (2d Cir. 1975).

43. *Silver Chrysler,* 518 F.2d 751.

the assumptions underlying the traditional notion of the lawyer-client relationship no longer apply.[44]

A "peripheral" lawyer may be one called in as a consultant on one aspect of a case, or an associate whose involvement in the matter was limited or sporadic. Such a lawyer's role would not be representation that would require disqualification.

Although some courts apply a rebuttable presumption if the lawyer was only "peripherally" involved,[45] a very strict standard of proof is normally needed to rebut the presumption.[46] The exception for peripheral involvement has been used in a case involving the disqualification of an "Of Counsel" lawyer. In *Atasi Corp. v. Seagate Technology*,[47] the conflict involved a classic case of a lawyer switching sides in the middle of the litigation. The court easily found that a substantial relationship existed between the lawyer's former and current representations. The lawyer involved had been "Of Counsel" to a firm representing the defendant, but, before the litigation concluded, became "Of Counsel" to a new firm representing the plaintiff. The "Of Counsel" attorney argued that he did not receive any confidential information while "Of Counsel" at the first firm.[48] But the court noted that the lawyer's disqualification did not rest upon proof of actual disclosure; the test "only depends on whether the former and current representations are substantially related."[49] Since the former representation was the very same action at law as the current representation, the substantial relationship test was satisfied.

Having found a substantial relationship, the court next considered whether the "Of Counsel" attorney's personal involvement in the former representation warranted mitigating the rebuttable presumption of shared confidences. The court noted that the "Of Counsel" attorney had personally signed a pleading, helped prepare a brief, and twice visited the defendant's

---

44. *See* Model Rules R. 1.9 cmt. 5 ("Paragraph (b) operates to disqualify the lawyer only when the lawyer involved has actual knowledge of information protected by Rules 1.6 and 1.9(c).").

45. *Silver Chrysler*, 518 F.2d at 756–57.

46. LaSalle Nat'l Bank v. Lake County, 703 F.2d 252 (7th Cir. 1983).

47. 847 F.2d 826 (Fed. Cir. 1988).

48. *Id.* at 829.

49. *Id.*

facility. As a result, the defense of peripheral representation failed, and the "Of Counsel" attorney and his new firm were disqualified from current representation.

Atasi illustrates that, by itself, the "Of Counsel" designation will not prevent disqualification under the exception for peripheral representation. The label attached to the relationship will not determine the success or failure of the defense. Rather, the lawyer's actual involvement, without regard to his or her status within the firm, is controlling. Where the "Of Counsel" attorney's signature appears on pleadings or briefs, or where personal appearances are made, it is unlikely that the involvement will be considered "peripheral."

The peripheral-representation exception is not limited to rebutting the presumption that the involved lawyer actually received confidential information. It has also been used to prevent firm-wide disqualification that is, where the firm seeks to rebut the presumption that confidential information was divulged to the firm's current affiliates.[50]

Advancing Inconsistent Positions

May a lawyer take inconsistent positions on a legal question when representing two or more parties in different cases? Rule 1.7 allows this, unless representation of either party would be adversely affected.[51] This may be proper in cases pending in different trial courts, but not in an appellate court.[52] Taking inconsistent positions in unrelated matters is improper if

---

50. *See infra,* Chapter 8.

51. Model Rules 1.7 cmt. [24], which states in part:

> A conflict of interest exists, however, if there is a significant risk that a lawyer's action on behalf of one client will materially limit the lawyer's effectiveness in representing another client in a different case; for example, when a decision favoring one client will create a precedent likely to seriously weaken the position taken on behalf of the other client. Factors relevant in determining whether the clients need to be advised of the risk include: where the cases are pending, whether the issue is substantive or procedural, the temporal relationship between the matters, the significance of the issue to the immediate and long-term interests of the clients involved and the clients' reasonable expectations in retaining the lawyer. If there is significant risk of material limitation, then absent informed consent of the affected clients, the lawyer must refuse one of the representations or withdraw from one or both matters.

52. *Id. See* Fiandaca v. Cunningham, 827 F.2d 825 (1st Cir. 1987) (applying New Hampshire ethics rules); Estates Theatres, Inc. v. Columbia Pictures Industries, Inc., 345 F. Supp. 93 (S.D.N.Y. 1972) (applying New York ethics rules).

there is a substantial risk that a lawyer will undercut the position taken for one of his clients.[53] The lawyer should first obtain the consent of both clients after making a full disclosure of the potential ramifications.[54]

Determining Of Counsel Disqualification

When a conflict arises from an "Of Counsel" attorney's involvement in a former and current representation, the approach is the same as it would be for any other lawyer. The inquiry focuses upon whether or not there is a substantial relationship between the subject matter of the two representations.[55] A substantial relationship may exist, for example, if the former representation is the same action at law as the current representation,[56] if there is a significant overlap between the services rendered in the two representations, or if the factual contexts of the two representations are similar.[57]

53. ABA Comm. on Ethics & Prof'l Responsibility, Legal Ethics Op. 377 (1993). Similar conclusions have been reached by several state ethics commissions. *See* Maine Ethics Op. 155 (January 15, 1997); D.C. Bar Legal Ethics Comm. Op. 265 (March 20, 1996); State Bar of Michigan Ethics Comm. Op. RI-108 (Dec. 3. 1991); State Bar of New Mexico, Advisory Opinions Comm., Op. 1990-3 (May 23, 1990); Association of the Bar of the City of New York, Comm. on Prof'l & Judicial Ethics, Formal Op. 1990-4 (May 22, 1990); Philadelphia Bar Association, Prof'l Guidance Comm., Op. 89-27 (Mar. 1990), State Bar of Michigan Ethics Comm. Op. CI-1194 (Apr. 6, 1988); Arizona State Bar, Comm. on the Rules of Prof'l Conduct, Op. 87-15 (July 27, 1987).

54. E.g. State Bar of California, Standing Comm. on Prof'l Responsibility & Conduct, Formal Op. 1989-108 (undated) ("Even where there is a substantial likelihood that one or both clients will be prejudiced by the representation, the attorney is not acting unethically by continuing the representation. The prudent attorney, however, will advise both clients of the other representation (if to do so will not violate the attorney/client relationship) and allow both an opportunity to seek new counsel.").

55. Niemi v. Girl Scouts of Minnesota & Wisconsin Lakes & Pines, 768 N.W.2d 385 (Minn. App. 2009).

56. Atasi Corp. v. Seagate Technology, 847 F.2d 826, 829 (Fed. Cir. 1988).

57. United States *ex rel.* Lord Elec. v. Titan Pacific Constr. Corp., 637 F. Supp. 1556, 1560 (W.D. Wash. 1986). The approaches taken by the courts are varied. *Compare* Phillips v. Haidet, 119 Ohio App. 3d 322, 327 (1997) (substantial relationship requires "commonality of issues"), *with* Rogers v. Pittston Co., 800 F. Supp. 350, 353 (W.D. Va. 1992), *aff'd*, 996 F.2d 1212 (4th Cir. 1993) (substantial relationship means "identical" or "essentially the same"). *See also* new comment [3] to 2002 Model Rule 1.9, which states that matters are "substantially related" for purposes of the rule "if they involve the same transaction or legal dispute or if there otherwise is a substantial risk that confidential factual information as would normally have been obtained in the prior representation would materially advance the client's position

A finding of a substantial relationship will give rise to the initial presumption that the "Of Counsel" attorney received confidences during the prior representation, potentially causing disqualification.

To prevent disqualification, the "Of Counsel" attorney must look at the subject matter of the two representations to determine whether the first presumption can be avoided altogether. This will turn on whether a substantial relationship exists. If a substantial relationship exists, the "Of Counsel" attorney must withdraw, unless the former client consents. However, if the former representation took place at the "Of Counsel" attorney's former law firm, the "Of Counsel" attorney and his or her new law firm may be able to avoid disqualification if the "Of Counsel" attorney did not acquire material information about the former firm's client that is protected by Rules 1.6 and 1.9(c). Thus, if the "Of Counsel" attorney was not involved, or was only peripherally involved, in the representation of his or her former firm's client, Model Rule 1.9(b) will not require disqualification.

For example, in *Niemi v. Girl Scouts of Minnesota and Wisconsin Lakes and Pines*,[58] the court refused to disqualify an attorney and his firm from representing the Girl Scouts in an action brought against the Girl Scouts by Niemi, a former client of the attorney and firm, on the grounds that:

> 25 years passed between the conclusion of [the attorney]'s representation of Niemi in the prior lawsuit and the beginning of his representation of the Girl Scouts in the present lawsuit. The facts that were relevant to Niemi's first lawsuit likely are irrelevant to the present lawsuit or have only limited, peripheral relevance because those facts are obsolete. The lack of relevance means that there is not "a substantial risk that confidential factual information" that presumably was communicated from Niemi to [the attorney] . . . during the first lawsuit "would materially advance [the Girl Scouts'] position in" the present lawsuit. Minn. R. Prof. Conduct 1.9 cmt. 3. Consequently, the prior lawsuit is not "so closely related to subject matter of present suit that it is readily apparent that it is substantially and essentially akin to the

in the subsequent matter."

58. 768 N.W.2d 385, 391–392 (Minn. App. 2009).

pending matter." (citation omitted). Thus, the present lawsuit is not a "substantially related matter" for purposes of rule 1.9(a). Because [the attorney] is not disqualified by rule 1.9(a), the [the attorney's law firm] is not disqualified by imputation by rule 1.10(a).[59]

Summary

While conflict of interest problems are common in all professional relationships of lawyers, the addition of an "Of Counsel" relationship increases the chances of encountering such problems. Most conflict problems arise from the lawyer's simultaneous or successive representation of multiple clients with adverse interests. If the conflict arises from simultaneously representing multiple clients with adverse interests, the lawyer is prohibited from undertaking the representation of such clients.

If the conflict arises from the lawyer's representation of a current client with interests adverse to those of a former client, the lawyer is prohibited from the current representation if the former and current matters are substantially related. If the matters are "substantially related," a presumption arises: Confidential information is deemed to have been obtained by the lawyer from the former client during the former representation. It is further presumed that the lawyer will use this information to the former client's disadvantage.

Some courts hold the substantial relationship presumption to be irrebuttable. But many recognize an exception where the lawyer was only "peripherally" involved in the former representation. A peripheral lawyer might be one called in as a consultant, or an associate whose involvement was limited to research in the library.

Lawyers who move between firms as "Of Counsel" attorneys or who maintain multiple "Of Counsel" relationships must guard against possible conflict of interest problems. Under these circumstances, the peripheral exception becomes important. "Of Counsel" lawyers are often used in

59. *Id.*

a limited capacity within a law firm. To force an "Of Counsel" attorney to withdraw would work a hardship on their desire to practice in an "Of Counsel" capacity, and preclude their moving between firms, without serving any useful social purpose. Similarly, requiring the law firm to withdraw might be of little social utility. Where the "Of Counsel" attorney's name appears on pleadings and other court documents, or where the "Of Counsel" attorney made personal appearances on behalf of a former client, the peripheral-lawyer exception cannot be used. And, in other situations, the courts should look closely at the extent of the actual involvement before requiring a withdrawal.

Thanks to the liberality of Formal Opinion 90-357, lawyers and law firms may now enter into multiple "Of Counsel" relationships. However, in view of the rules with regard to imputed disqualification, all parties to a prospective "Of Counsel" arrangement should carefully consider the effects of the relationship before finalizing an agreement. In the next chapter, we shall consider the effects of the "Of Counsel" relationship on imputed disqualification.

Checklists for Issue Spotting

Simultaneous Representation

(1) Is the "Of Counsel" attorney or firm simultaneously representing clients with adverse interests?

(2) Are the clients coplaintiffs? Are they codefendants? Is it likely that the clients' interests will become adverse during litigation?

Successive Representation

(1) Are there any facts that might cause the former client to be considered to be a current client?

(2) Is the "Of Counsel" attorney or firm representing a client who has a direct conflict with a former client of the "Of Counsel" attorney or the "Of Counsel" attorney's former firm?

(3) Are the former and current representations substantially related? Are the representations related to the same controversy? Does it appear

that the "Of Counsel" attorney had access to confidential information of the former client? Are the legal or factual issues of the two matters related?

The Peripheral-Representation Exception

(1) If the matters are substantially related, can the "Of Counsel" attorney take advantage of the peripheral-representation exception?

(2) Was the "Of Counsel" attorney actively involved in the former representation? Did he or she personally sign pleadings, briefs, or opinion letters? Did the "Of Counsel" attorney make personal appearances on behalf of the client? Was there participation in private conferences with the former client?

(3) Was the "Of Counsel" attorney's involvement in the former representation peripheral? Was this involvement brief and for a limited purpose? Was the "Of Counsel" attorney called in as a consultant on one aspect of the case? Was this involvement limited to legal research or technical advice?

CHAPTER 8

IMPUTED DISQUALIFICATION

In general, when a lawyer is disqualified by a conflict, all lawyers "associated" with this lawyer are vicariously disqualified. As the ABA Standing Committee on Ethics and Professional Responsibility pointed out in Formal Opinion 90-357, "[t]here can be no doubt that an of counsel lawyer (or firm) is 'associated in' and has an 'association with' the firm (or firms) to which the lawyer is of counsel,"[1] for purposes of the rules of imputation of disqualification. But a broad and inflexible rule of vicarious disqualification may work hardship on lawyers in general, and on lawyers who are "Of Counsel" in particular. As the following sections illustrate, the general rule of imputed disqualification is subject to exceptions and modifications.

Rules Governing Imputed Disqualification

The ABA Model Code of Professional Responsibility applied a sweeping rule to disqualify all members of an affected lawyer's firm from continuing in the representation once a conflict had been found. If one lawyer was disqualified from representing a client because of a conflict of interest, every partner and associate in the law firm was also disqualified.[2]

---

1. ABA Comm. on Ethics & Prof'l Responsibility, Formal Op. 90-357, at 13.

2. MODEL CODE OF PROF'L RESPONSIBILITY [hereinafter MODEL CODE] DR 5-105(D) (1969, amended 1980) provides:

> If a lawyer is required to decline employment or to withdraw from employment

The Model Rules of Professional Conduct modified this approach somewhat by imposing firm-wide disqualification only where there is a special danger of conflicting representation by present or past associates of the same firm.[3] Model Rule 1.10(a) provides that, while lawyers are currently "associated" in a firm, none of them can represent a client if any one of them practicing alone would be disqualified from representing a client.[4] The application of this rule is limited to circumstances where a lawyer is disqualified on the grounds that the representation would offend the conflict of interest rule with regard to a present client (Model Rules, R 1.7), and where a lawyer is disqualified on the grounds that the representation would offend the conflict of interest rule with regard to a former client (Model Rules, R 1.9). However, if the disqualification of the specific lawyer is based on such lawyer's personal interests, and the such interests would not be an impediment to the remaining lawyers in the firm, disqualification is not imputed to the rest of firm.[5]

> under a Disciplinary Rule, no partner or associate, or any other lawyer affiliated with him or his firm may accept or continue such employment.

3. Model Rules of Prof'l Conduct [hereinafter Model Rules] R. 1.10.
4. Model Rules R. 1.10(a) provides:

> While lawyers are associated in a firm, none of them shall knowingly represent a client when any one of them practicing alone would be prohibited from doing so by Rules 1.7 or 1.9, unless
>
> (1) the prohibition is based on a personal interest of the disqualified lawyer and does not present a significant risk of materially limiting the representation of the client by the remaining lawyers in the firm; or
>
> (2) the prohibition is based upon Rule 1.9(a) or (b) and arises out of the disqualified lawyer's association with a prior firm, and
>
> (i) the disqualified lawyer is timely screened from any participation in the matter and is apportioned no part of the fee therefrom;
>
> (ii) written notice is promptly given to any affected former client to enable the former client to ascertain compliance with the provisions of this Rule, which shall include a description of the screening procedures employed; a statement of the firm's and of the screened lawyer's compliance with these Rules; a statement that review may be available before a tribunal; and an agreement by the firm to respond promptly to any written inquiries or objections by the former client about the screening procedures; and
>
> (iii) certifications of compliance with these Rules and with the screening procedures are provided to the former client by the screened lawyer and by a partner of the firm, at reasonable intervals upon the former client's written request and upon termination of the screening procedures.

5. *Id.*

Imputed-disqualification issues frequently arise when there is a substantial relationship between representations that are adverse to a current or former client. We shall focus on the rules that have developed in this area, with emphasis on conflicts that arise due to a firm's multiple representation or conflicts that arise after a lawyer has left one firm and joined another that represents a client with interests adverse to a client of the former firm.

The Presumption of Shared Confidences

The substantial-relationship test (described in Chapter 7) triggers two presumptions. The first, related to the receipt of confidential information, causes disqualification of the individual lawyer. Under the second presumption, the disqualified lawyer is presumed to have conveyed the confidential information to all of the lawyers in the current firm, causing the disqualification of the entire firm. But whether this latter presumption is irrebuttable depends upon whether the lawyers are currently or formerly affiliated.

Present Affiliates: Presumption of Shared Confidences

When lawyers work together, they are presumed to share confidences. The threat that confidential information may be disclosed raises a presumption of conflict.

However, under Model Rule 1.10(a) conflicts that arise among currently associated attorneys are not bar to representation where the conflict arises out of an attorney's personal interest and does not present a significant risk of materially limiting the representation by other attorneys in the firm, or is based on an attorney's prior firm affiliation, provided the disqualified lawyer is timely screened and the client is given written notice and periodic certifications of compliance by the firm.[6]

Prior to recent Model Rule amendments, a number of courts imposed an irrebuttable presumption of shared confidences,[7] the majority of which

6. *Id.*

7. *See* Westinghouse Elec. Corp. v. Kerr-McGee Corp., 580 F.2d 1311 (7th Cir.), *cert. denied*, 439 U.S. 955 (1978); International Business Mach. Corp. v. Levin, 579 F.2d 271 (3d Cir. 1978); Fund of Funds, Ltd. v. Arthur Andersen & Co., 567 F.2d 225 (2d Cir. 1977).

did not inquire into whether confidential information was in fact shared between the lawyers, reflecting the general notion that the risk of even casual sharing was too great.[8] As long as the matters were substantially related, the lawyer and the entire firm were disqualified. To prevent disqualification, the lawyer and firm had to show that there was no substantial relationship between the multiple representations. For example, in *Department of Corporations v. Speedee Oil Change Systems, Inc.*,[9] the court disqualified an "Of Counsel" attorney's firm from representing litigants against a client because the client had simultaneously consulted the "Of Counsel" attorney concerning the same matter. Although the court recited the facts concerning the simultaneous consultation, and discussed whether confidences might have been shared, the court's statements with respect to its holding in the opinion seem to promulgate a bright-line rule with respect to imputation of an "Of Counsel" attorney's conflicts to a law firm.[10] The court stated that "[t]he fundamental nature of the [of counsel] relationship makes a presumption of shared confidences as appropriate for the of counsel attorney as it is for partners, associates, and members of law firms."[11] The court noted that from the perspective of clients and the public, the "Of Counsel" attorney is hardly distinguishable from such other attorneys. Thus, the court held that "the need to preserve confidentiality and public confidence in the integrity of the legal profession and judicial process require that of counsel attorneys be regarded as the same as partners, associates and members of the law firms for conflict of interest issues."[12]

On the other hand, in *Regal Marketing Corp. v. Sonny & Son Product Corp.*,[13] the court declined to apply the imputed-disqualification rule because

---

8. Note, *Developments in the Law: Conflicts of Interest in the Legal Profession*, 94 HARV. L. REV. 1243, 1372 (1981).

9. 20 Cal. 4th 1135, 86 Cal. Rptr. 816 (1999).

10. Indeed, in a concurring opinion, Justice Mosk was critical of the majority for seeming to suggest, by its extensive recitation of the facts, that the holding hinged on the particular facts:

> An attorney who is designated of counsel to a law firm should be subject to the same rules as a partner or associate of the firm for conflicts purposes. This is a bright-line rule. We need not inquire into the particulars of the of counsel relationship in question. *Id.*

11. *Id.*, 86 Cal. Rptr. at 831.

12. *Id.*

13. No. 01 Civ.1911, 2002 WL 1788026, 2002 U.S. Dist. LEXIS 14069 (S.D.N.Y. Aug.1,

of the lack of a close relationship between the "Of Counsel" attorney and the law firm in question. The "Of Counsel" attorney leased space on the same floor in the same building as the law firm, but the "Of Counsel" attorney had separate phone, fax, and billing systems, was not included in the firm's professional liability insurance policy, only occasionally relied on the firm for secretarial assistance, handled only a few cases a year for the firm in an "Of Counsel" capacity, and was not listed on the firm's letterhead. The court held that the "Of Counsel" attorney's relationship with the law firm was too attenuated to merit the imputation of the law firm's conflicts of interest to the "Of Counsel" attorney.

Rule 1.10(a) can also result in disqualification of the "Of Counsel" attorney because of the imputation to the "Of Counsel" attorney of a conflict of another lawyer in his or her firm. In *Monroe v. City of Topeka*,[14] the court held that an "Of Counsel" attorney should be disqualified (assuming that, on remand, the lower court found that the substantial-relationship test was satisfied) because a partner in the firm with which she had an "Of Counsel" relationship had previously represented the client who was now adverse to the "Of Counsel" attorney's client. The court based the imputed disqualification on the grounds that the "Of Counsel" attorney and the law firm with which she had an "Of Counsel" relationship had presented themselves to the public in ways strongly suggesting that they conducted themselves as a firm. There was no internal sharing of fees or other management facets of the law practice, and the "Of Counsel" attorney had separate professional liability insurance. However, the "Of Counsel" attorney shared office space and telephone numbers with the firm, was listed as "Of Counsel" on the firm's letterhead, had used the firm name with her signature on her entry of appearance in the lawsuit in question, and had used the firm name with her signature on a letter to the judge regarding the lawsuit.

Former Affiliates: Rebuttable Presumption

When a lawyer leaves one firm and joins another, the problem of disqualification becomes more complicated. Then all of the disqualifications that

---

2002).

14. 267 Kan. 440, 988 P.2d 228 (1999).

afflicted every lawyer in the first firm are potentially spread to all of the lawyers in the second firm.[15]

As the prohibition against representation is extended, the wisdom of an absolute rule of imputed disqualification becomes questionable. Competing interests must be considered. First, the client must be assured that a departing lawyer will maintain the duties of loyalty and confidentiality. Second, a lawyer should not be precluded from taking on new clients, particularly when the lawyer's involvement in a matter was limited or peripheral. A broad disqualification rule would hamper a lawyer's career opportunities with no substantial benefit to the client. Third, a broad rule of disqualification would preclude prospective clients from their first choice of counsel.[16]

The courts are divided on the extension of the rule of imputed disqualification and whether a rebuttable or an irrebuttable presumption should be applied when the conflict involves a departing lawyer. The traditional rule was to apply an irrebuttable presumption that client confidences were shared between the departing lawyer and his or her current affiliates, and impose a firm-wide disqualification of the second firm.[17] The trend now is to use a flexible approach and allow the firm an opportunity to rebut the presumption of shared confidences.[18] This trend is reflected in Model Rules 1.9(b) and 1.10(b).

---

15. Wolfram, *supra* note 5, at § 7.6. It is sometimes helpful to separate out the possible situations that tend to give rise to problems involving imputed disqualification:

(1) a disqualification spread from an individual lawyer to another;

(2) a disqualification spread from an individual lawyer to the entire firm;

(3) a disqualification spread from the firm to its individual members, associates, or other affiliates; and

(4) a disqualification spread from one firm to another. *Id.*

16. *See* Model Rules R. 1.9 cmt. [4].

17. Emle Indus., Inc. v. Patentex, Inc., 478 F.2d 562 (2d Cir. 1973); Marketti v. Fitzsimmons, 373 F. Supp. 637 (W.D. Wis. 1974); T.C. Theatre Corp. v. Warner Bros. Pictures, 113 F. Supp. 265 (S.D.N.Y. 1953).

18. *See* Panduit Corp. v. All States Plastic Mfg. Co., 744 F.2d 1564, 1580 (Fed. Cir. 1984); Schiessle v. Stephens, 717 F.2d 417 (7th Cir. 1983); Novo Terapeutisk Laboratorium A/S v. Baxter Travenol Laboratories, Inc., 607 F.2d 186 (7th Cir. 1979); Akerly v. Red Barn Sys., Inc., 551 F.2d 539 (3d Cir. 1977); City of Cleveland v. Cleveland Elec. Illuminating Co., 440 F. Supp. 193, 209 (N.D. Ohio 1976), *aff'd*, 537 F.2d 1310 (6th Cir. 1977), *cert. denied*, 435 U.S. 996 (1978); Silver Chrysler Plymouth, Inc. v. Chrysler Motors Corp., 518 F.2d 751 (2d Cir. 1975); United States *ex rel.* Lord Elec. Co. v. Titan Pac. Constr. Corp., 637 F. Supp. 1556 (W.D. Wash. 1986); Hempstead Video, Inc. v. Incorporated Village of Valley Stream 409 F. 3d. 127 (2d Cir. 2005) (the following elements must be shown before an attorney can be disqualified

As discussed in Chapter 7,[19] Model Rule 1.9(b)[20] provides that when a lawyer moves to a new firm, he or she is not prohibited from representing a current client adversely to a former client of the lawyer's old firm, unless the lawyer had acquired protected information about the former client while he or she was affiliated with the old firm. Thus, if the lawyer had no or a limited role in the representation of the former client at his or her old firm, the lawyer will avoid disqualification under Rule 1.9(b) with regard to duties to former clients. And, in this circumstance, the lawyer's new firm will avoid imputed disqualification under Rule 1.10(a).

The imputed disqualification rules applicable to a departed lawyer's old firm are found in Model Rule 1.10(b) with regard to imputation of conflicts of interest.[21] That rule provides that when a lawyer leaves a firm, the lawyer's old firm is not prohibited from representing a client adversely to a client represented by the departed lawyer and not currently represented by the firm (regardless of when the departed lawyer represented the client), unless (1) the representation of the client by the firm is in a matter that is the same or substantially related to the matter in which the departed lawyer represented his or her client, and (2) any lawyer remaining in the

---

in a case of successive representation: (1) the moving party is a former client of the adverse party's counsel; (2) there is a substantial relationship between the subject matter of the counsel's prior representation of the moving party and the issues in the present lawsuit; and (3) the attorney whose disqualification is sought had access to, or was likely to have had access to, relevant privileged information in the course of his prior representation of the client.).

19. *Supra* in Chapter 7.

20. The text of Model Rule 1.9(b) is as follows:

> A lawyer shall not knowingly represent a person in the same or a substantially related matter in which a firm with which the lawyer formerly was associated had previously represented a client,
>
> (1) whose interests are materially adverse to that person; and
>
> (2) about whom the lawyer has acquired information protected by Rule 1.6 and 1.9(c) that is material to the matter; unless the former client gives informed consent confirmed in writing.

21. The text of Model Rule 1.10(b) is as follows:

> When a lawyer has terminated an association with a firm, the firm is not prohibited from thereafter representing a person with interests materially adverse to those of a client represented by the formerly associated lawyer and not currently represented by the firm, unless:
>
> (1) the matter is the same or substantially related to that in which the formerly associated lawyer represented the client; and
>
> (2) any lawyer remaining in the firm has information protected by Rules 1.6 and 1.9(c) that is material to the matter.

departed lawyer's old firm has information protected by Model Rules 1.6 and 1.9(c) that is material to the matter. Thus, if the departed lawyer was responsible for the representation of the client, and other lawyers remaining in the departed lawyer's old firm had no or limited roles in the representation, the firm will avoid disqualification under Rule 1.10(b).

When the lawyer who has moved to a new firm is "Of Counsel" to the firm, the question of whether the firm will incur imputed disqualification may depend upon several factors:[22]

- The nature and extent of the "Of Counsel" attorney's former representation of the client;
- The time lapse between that representation and the present controversy;
- The nature of the "Of Counsel" attorney's arrangement, including work assignments and salary arrangements;
- The likelihood that the "Of Counsel" attorney has had contact with the firm's lawyers responsible for handling the present controversy; and
- The presence of any "specific institutional mechanisms" designed to prevent the passage of information between the tainted lawyer and the lawyers responsible for handling the instant controversy.

Several cases illustrate how these factors are applied. In *Smith & Nephew v. Ethicon, Inc.*[23] a law firm was disqualified from representing a client in a dispute over ownership interests in patents issued to the client's former employees, where an attorney who was currently "Of Counsel" to the law firm had previously represented those employees adversely to the client in connection with negotiating and drafting their employment agreements. The "Of Counsel" attorney's representation of the employees in connection with the contracts giving rise to the dispute occurred fifteen years ago and in another state, the "Of Counsel" attorney was on a "semi-retired part-time basis" with the law firm, and the law firm had instituted procedures to screen him from the firm's attorneys who were representing the client. Nevertheless, the court found that disqualification of the law firm was

22. *Lord Elec. Co.*, 637 F. Supp. at 1565–66.
23. 98 F. Supp. 106 (D. Mass. 2000).

warranted. The court said that to say now that the "Of Counsel" attorney's role in drafting the contracts was not substantial because of the passage of time is akin to saying that Julius Caesar had no substantial involvement in the conquest of Gaul "because it happened a long time ago."[24]

In *United States ex rel. Lord Electric v. Titan Pacific Construction Corp.*,[25] the court refused to disqualify the entire firm because of a conflict involving an "Of Counsel" attorney. Several factors were important in the court's decision. Not only had the court found that the movants were using the motion to disqualify as a tool for harassment and delay, but the nature of the "Of Counsel" attorney's relationship with his current firm indicated that the other lawyers in the firm were not exposed to confidential information. The "Of Counsel" attorney worked less than full-time at the firm — he averaged approximately 70 hours per month[26] — and he did not participate in the general earnings of the firm. In describing the nature of the "Of Counsel" attorney's relationship, the court stated:

> ["of counsel" attorney's] involvement in the firm as a non-participating attorney makes it less likely that he has disclosed confidences to other lawyers working on this and related suits against [the defendant].[27]

Another relevant factor was the prolonged time lapse between the current and former representations. The "Of Counsel" attorney had ceased working on matters related to the former client over a year before he left the firm. He then left the practice for a period of four years, after which he returned and joined his current firm as "Of Counsel." This time lapse made it less likely that the "Of Counsel" attorney had retained any significant recollection of his former client's affairs, particularly since he had not taken any files or notes with him when he left his former firm.

In *Atasi Corp. v. Seagate Technology*,[28] the Ninth Circuit also focused on the nature of the "Of Counsel" attorney relationship with his current firm.

24. *Id.* at 110.
25. *Id.*
26. *Id.* at 1559, 1566.
27. *Id.* at 1566.
28. 847 F.2d 826 (Fed. Cir. 1988).

According to the court, the "Of Counsel" agreement revealed an "active and very close relationship with the firm."[29] The agreement provided in part that:

- a full time secretary would be provided to [the "of counsel" attorney] if necessary and that an office would be provided to him;
- billing would be done by the firm;
- the firm's medical and dental insurance policies would cover [the "of counsel" attorney], at his option;
- his mail would be received through the firm's office;
- he would do "all of his legal work through and in the name of the firm";
- miscellaneous costs such as postage, telephone, copying, etc., would be billed to his clients by the firm;
- backup help would be provided when he was overloaded with work;
- legal work of the firm's clients would be sent to him;
- [the "of counsel" attorney's] work would be billed for him by the firm at the rate of $160 per hour; and
- the firm would reimburse [the "of counsel" attorney] for dues and fees paid for state bars and law associations.[30]

Based on the terms of this contract, the court concluded the "Of Counsel" attorney "had an active and very close relationship with the firm."[31]

Since there was a significant relationship between the former and current controversies, a rebuttable presumption arose that the "Of Counsel" attorney had shared those secrets with his current affiliates. The entire firm was disqualified because it could not show that each lawyer in the firm had been notified of screening procedures before the "Of Counsel" attorney joined the firm.

Another relevant factor relied on by the courts is the nature and extent of the "Of Counsel" attorney's involvement in the prior controversy. The firm may be able to escape disqualification if it can show that the "Of Counsel" attorney was only "peripherally" involved in the former representation.[32]

---

29. *Id.* at 831.
30. *Id.* at 831.
31. *Id.*
32. In this approach, the inquiry focuses upon whether the first presumption — whether

Even if the "Of Counsel" attorney is found to have been only peripherally involved in the prior representation, the firm might still be required to demonstrate that appropriate screening mechanisms are established.

In re Mortgage & Realty Trust[33] illustrates the principle that when a conflict of interest requires the disqualification of an "Of Counsel" attorney, all attorneys in all offices of the firm such attorney is affiliated with must be disqualified, no matter how large the firm. There, an "Of Counsel" attorney in a law firm of approximately 400 attorneys with offices in nine cities in the United States and seven foreign countries was disqualified from representing a client in a contract dispute with a Chapter 11 bankruptcy debtor because the "Of Counsel" had been a member of the board of trustees of the debtor when it approved the transaction in question. Although the "Of Counsel" attorney had acquired confidential information about the debtor in his capacity as a member of the board of trustees rather than as a lawyer, his representation of another client adversely to an entity to which he had a continued fiduciary duty of confidentiality would have been a disqualifying conflict of interest under legal ethics principles. The court held that it was of no consequence that the disqualified attorney was "Of Counsel" rather than a partner or associate, or that he was affiliated with the firm's Washington office and the litigation was handled in California by the firm's St. Louis office. The court noted that, even if California had permitted screening as a remedy for imputed conflicts, the law firm still would have been disqualified because it made no attempt to institute screening procedures when the conflict arose.

Screening

When a lawyer cannot show that his prior involvement in a client's representation was limited, other methods of rebuttal may still prevent firm-wide disqualification, such as screening pursuant to Model Rule 1.10(a)(1) and (2) to prevent the "spread" of confidential information to the rest of the

---

shared confidences were received by the lawyer in question — can be rebutted.

33. 195 B.R. 740 (Bankr. C.D. Cal. 1996).

firm.[34] The lawyer is, in effect, screened from discussing confidential information with the other members of the firm.

In many jurisdictions, screening is now a recognized approach to conflict management, in accordance with the Model Rules. For example, Delaware Professional Conduct Rule 1.10(c) provides:

> When a lawyer becomes associated with a firm, no lawyer associated in the firm shall knowingly represent a client in a matter in which that lawyer is disqualified under Rule 1.9 unless:
>
> (1) the personally disqualified lawyer is timely screened from any participation in the matter and is apportioned no part of the fee therefrom; and
>
> (2) written notice is promptly given to the affected former client.[35]

Prior to the recent amendment to Model Rule 1.10, use of screening in the private sector in general and in the "Of Counsel" context in particular had not met with widespread approval by the courts. Although it has been recognized in the limited area of conflicts involving former government lawyers, it has generally been characterized as a self-serving defense to escape the lawyer's ethical obligations. Even when the most stringent barriers are in place,[36] screening cannot assure the client that confidential information will not be leaked. Although there had been a split of authority on screening as a viable defense, the trend had been to allow it in principle[37] but to require

34. Wolfram, *supra* note 5, at § 7.6.4.

35. Delaware Rule 1.10(c); *see also* Illinois Rules 1.10(e); Kentucky Rule 1.10(d); Maryland Rule 1.10(c); Massachusetts Rule 1.10(d)(2); Michigan Rule 1.10(b)(1); Minnesota Rule 1.10(b); Montana Rule 1.10(c)(1); North Carolina Rule 1.10(c); Oregon Rule 1.10(c); Pennsylvania Rules 1.10(b); Tennessee Rule 1.10(c); and Washington Rule 1.10(e) among others.

36. Effective screening methods include both internal procedures and structural barriers. These include separating the affected lawyers to different offices or even cities, placing limitations on all interoffice correspondence and memoranda, and files. *See* Note, *Developments in the Law: Conflicts of Interest in the Legal Profession*, 94 HARV. L. REV. 1243, 1368–69 (1981).

37. Courts that have accepted the screening defense include County of L.A. v. U.S. Dist. Court for the Cent. Dist. of Cal. (In re County of L.A.), 223 F.3d 990 (9th Cir. 2000); Manning v. Waring, Cox, James, Sklar & Allen, 849 F.2d 222 (6th Cir. 1998), criticized in SLC Ltd. V v. Bradford Group West, Inc., 147 B.R. 586 (D. Utah 1992), for permitting the institution of screening some period time after the tainted lawyer joined the firm (in preference of

such stringent proof of "specific institutional mechanisms" that the defense rarely succeeded, thereby necessitating a change to the Model Rules.[38]

At least one court allowed screening as a viable defense specifically in the context of an "Of Counsel" relationship. In *United States ex rel. Lord Electric v. Titan Pacific Construction Corp.*,[39] the court was satisfied that no disclosures had taken place between the tainted lawyer and his current firm. The court found that appropriate screening measures had been in place when the "Of Counsel" attorney first joined the firm. Once the "Of Counsel" attorney's current firm learned of the conflict, the lead counsel instructed all lawyers at the firm to have no conversations with the "Of Counsel" attorney regarding the current matter. In addition, the lead counsel revealed the conflict to opposing counsel and requested their consent to allow the firm to work on the matter. Screening mechanisms that are established at the time a tainted lawyer joins a firm are the most reliable objective evidence available to rebut the presumption of shared confidences. Satisfied that the "Of Counsel" attorney and his firm had acted in an ethical manner, the court refused the motion to disqualify. As a precaution that no confidences would be disclosed in the future, it decided that additional measures would be necessary. Each lawyer at the firm would be required to certify he or she had no conversation on the matter in the past with the "Of Counsel" attorney, and would not speak of the matter in the future with him.

Although the *Titan* court allowed screening to rebut the presumption of shared confidences, other courts have not only disagreed with its reasoning but have ruled that *Titan* did not adequately reflect the trend in the Ninth Circuit.[40] In applying the law of the Ninth Circuit, the Federal Circuit found

---

the bright-line requirement for establishing screening mechanisms contemporaneously with a new attorney's arrival); EZ Paintr Corp. v. Padco, Inc., 746 F.2d 1459 (Fed. Cir. 1984); LaSalle Nat'l Bank v. Lake County, 703 F.2d 252 (7th Cir. 1983); Nemours Found. v. Gilbane, Aetna, Fed. Ins., 632 F. Supp. 418, 429 (D. Del. 1986); Kovacevic v. Fair Automotive Repair, Inc., 641 F. Supp. 237, 244 (N.D. Ill. 1986); *Lord Elec. Co.*, 637 F. Supp. 1556.

38. United States Filter Corp. v. Ionics, Inc., 68 F. Supp. 2d 48 (D. Mass. 1999) (Massachusetts screening requirements not met); Nelson v. Green Builders, Inc., 823 F. Supp. 1439 (E.D. Wis. 1993) (screen erected too late); Kassis v. Teacher's Insurance & Annuity Association, 695 N.Y.S.2d 515, 717 N.E.2d 674 (1999) (screen not permitted when tainted lawyer has significant or material information); *EZ Paintr Corp.*, 746 F.2d at 1462 (wall must be timely implemented); *Schiessle*, 717 F.2d 417 (there must be a formal, institutionalized wall).

39. 637 F. Supp. 1556 (W.D. Wash. 1986).

40. *See Atasi*, 847 F.2d at 832, n.7.

that the Ninth Circuit had not yet ruled on the availability of screening as a defense.[41] But even if the defense were available, the Federal Circuit found that the presumption could not be overcome because timely screening procedures were not established:

> [T]here is a complete lack of evidence before the court indicating that the *entire* . . . firm was also notified of this oral screening *before* [the "of counsel" attorney] assumed his "of counsel" position.[42] (Emphasis in original.)

Affiliated Law Firms

A difficult series of questions is presented in the conflict area raised by relationships between law firms. For the reasons described above, no hard and fast rule applies to all situations in which law firms become "Of Counsel" to one another. However, as a general proposition, where two law firms have a close, regular, and continuing relationship, it is highly unlikely that one could represent a client whose interests are adverse to clients of the other firm without following the procedure prescribed in Model Rule 1.7(b). In such a case, the law firm must make a good faith determination that the representation will not be adversely affected and, if that determination can be made, secure the informed consent of the client, confirmed in writing, if the representation is to go forward.

Several examples from published opinions are instructive in evaluating the conflict situations raised by "Of Counsel" relationships between law firms.

In *Mustang Enterprises v. Plug-In Storage, Inc.*[43] Hill, Steadman & Simpson (the Hill Firm), a Chicago-based intellectual property law firm of some

41. *Id.* at 831. The decision noted that two district courts in the Ninth Circuit had previously allowed the defense in *Lord Elec. Co.*, 637 F. Supp. 1556, and Haagen-Dazs Co., 639 F. Supp. at 282, 287 (N.D. Cal. 1986). Subsequently, the Ninth Circuit permitted screening in In re In Re: Hoglund County of Los Angeles v. United States District Court, 223 F.3d 990 (9th Cir. 2000).

42. *Id.* at 831.

43. 874 F. Supp. 881 (N.D. Ill. 1995).

thirty lawyers and "Of Counsel" to Bachman & Lapointe, P.C. (the Bachman Firm), defendant's patent counsel, was disqualified from representing the plaintiff in the same patent action. Since 1991, the Bachman Firm, which consisted of four lawyers, had been retained by Plug-In as its patent counsel. When all the legal files were transferred to the Bachman Firm from the firm that had previously represented Plug-In, the files included a substantial number of documents dealing with patents currently in suit.

There was no question that the Bachman Firm could not take on the current lawsuit on behalf of Mustang against its current client, Plug-In. What remained for the court's resolution was whether that disqualification was also imputed to its "affiliated" law firm, the Hill Firm. For that purpose, the existence or nonexistence of a screen would make no difference whatsoever if the Hill Firm and Bachman Firm were regarded as the equivalent of two offices of the same law firm, because in that event the firm itself would be regarded as having switched sides.[44]

In legal terms, the question before the court was whether "affiliated firms" are to be treated as the equivalent of two offices of the same firm as a matter of law. Relying on ABA Formal Opinion 84-351, the court noted that the question would be answered in the affirmative unless the "affiliated" designation was available on a limited basis.[45]

For example, availability may be limited if the "affiliated" or "associated" firm performs all of the tax, labor, patent, or other specialized work for the other firm. Availability may also be limited to performing legal services that have a relationship to or must be performed in another state.[46]

In this case, the court noted that the Hill Firm and the Bachman Firm used the "affiliated firm" designation without limiting it in any respect. Having chosen to obtain those benefits that flowed from the public listings, the Hill Firm could not now complain if the firms are treated as a two-office law firm for conflict of interest purposes:

---

44. *Id.* at 887.
45. *Id.* at 888.
46. *Id.* (quoting ABA Comm. on Ethics & Prof'l Responsibility, Formal Op. 84-351).

> Whatever benefits Hill Firm and Bachman Firm may view themselves as deriving from holding each other out as an "affiliated firm," the price that must be paid for deriving those benefits is the inability of either firm to litigate against clients of the other firm under circumstances such as those presented here.[47]

Difficult questions are also raised when the professional relationship between the firms becomes more substantial. In *Complaint of Maritima Aragua, S.A.*,[48] an action involving parties with an interest in a vessel involved in a collision, the court refused to disqualify the law firms representing plaintiffs due to their prior representation of defendants' related entity. The plaintiffs' law firm, Watson Farley & Williams (WFW) of New York, was part of a Jersey Island partnership (WFW Jersey). The partners of the affiliated firm of WFW, with offices in London, England (WFW UK), were also members of WFW Jersey, but the New York partners of WFW Jersey were not members of WFW UK.

The underlying matter involved the collision in Venezuela between two vessels, the *Mar Coral* and the *Trade Resolve,* and a claim for damages filed by Maraven, a pipeline owner whose pipeline was damaged in the collision. The *Trade Resolve* was owned by a Panamanian corporation related in ownership to Gregory Callimanopulos, a well-known Greek ship owner. The complaint in the *Trade Resolve* litigation was answered by WFW Jersey. The *Trade Resolve* defendants filed a motion to disqualify WFW Jersey due to prior representation its affiliated firm, WFW UK, had given to Callimanopulos. WFW UK's prior representation included advice to in-house counsel of Brokerage & Management Corp., one of the *Trade Resolve* defendants, on the manner in which Callimanopulos's international holdings and activities should be structured in light of questions concerning legal responsibilities and liabilities. Confidences and secrets were imparted to WFW UK concerning Callimanopulos's business interests. In addition, the companies' in-house counsel met with partners of the New York office of WFW Jersey to discuss implications of the Oil Pollution Act of 1990 and

47. Mustang Enterprises v. Plug-In Storage, Inc., 874 F. Supp. 881, 890 (N.D. Ill. 1995).
48. 847 F. Supp. 1177 (S.D.N.Y. 1994).

certain taxation matters for companies associated with Callimanopulos, including the various entities that compose the *Trade Resolve* defendants.

The court acknowledged that there was a trend for lawyers and firms to practice in multiple states, and that this is often not done as a single firm with multiple offices but rather through the structure of "associated" or "affiliated" law firms. With regard to the confidentiality that must be maintained between "affiliated" or "associated" firms, the court relied on ABA Formal Opinion 84-351 (October 20, 1984), which noted that potential clients are led to believe that lawyers of the "affiliated" or "associated" firms will not simultaneously represent persons whose interests conflict with the client's interests.

When a firm elects to affiliate or associate another with it and to communicate that fact to the public and clients, there is no practical distinction between the relationship of affiliates under that arrangement and the relationship of separate offices in a law firm.[49]

The partners of WFW UK were partners of WFW Jersey, but the partners of the New York office of WFW Jersey were not partners of WFW UK. Although the law firms were not in an "Of Counsel" relationship, partners at each firm admitted the firms were, at a minimum, an affiliated partnership. As such, the court determined that WFW UK's prior representation of Trade & Transport and Brokerage & Management must be considered representation by WFW Jersey for which confidences were presumed to have been transmitted.

Disqualification would not follow unless the *Trade Resolve* defendants could demonstrate that the relationship between the two actions was "patently clear" or that the actions were "identical" or "essentially the same." Applying the substantial relationship test in this case, the court determined that the *Trade Resolve* defendants had not satisfied their burden of demonstrating that WFW's prior representation of Callimanopulos's interests was "substantially related" to the present matters. WFW UK's prior advice to Brokerage & Management was completely unrelated to the present action. Moreover, the meetings between Baldwin and various WFW lawyers discussed only general matters related to the Oil Pollution

49. *Id.* at 1181.

Act of 1990, citizenship, and taxes, and included no discussion of confidential information.

Whether conflicts have to be cleared between law firms and whether relationships have to be disclosed to clients of either firm turns on the substance of the relationship, not the terminology assigned to the relationship by the law firms. But if a particular representation may be materially limited by an existing relationship, the lawyer must decline the representation unless the lawyer believes the representation will not be adversely affected and the client consents after consultation.[50]

Former Government Employees

Another type of conflict of interest problem, a result of the classic "revolving door" situation,[51] arises frequently in the case of a retiring judge or other government employee who wishes to leave government employment and become affiliated with a law firm in an "Of Counsel" capacity. While in the role of prosecutor, a lawyer may have prosecuted an individual who is a client of the firm. Or a former judge may have participated in a court matter involving a client regularly represented by the firm.

Although conflicts problems are inherent in these situations, competing interests, such as the need to encourage government service by lawyers and the public's desire to avoid professionalization of government service, have resulted in the development of special rules.[52] The effect of the rules

50. ABA Comm. on Ethics & Prof'l Responsibility, Formal Op. 94-388 (1994), *reprinted in* Appendix I.

51. *See* Note, *Developments in the Law, supra* note 6, at 1425 n.43.

52. As to government employees in general, Rule 1.11 of the Model Rules provides in pertinent part:

> (a) Except as law may otherwise expressly permit, a lawyer who has formerly served as a public officer or employee of the government:
>
> (1) is subject to Rule 1.9(c); and
>
> (2) shall not otherwise represent a client in connection with a matter in which the lawyer participated personally and substantially as a public officer or employee, unless the appropriate government agency gives its informed consent, confirmed in writing, to the representation.
>
> (b) When a lawyer is disqualified from representation under paragraph (a), no lawyer in a firm with which that lawyer is associated may knowingly undertake

or continue representation in such a matter unless:

(1) the disqualified lawyer is timely screened from any participation in the matter and is apportioned no part of the fee therefrom; and

(2) written notice is promptly given to the appropriate government agency to enable it to ascertain compliance with the provisions of this rule.

(c) Except as law may otherwise expressly permit, a lawyer having information that the lawyer knows is confidential government information about a person acquired when the lawyer was a public officer or employee, may not represent a private client whose interests are adverse to that person in a matter in which the information could be used to the material disadvantage of that person. As used in this Rule, the term "confidential government information" means information that has been obtained under governmental authority and which, at the time this Rule is applied, the government is prohibited by law from disclosing to the public or has a legal privilege not to disclose and which is not otherwise available to the public. A firm with which that lawyer is associated may undertake or continue representation in the matter only if the disqualified lawyer is timely screened from any participation in the matter and is apportioned no part of the fee therefrom.

(d) Except as law may otherwise expressly permit, a lawyer currently serving as a public officer or employee:

(1) is subject to Rules 1.7 and 1.9; and

(2) shall not:

(i) participate in a matter in which the lawyer participated personally and substantially while in private practice or nongovernmental employment, unless the appropriate government agency gives its informed consent, confirmed in writing; or

(ii) negotiate for private employment with any person who is involved as a party or as lawyer for a party in a matter in which the lawyer is participating personally and substantially, except that a lawyer serving as a law clerk to a judge, other adjudicative officer or arbitrator may negotiate for private employment as permitted by Rule 1.12(b) and subject to the conditions stated in Rule 1.12(b).

Rule 1.12 of the Model Rules provides:

(a) Except as stated in paragraph (d), a lawyer shall not represent anyone in connection with a matter in which the lawyer participated personally and substantially as a judge or other adjudicative officer or law clerk to such a person or as an arbitrator, mediator or other third-party neutral, unless all parties to the proceeding give informed consent, confirmed in writing.

(b) A lawyer shall not negotiate for employment with any person who is involved as a party or as lawyer for a party in a matter in which the lawyer is participating personally and substantially as a judge or other adjudicative officer or as an arbitrator, mediator or other third-party neutral. A lawyer serving as a law clerk to a judge or other adjudicative officer may negotiate for employment with a party or lawyer involved in a matter in which the clerk is participating personally and substantially, but only after the lawyer has notified the judge, or other adjudicative officer.

(c) If a lawyer is disqualified by paragraph (a), no lawyer in a firm with which that lawyer is associated may knowingly undertake or continue representation in the matter unless:

is to require that the former government employee be disqualified only in matters with which the lawyer was associated, or in which the lawyer had "substantial" responsibility,[53] while employed by the government.

These rules have not been interpreted literally, and resolution of the matter has been left for the courts.[54] Even if a former government employee is disqualified, it may be possible to avoid imputed disqualification of his or her firm through screening the former government employee from the matter.[55] This procedure has been endorsed by the ABA ethics committee and in the Model Rules and, unlike the case of private sector employment, accepted by most courts.[56] The screening technique has been incorporated into the Model Rules to prevent the imputed-disqualification rules from imposing too severe a deterrent against entering public service.[57]

Imputed Disqualification and the Lawyer as Witness

Another conflict of interest problem arises when the lawyer is asked to testify as a witness at a trial in which one of the parties is represented by the lawyer or a member of the firm. The lawyer, in the role of witness called by the opposing party, may present testimony directly adverse or prejudicial to the interests of the client. Or the lawyer may be called to act as witness on behalf of the client. In this situation, the lawyer's credibility may be called into question, thereby compromising and prejudicing the interests of the client. In Formal Opinion 90-357, the committee stated:

---

(1) the disqualified lawyer is screened from any participation in the matter and is apportioned no part of the fee therefrom; and

(2) written notice is promptly given to the parties and any appropriate tribunal to enable them to ascertain compliance with the provisions of this rule.

(d) An arbitrator selected as a partisan of a party in a multimember arbitration panel is not prohibited from subsequently representing that party.

53. For a discussion of the substantial-relationship test in the context of former government officials, *see* Note, *Developments in the Law, supra* note 6, at 1433–39 (1981).

54. *Id.* at 1439–40.

55. Model Rules R. 1.11(b) and 1.12(c).

56. ABA Comm. on Ethics & Prof'l Responsibility, Formal Op. 342, at 10 (1975); Model Rules 1.11 and 1.12.

57. *See* Model Rules R 1.11 cmt. [4].

> [An "of counsel" attorney] is a lawyer in the firm for purposes of Rule 3.7(b), regarding circumstances in which, when a lawyer is to be a witness in a proceeding, the lawyer's colleague may nonetheless represent the client in that proceeding.[58]

Model Rule 3.7 prohibits an attorney from representing a client at a trial where such attorney is likely to be a witness unless the testimony is with regard to an uncontested matter, relates to the nature and value of legal services in the case, or disqualification of the attorney would be a substantial hardship for the client.[59] Most states prohibit an "Of Counsel" attorney from accepting employment where the likelihood of being called as a witness exists.

When the lawyer-witness must withdraw from representing a client because of a conflict, the firm must also withdraw from representation. The Model Rules permit an attorney's representation of a client at a trial where another member of the firm will be required to act as a witness unless prohibited by Rule 1.7 Rule 1.9.[60] The Model Rules provide for imputed disqualification of the firm where a member of the firm is precluded from

---

58. ABA Comm. on Ethics & Prof'l Responsibility, Formal Op. 90-357, at 13 (1990).

59. Rule 3.7 of the Model Rules provides:

> (a) A lawyer shall not act as advocate at a trial in which the lawyer is likely to be a necessary witness unless:
>
> (1) the testimony relates to an uncontested issue;
>
> (2) the testimony relates to the nature and value of legal services rendered in the case; or
>
> (3) disqualification of the lawyer would work substantial hardship on the client.
>
> (b) A lawyer may act as advocate in a trial in which another lawyer in the lawyer's firm is likely to be called as a witness unless precluded from doing so by Rule 1.7 or Rule 1.9.

Although the Model Rules have become virtually ubiquitous, under the Model Code, DR 5-102(A) prohibited a lawyer or the lawyer's firm from representing a client if he or a lawyer in his firm should be called as a witness on behalf of his client. DR 5-102(B) provided that a lawyer may continue the representation if the lawyer learns or it is obvious that he or a lawyer in his firm may be called as a witness other than on behalf of the client unless or until it is apparent that such testimony is or may be prejudicial to his client. DR 5-101(B) permitted a lawyer to testify while representing a client under certain circumstances.

60. *See* MODEL RULES R. 3.7(b) ("(b) A lawyer may act as advocate in a trial in which another lawyer in the lawyer's firm is likely to be called as a witness unless precluded from doing so by Rule 1.7 or Rule 1.9").

representing a client by virtue of a conflict resulting from the combination of roles.[61] Whether the combination of roles involves an improper conflict is determined by the general conflict of interest rule,[62] which prohibits a lawyer from representing a client with interests adverse to those of another client, and the rule that prohibits a lawyer from representing a client with interests adverse to those of a former client.[63] For example, the lawyer's representation is improper where the testimony of the lawyer will substantially conflict with that of the client.[64]

The few state bar ethics panels that have addressed the issue in the context of an "Of Counsel" attorney have imposed imputed disqualification under the reasoning found in the Model Code or the Model Rules.[65]

Summary

If one lawyer is disqualified because of a conflict, all affiliated lawyers are typically also disqualified. This rule is the result of the following presumption: a disqualified lawyer is presumed to have conveyed confidential information to all of the lawyers with whom the lawyer is or has been affiliated. If the conflict arises between clients represented by lawyers currently affiliated in the same firm, the presumption is irrebuttable. But if the conflict arises between clients of lawyers who were once affiliated, the Model Rules and many courts apply a rebuttable presumption. To rebut the presumption, the firm must show by clear and convincing evidence that confidential information was not and is not likely to be disclosed.

Imputed disqualification frequently arises in the context of "Of Counsel" relationships. "Of Counsel" attorneys often move between firms; in some cases, "Of Counsel" attorneys are simultaneously affiliated with more than one firm. Where the conflict arises because the "Of Counsel" attorney and

61. *Id.*

62. *See* Model Rules R. 1.7.

63. *See* Model Rules R. 1.9.

64. *See* Model Rules R. 3.7 cmt. [6].

65. Michigan State Bar Ethics Op. CI-1071 (undated); Texas State Bar Ethics Op. 445 (1987).

the affiliated firm are simultaneously representing clients with adverse interests, the "Of Counsel" attorney and the firm must both withdraw.

Where the "Of Counsel" attorney is representing a client with interests adverse to those of a client of a former firm, the Model Rules and many courts allow the "Of Counsel" attorney's present firm to rebut the presumption. For a successful rebuttal, the "Of Counsel" attorney must show by clear and convincing evidence that confidential information was not shared. This includes evidence in the form of testimony, affidavits, or oral or documentary evidence of effective screening procedures.

Checklist for Issue Spotting

Is Of Counsel's Present Firm Vicariously Disqualified?

(1) Does the conflict arise between clients of lawyers presently affiliated? If so, there is an irrebuttable presumption that confidences were disclosed.

(2) Does the conflict arise between clients of lawyers who were at one time affiliated? If so, is the presumption rebuttable?

(3) If the presumption is rebuttable, is there clear and convincing evidence that confidences were not disclosed? If screening is permitted by the applicable ethics rules or court decisions, were effective screening procedures in place at the time the "Of Counsel" attorney joined the firm? At the time the conflict first arose? Are institutional screening procedures currently in place?

(4) How effective are the screening procedures? Is there restricted access to the client's file? Is there a physical separation between the "Of Counsel" attorney and the rest of the firm? Does the "Of Counsel" attorney practice in a different city or office of the firm? How large is the firm?

CHAPTER 9

Lawyer Advertising and Solicitation

Because advertising plays a significant role in every "Of Counsel" relationship, this chapter considers the history and interrelationship of the rules governing lawyer advertising and solicitation, in addition to considerations specific to the "Of Counsel" relationship.

The American Bar Association's Model Rules of Professional Conduct, Rule 7.1 (Communications Concerning a Lawyer's Services) provides simply:

> A lawyer shall not make a false or misleading communication about the lawyer or the lawyer's services. A communication is false or misleading if it contains a material misrepresentation of fact or law, or omits a fact necessary to make the statement considered as a whole not materially misleading.

However, the comments to the Rule provide a bit more detail.[1] Rule 7.1 requires that communications regarding a lawyer's services be truthful,

1. The following are the Comments to the Model Rules of Professional Conduct, Rule 7.1:

> [1] This Rule governs all communications about a lawyer's services, including advertising permitted by Rule 7.2. Whatever means are used to make known a lawyer's services, statements about them must be truthful.
> [2] Truthful statements that are misleading are also prohibited by this Rule. A truthful statement is misleading if it omits a fact necessary to make the lawyer's

including advertising permitted under Model Rule 7.2.[2] Under Model Rule 7.1, a communication is false and misleading if it contains a material misrepresentation of fact or law, is likely to create an unjustified expectation about results the lawyer can achieve, or compares the lawyer's services with other lawyers' services, unless the comparison can be factually substantiated.

Model Rule 7.2 (Advertising) authorizes attorney advertising under specified conditions, namely:

> (a) Subject to the requirements of Rules 7.1 and 7.3, a lawyer may advertise services through written, recorded or electronic communication, including public media.
> (b) A lawyer shall not give anything of value to a person for recommending the lawyer's services except that a lawyer may
> (1) pay the reasonable costs of advertisements or communications permitted by this Rule;
> (2) pay the usual charges of a legal service plan or a not-for-profit or qualified lawyer referral service. A qualified lawyer referral service is a lawyer referral service that has been approved by an appropriate regulatory authority; and
> (3) pay for a law practice in accordance with Rule 1.17; and

---

communication considered as a whole not materially misleading. A truthful statement is also misleading if there is a substantial likelihood that it will lead a reasonable person to formulate a specific conclusion about the lawyer or the lawyer's services for which there is no reasonable factual foundation.

[3] An advertisement that truthfully reports a lawyer's achievements on behalf of clients or former clients may be misleading if presented so as to lead a reasonable person to form an unjustified expectation that the same results could be obtained for other clients in similar matters without reference to the specific factual and legal circumstances of each client's case. Similarly, an unsubstantiated comparison of the lawyer's services or fees with the services or fees of other lawyers may be misleading if presented with such specificity as would lead a reasonable person to conclude that the comparison can be substantiated. The inclusion of an appropriate disclaimer or qualifying language may preclude a finding that a statement is likely to create unjustified expectations or otherwise mislead the public.

[4] See also Rule 8.4(e) for the prohibition against stating or implying an ability to influence improperly a government agency or official or to achieve results by means that violate the Rules of Professional Conduct or other law.

2. *Id.*

(4) refer clients to another lawyer or a nonlawyer professional pursuant to an agreement not otherwise prohibited under these Rules that provides for the other person to refer clients or customers to the lawyer, if

(i) the reciprocal referral agreement is not exclusive, and

(ii) the client is informed of the existence and nature of the agreement.

(c) Any communication made pursuant to this rule shall include the name and office address of at least one lawyer or law firm responsible for its content.

Although not directly binding, the ABA's Model Rules have been adopted in whole or in part by virtually every U.S. jurisdiction.[3] It is important to review the applicable state versions of these rules to ensure compliance. For example, in California, a communication is considered misleading if it:

> contains testimonials about or endorsements of a [lawyer] unless such communication also contains an express disclaimer such as "this testimonial or endorsement does not constitute a guarantee, warranty, or prediction regarding the outcome of your legal matter."[4]

Similar restrictions on testimonials have been included in the Rules of Professional Conduct adopted in Louisiana, Missouri, New York, Oregon, Rhode Island, South Dakota, Virginia, and Wisconsin.[5] Other common modifications to Model Rule 7.1 include restrictions on statements regarding

---

3. The ABA maintains a set of links to the Rules of Professional Conduct and formal ethics opinions of each state, along with other resources, at http://www.americanbar.org/groups/professional_responsibility/resources/links_of_interest.html#States, last visited Dec. 4, 2012.

4. California Rules of Prof'l Conduct R. 1-400 (Standards) (2).

5. *See* Rules of Prof'l Conduct, Louisiana Rule 7.2(c)(1)(H), Missouri Rule 4-7.1(h), New York Rule 7.1(c)(2), Oregon Rule 7.1(a)(6), Rhode Island Rule 7.1(b), South Dakota Rule 7.1(c)(12), (13) & (14), Virginia Rule 7.2(a)(1), and Wisconsin Rule 20:7.1(a)(4).

past success,[6] and disclaimers and disclosures regarding contingent fees,[7] among others.

The use of general advertising to transmit information about a lawyer's services to a prospective client is viewed differently from the direct solicitation of prospective clients. While advertising makes it possible to inform clients about the need for legal services, direct solicitation causes a potential risk of undue influence, intimidation, overreaching, and even abuse.[8]

The methods of solicitation are varied. A lawyer might attempt to persuade a client known to need legal services by using a direct, personal approach. Other forms of solicitation can be indirect, although its impact is similar to the face-to-face approach. Indirect solicitations can be effected via mail, brochures, telephone, fax, email, text, television, radio, or a third party.

It is here that constitutional questions, such as whether lawyer advertising is worthy of First Amendment protection, often arise.[9] Model Rule 7.3 (Direct Contact with Prospective Clients) contains a fairly broad prohibition on in-person solicitation, live telephone, and real-time electronic communication.[10] However, the Model Rule does provide an exception

---

6. *See* Rules of Prof'l Conduct, Florida Rule 4-7.2(c)(1)(F), Indiana Rule 7.1 Comment [2], Louisiana Rule 7.2(c)(1)(D), Missouri Rule 4-7.1(c), New Mexico Rule 16-701(A)(4), New York Rule 7.1(e), South Dakota Rule 7.1(c)(4), Texas Rule 7.02(a)(2), and Virginia Rule 7.2(a)(3).

7. *See* Rules of Prof'l Conduct, California Rule 1-400 (Standards) (14), Colorado Rule 7.1(d), Connecticut Rule 7.2(f), Florida Rule 4-7.2(c)(7), Georgia Rule 7.1(a), Kentucky SCR 3.130 (7.05) (1) (a) (22), Louisiana Rule 7.2(c)(6), Missouri Rule 4.7.1(k), Nevada Rule 7.2(e), New York Rule 7.1(p), Pennsylvania Rule 7.2(g), Rhode Island Rule 7.2(e), and Texas Rule 7.04(h).

8. *See* Model Rules R. 7.3 cmts. [1] and [2].

9. *See* Shapero v. Kentucky Bar Ass'n, 486 U.S. 466 (1988), discussed *infra* in detail under "History of Lawyer Advertising."

10. Model Rules R. 7.3 provides as follows:

> (a) A lawyer shall not by in-person, live telephone or real-time electronic contact solicit professional employment when a significant motive for the lawyer's doing so is the lawyer's pecuniary gain, unless the person contacted:
>
> (1) is a lawyer; or
>
> (2) has a family, close personal, or prior professional relationship with the lawyer.
>
> (b) A lawyer shall not solicit professional employment from a prospective client by written, recorded or electronic communication or by in-person, telephone or real-time electronic contact even when not otherwise prohibited by paragraph (a), if:
>
> (1) the target of the solicitation has made known to the lawyer a desire not

for communication with a prospective client who is also a lawyer and for communication with a prospective client that has a family, close personal, or prior professional relationship with the lawyer.[11]

Advertising the Of Counsel Relationship

Meticulous rules governing use of the "Of Counsel" designation in public communications have developed among the states, generally following the liberal approach to lawyer communication advocated by the Model Rules. Most forms of communication may be made as long as they are not false or misleading.

The Model Rules provide that a lawyer's letterhead is a form of public communication and is subject to the Model Rule 7.1 stipulation that it not be false and misleading. But even as a form of solicitation targeted to a person known to be in need of legal services, communication contained on letterheads cannot be categorically prohibited unless it is false and misleading.[12] What this means in terms of the "Of Counsel" relationship is that the lawyer or firm cannot be designated as "Of Counsel" on the law firm's letterhead, business cards, advertising, and related communications unless there is a "close, regular, personal" relationship.[13]

---

to be solicited by the lawyer; or

(2) the solicitation involves coercion, duress or harassment.

(c) Every written, recorded or electronic communication from a lawyer soliciting professional employment from anyone known to be in need of legal services in a particular matter shall include the words "Advertising Material" on the outside envelope, if any, and at the beginning and ending of any recorded or electronic communication, unless the recipient of the communication is a person specified in paragraphs (a)(1) or (a)(2).

(d) Notwithstanding the prohibitions in paragraph (a), a lawyer may participate with a prepaid or group legal service plan operated by an organization not owned or directed by the lawyer that uses in-person or telephone contact to solicit memberships or subscriptions for the plan from persons who are not known to need legal services in a particular matter covered by the plan.

11. *Id.*

12. *Shapiro*, 486 U.S. at 466.

13. ABA Comm. on Ethics & Prof'l Responsibility, Formal Op. 90-357 (1990), *reprinted in* Appendix G.

As long as there is an actual "Of Counsel" relationship, that fact can be included on all written communications by the lawyer, and by the law firm regarding the firm's services.[14] But what other information can be included? Can information about the "Of Counsel" attorney's experience be included on letterheads, professional announcement cards, and firm brochures? Must the out-of-state "Of Counsel" attorney's or firm's jurisdictional limitations be indicated on the firm's letterhead? Can an "Of Counsel" attorney's name be included in the firm's name?

Using Of Counsel's Name in the Firm Name

The law firm's ability to use a retired partner's name in the firm's name is governed by Model Rules 7.1 (Communications Concerning a Lawyer's Services) and 7.5 (Firm Names and Letterheads), which state in pertinent part:

> Rule 7.1: A lawyer shall not make a false or misleading communication about the lawyer or the lawyer's services. A communication is false or misleading if it contains a material misrepresentation of fact or law, or omits a fact necessary to make the statement considered as a whole not materially misleading.
>
> Rule 7.5 (a): A lawyer shall not use a firm name, letterhead or other professional designation that violates Rule 7.1. . .
>
> Rule 7.5 (d): Lawyers may state or imply that they practice in a partnership or other organization only when that is the fact.[15]

In general, the rules require that lawyers be honest and clear in the representations they make to the public regarding the nature of their practice. Where a named partner of a law firm retires, but remains associated with the firm as "Of Counsel," the firm may continue to use the partner's name in the firm name, provided that (1) the firm name retained has been long-established

14. Model Rules Rules 7.1, 7.2, and 7.5.

15. *See* Appendix J for a complete copy of ABA Model Rules of Professional Conduct, Rule 7.5, and a chart listing the state-by-state variations of the same.

and well-recognized; (2) the retiring partner maintains an "Of Counsel" relationship with the firm that is close, regular, and frequent; and (3) the retiring partner's "Of Counsel" status is clearly designated in the law firm's letterhead, signs, advertising, and the like. For example, in Opinion RI-90 (June 25, 1991), the Michigan State Bar Standing Committee on Professional and Judicial Ethics allowed a law firm to retain the name of a named shareholder after he had withdrawn from the firm and the active practice of law, where he remained associated with the firm in an "Of Counsel" status. The committee found that the firm name had been long established and well recognized and that communications about the lawyer's status would clearly indicate that he was retired.

In some cases, partnerships may even retain in their firm name the name of the retired partner who remains active practicing in a related firm located in another jurisdiction. One such case involved a New York law firm whose name consisted of three partners, one of whom resided in Washington, D.C. The District of Columbia partner, motivated by tax considerations, wanted to retire from the New York firm, become "Of Counsel" to the firm, and become a partner in a newly formed partnership in Washington, D.C. The Washington, D.C., law firm would consist of all of the partners of the New York law firm and retain the same firm name designated by its District of Columbia rather than New York location. Before opening the District of Columbia office, the law firm asked the New York City Ethics Committee whether it was permissible to form a second law firm while retaining the retiring partner's name in both.[16] Citing DR 2-102(B), the committee noted that a lawyer may not practice under a firm name that is misleading about the identity of the lawyers practicing under the name. The committee further noted that the proposed arrangement was a departure from the usual principle that inclusion in a partnership's name of a partner who is not "deceased" and who, although nominally "retired," is still practicing

16. The Association of the Bar of the City of New York, Comm. on Prof'l & Judicial Ethics, Formal Op. 1995-9 (May 31, 1995) (Partners of one law firm may form a second law firm bearing the same name in another jurisdiction. A lawyer may be "Of Counsel" to one law firm while an active name partner in another law firm. A law partnership may retain in its firm name the name of a partner who has retired from the partnership but remains "Of Counsel" while actively practicing in a firm having the same partners in another jurisdiction.).

law elsewhere, is likely to violate DR 2-102(B) because the firm title may be misleading. However, after considering the scenario presented, the committee concluded that the proposed name would not be misleading for several reasons. First, the committee held that naming the Washington, D.C., law firm with the three partners' names was accurate, since all three named partners would be members of the firm. Second, the committee concluded that the New York law firm should be able to keep the retiring partner's name, even though he would no longer be a partner of that firm, since the retiring partner would remain as "Of Counsel" to the New York law firm. In the committee's opinion, there was no requirement that a firm's name consist exclusively of partners; a partner's continuing "Of Counsel" relationship with the firm is enough. Here, the committee made clear that as long as the retiring partner continued to maintain a close, regular, personal relationship with the New York law firm, the New York law firm could continue to include him in its name.

Listing Out-of-State Of Counsel on Letterhead

The rules among the states differ also with regard to whether the name of a nonresident "Of Counsel" attorney or firm may be included on the firm's letterhead. As a general matter, as long as the relationship with the out-of-state attorney or law firm is close and ongoing and involves frequent contact for the purpose of providing consultation and advice, the attorney or firm may be designated as "Of Counsel" on the law firm's letterhead, business cards, advertisements, and related communications. For example, in Opinion 522 (October 6, 1983), the New Jersey Supreme Court Committee on Attorney Advertising denied a New Jersey firm's request to list a Pennsylvania law firm on its letterhead as "Of Counsel" because the relationship between the firms was one of each firm referring legal matters to the other. The committee held that listing the Pennsylvania firm as "Of Counsel" would be misleading by indicating that the out-of-state firm had some relationship with the New Jersey firm, which was not the case. The committee could see "no valid reason for attorneys to include on their letterheads referral attorneys or firms . . . to whom they refer legal matters."[17]

17. N.J. Eth. Op. 522, 122 N.J.L.J. 384, 1983 WL 106232 (N.J. Adv. Comm. Prof. Ethics).

Assuming the relationship is close, continuing, and regular, most jurisdictions allow the law firm to list on its letterhead names of out-of-state "Of Counsel," even if the "Of Counsel" lawyers are not licensed to practice in that jurisdiction.[18] But, in most of these same jurisdictions, the letterhead must state the "Of Counsel" attorney or firm's jurisdictional limitations.[19] Under Model Rules, Rule 7.5 (b), "[a] law firm with offices in more than one jurisdiction may use the same name or other professional designation in each jurisdiction, but identification of the lawyers in an office of the firm shall indicate the jurisdictional limitations on those not licensed to practice in the jurisdiction where the office is located." However, some jurisdictions prohibit the letterhead from including the name of an out-of-state "Of Counsel" who is not licensed to practice in that jurisdiction.[20] Although Formal Opinion 330 did not address the issue, the ABA committee in Formal Opinion 90-357 stated:

> An additional ethical consequence of the relationship implied by the term "of counsel" is that in any listing, on a letterhead, shingle, bar listing or professional card, which shows the of counsel lawyer's name, any pertinent jurisdictional limitations on the lawyer's entitlement to practice must be indicated.[21]

Listing Areas of Specialization on Letterhead

There is little divergence of opinion on whether an "Of Counsel" attorney or firm's areas of specialization may be included on the letterhead. Most

18. Iowa State Ethics Op. 85-6 (1986); Michigan State Ethics Op. CI-749 (April 1, 1982) (Letterhead indicating "Of Counsel" for relationships with out-of-state lawyers is not improper so long as the relationship is close, regular, and involving frequent contact. Such letterhead may indicate designations as to the areas of expertise such as legal consulting in a given filed so long as: (1) The designations are not false, misleading, fraudulent or deceptive; (2) The designations clearly indicate that out-of-state "Of Counsel" is limited to legal consulting work in his or her own jurisdiction only and not within the State of Michigan; and (3) The underlying relationship does not allow out-of state counsel to practice law within Michigan nor that the public is mislead in the same regard.

19. Iowa State Ethics Op. 85-6 (1986).

20. *See* Appendix J for state-by-state variations.

21. ABA Comm. on Ethics & Prof'l Responsibility, Formal Op. 90-357, at 13 (1990) (citations omitted).

jurisdictions hold that if only particular services or areas of law are subject to the "Of Counsel" relationship, the letterhead may contain more descriptive language to explain the true nature of the "Of Counsel" relationship.[22] For example, Arizona allows the letterhead of a firm to list a lawyer as "of counsel for litigation purposes only" where there is a substantial and continuing relationship.[23] In Philadelphia, a lawyer may be designated as "Tax Counsel" on the letterhead of two separate firms, provided both associations meet the requirements of an "Of Counsel" relationship.[24]

In some states, the phrase "Of Counsel" may be modified slightly to reflect accurately the true nature of the "Of Counsel" relationship. The phrase "Special Counsel" can be used on the firm's letterhead where the "Of Counsel" has been employed by the firm for a number of years as an associate and has acquired a high standing within the firm and the legal community.[25] Adding the word "special" to "counsel" is not a problem since it does not modify the word "counsel" in a misleading way.[26]

---

22. Arizona State Ethics Op. 87-24 (1987); Michigan State Ethics Op. CI-749 (1982) (letterhead may include designations of areas of expertise, but designations must not be false, deceptive, or misleading); New York City Ethics Op. 81-54 (undated) (Of Counsel's areas of specialization may be listed); Suffolk County Ethics Op. 88-1 (undated) (a lawyer may list the name of another lawyer who is not a partner or associate as "Of Counsel" for tax matters, as long as the lawyers have an actual and continuing relationship).

23. Arizona State Ethics Op. 82-6 (1982).

24. Philadelphia Ethics Op. 86-143 (1986).

25. *See* ABA Comm. on Ethics & Prof'l Responsibility, Formal Op. 90-357 (1990); *see also* New York City Ethics Op. 1995-8 (May 31, 1995) (Unaffiliated group of lawyers may not advertise themselves collectively as "The Law Offices at X Square." A law firm may be "Of Counsel" to another law firm or to individual lawyers. Lawyers or law firms may state in advertisements or on letterhead that they are "associated" or "affiliated" with each other, so long as their relationship is akin to an "Of Counsel" relationship and the precise nature of the relationship is fully disclosed in communications with specific prospective clients whenever such disclosure could be relevant to the clients.). *But see* Minnesota Informal Ethics Op. 12 (undated) (a law firm may not list a lawyer as "Of Counsel" on its letterhead; lawyer's role is similar to that of an associate).

26. *Id.*

History of Lawyer Advertising

The 1908 Canons of Professional Ethics contained provisions that, although not completely prohibitive, discouraged lawyer advertising. Canon 27 of the ABA Canons of Professional Ethics maintained that it was "unprofessional" for a lawyer to advertise or solicit professional employment. This canon prohibited most forms of advertising, whether in the form of "circulars, advertisements, or through touters."[27] But the same canon permitted professional cards, stating that the "publication or circulation of ordinary simple business cards, being a matter of personal taste or local custom, is not per se improper."[28]

The ban against lawyer advertising was justified in part on the ground that lawyer advertising and solicitation denigrated the profession and treated it as a business.[29] But as communities began to grow, the number of lawyers who began to ignore the 1908 ban also increased. The organized bar reacted by fighting back vigorously, issuing stern disciplinary rulings that solidified the organized bar's ban on overt lawyer advertising.[30]

By the late 1960s and early 1970s, developments in the law began to occur when lawyers and the Justice Department, on free expression and antitrust grounds, questioned the advertising ban.[31]

During the 1970s and 1980s, radical changes in the rules, brought on by decisions of the United States Supreme Court, resulted in an expansion of commercial advertising and other formal means of communication with potential clients.

In Formal Opinion 330 (1972) [since withdrawn][32], the ABA Standing Committee on Ethics and Professional Responsibility considered whether

---

27. Model Code EC 2-1 (1969, amended 1980); *see also* Model Code EC 2-2 (1969, amended 1980).

28. Canons of Prof'l Ethics Canon 27 (1908). For the original wording of the 1908 Canons of Professional Ethics, *see* ABA Opinions of the Committee on Prof'l Ethics with the Canons of Prof'l Ethics Annotated and Canons of Judicial Ethics Annotated 75 (American Bar Foundation 1967).

29. *See* Canons of Prof'l Ethics Canon 27 (1908).

30. *See* D. Calhoun, Professional Lives in America 82 (1965).

31. *See* Lawpoll, 63 A.B.A. J. 1541 (1977).

32. *See* ABA Comm. on Ethics & Prof'l Responsibility, Formal Op. 330 (1972), *reprinted in* Appendix K.

the "Of Counsel" designation could be used on letterheads, professional announcement cards, and office shingles. Consideration was necessary, the committee wrote, because:

> [T]he Code of Professional)(Responsibility uses the term "Of Counsel" only in DR 2-102(A)(4) relating to letterheads, yet the problems concerning "Of Counsel" arise in connection with other professional notices.

Formal Opinion 330 held)(that where an "Of Counsel" relationship existed, that fact could be shown on professional announcement cards and shingles.[33] The committee also considered whether DR 2-102(A)(6) (a provision that was subsequently deleted from the Model Code of Professional Responsibility) authorized use of the term in law lists or legal directories. Subdivision 6 had stated that data published in a law list or legal directory could include only the name of the lawyer, the lawyer's firm, and "names of professional associates." The existence of an "Of Counsel" relationship was not among the items of information that were expressly permitted to be published. Nevertheless, the committee construed the phrase "names of professional associates" to include lawyers who were "Of Counsel."[34]

Unfortunately, Formal Opinion 330 failed to consider many other significant issues that arise by virtue of the "Of Counsel" relationship. The committee did not discuss whether the name of a lawyer who is "Of Counsel" may ethically be included in the firm name. Nor did the committee consider whether the out-of-state "Of Counsel" attorney and law firm's jurisdictional limitations must be listed on professional announcement cards, letterheads, directories, and law lists. After Formal Opinion 330 was issued, the ABA

---

33. *Id.* Formal Opinion 330 held that use of the term "Of Counsel" was permissible on professional announcement cards because of the language contained in DR 2-102(A)(2), which permits professional announcement cards to state "changed associations . . . or similar matters. . . ." The committee wrote, "The change of a lawyer's status to 'Of Counsel' or the addition to the firm's ranks of a lawyer whose status factually will be 'Of Counsel' falls within the quoted language and is permissible." ABA Comm. on Ethics & Prof'l Responsibility, Formal Op. 330 (1972). Moreover, the committee found that subdivision (3) of DR 2-102(A) contained general language that permitted a lawyer to use a shingle.

34. ABA Formal Op. 330, at 71.

Model Rules of Professional Conduct were developed to displace the ABA Model Code of Professional Responsibility. Constitutional law affecting lawyer advertising underwent a radical change. Some of these changes were reflected in Formal Opinion 90-357 (1990).[35]

The ban on lawyer advertising was first assaulted in 1975, in *Goldfarb v. Virginia State Bar*,[36] an antitrust case in which the plaintiff challenged a state bar's promulgation and enforcement of minimum fee schedules. Though the *Goldfarb* case applied to restrictions on fees, the rationale of *Goldfarb* was quickly applied to lawyer advertising. A second attack came in 1976, when the Justice Department commenced a suit against the American Bar Association under the Sherman Act in *United States v. American Bar Association.*[37] Shortly after the *Goldfarb* case was handed down, the ABA liberalized the Model Code's advertising rules.[38]

In *Virginia State Board of Pharmacy v. Virginia Citizens Consumer Council*,[39] the United States Supreme Court held that commercial speech is entitled to an intermediate level of constitutional protection. But the extension of this doctrine, and the radical liberalization of the Model Rules on lawyer advertising, was not to occur until 1977 when the Supreme Court rendered its now famous decision in *Bates v. Arizona Bar Association.*[40]

The controversy in *Bates* arose after two recent law school graduates decided to place an advertisement in a newspaper announcing their new legal clinic and stating the fees they would charge for certain routine services.[41] The Arizona Bar attacked the advertisement as a violation of the disciplinary rule prohibiting lawyer advertising. The Supreme Court, in a 5–4 decision, held that the disciplinary rule was an unconstitutional abridgement on free speech. The Court held that "blanket suppression of legal advertising does not violate the Sherman Act, but does abridge first amendment rights."[42]

---

35. Model Code of Prof'l Responsibility [hereinafter Model Code] EC 8-3 (1969, amended 1980).

36. 421 U.S. 773 (1975).

37. United States v. American Bar Ass'n, Civil No. 76-1182 (D.D.C. 1976).

38. The August 1976 amendments were criticized in Justice Powell's opinion in *In re R.M.J.*, 455 U.S. 191 (1982).

39. 425 U.S. 748 (1976).

40. 433 U.S. 350 (1977).

41. *Bates*, 433 U.S. 350 (1977).

42. *Id.* at 384.

The holding in *Bates* was actually quite narrow: A state may not prevent a truthful advertisement concerning the availability and terms of routine legal services. Many questions went unanswered in *Bates.* What was the constitutional status of lawyer advertising concerning services other than routine legal services? May a state prohibit in-person solicitation by a lawyer? What standards should a state follow in adopting new codes of ethics allowing lawyer advertising?

After the *Bates* decision, all states and the District of Columbia altered their ethics codes to allow lawyers to engage in some form of advertising. But, since the *Bates* court left open the question of which standards to follow, many ethics codes continued to prohibit the very kind of advertising the Court felt was most needed by the public.

In 1982, the Supreme Court further refined its analysis of First Amendment protection for lawyer advertising in *In re R.M.J.*[43] In this case, the Court provided states with a standard to follow when determining the constitutionality of their own rules concerning lawyer advertising. In R.M.J., the Court reversed a Missouri court that had reprimanded a lawyer for publishing newspaper advertisements that listed areas of practice using language other than that allowed by the rules, and for listing courts in which he was permitted to practice even though such information was not among the information authorized by the rules. He was also reprimanded for sending professional announcement cards to persons other than those permitted by the rules.

In striking down the Missouri rules as unconstitutional, the Court utilized the four-part commercial speech test developed in *Central Hudson Gas & Electric Corp. v. Public Service Commission of New York.*[44] The Court asked whether (1) the commercial speech in question was misleading or proposed a lawful activity; (2) there was a substantial governmental interest at stake; (3) the regulation directly advanced that governmental interest; and (4) the regulation was no more extensive than necessary to serve that interest. It held that the advertisement was not unlawful or misleading. It

43. 455 U.S. 191 (1982).
44. 447 U.S. 557 (1980).

further determined that the state did not show that there was at stake a substantial state interest that justified an absolute ban. The Court stated:

> [W]hen the particular content or method of the advertising suggests that it is inherently misleading or when experience has proven that in fact such advertising is subject to abuse, the states may impose appropriate restrictions. Misleading advertising may be prohibited entirely. But the states may not place an absolute prohibition on certain types of potentially misleading information, e.g., a listing of areas of practice, if the information also may be presented in a way that is not deceptive.[45]

Though the *R.M.J.* decision established an analytical framework for states to use in implementing rules concerning lawyer advertising, the decision left unanswered questions regarding which state interests are so "substantial" that the state can regulate lawyer communications affecting those interests.

In *Zauderer v. Office of Disciplinary Counsel*,[46] the Court addressed the question of whether a state can regulate newspaper advertisements that are targeted to a specific class of litigants. Zauderer, an Ohio attorney, placed several newspaper advertisements featuring drawings of intrauterine devices, accompanied by a headline asking, "Did You Use This IUD?"[47] The advertisement went on to state that Zauderer was available to handle lawsuits for individuals who were injured by using the device, and that no legal fees would be charged unless there was a recovery. The Ohio disciplinary panel's finding that Zauderer had violated a rule against false and misleading statements was affirmed by the Ohio Supreme Court.

The United States Supreme Court found that the Ohio prohibition on lawyer advertising targeted at particular clientele regarding specific legal problems was unconstitutional. In its analyses, the Supreme Court restated the rule that commercial speech is entitled to limited First Amendment protection. The Court reaffirmed the rule allowing states to regulate false and

45. Note, *supra* note 17, at 203.
46. 471 U.S. 626 (1985).
47. *Id.*

misleading advertising, advertising that promulgates illegal transactions, or even non-deceptive, truthful advertising if the state's interest is substantial, as long as the means directly advance that interest. But here the Court made it more difficult for the states to restrict the content of commercial speech that is not misleading, deceptive, or untruthful.

Since *Zauderer,* lawyers are generally permitted to solicit business through print media as long as the advertisements are truthful and non-deceptive, and do not propose involvement in an illegal transaction. No longer are the state's interests in dignity and decorum substantial enough to warrant an absolute ban on all advertising.

The accepted view, as enunciated in *Bates* and followed in *Zauderer, is* that dissemination of information to the public is of primary importance. The holdings of *Zauderer* and *Bates* are narrowly limited to the facts of those cases, but since *Zauderer* there has been a steady increase in lawyer advertising.[48]

The *Zauderer* decision was also significant in that it addressed both the problem of lawyer advertising and the problem of lawyer solicitation of legal business. Lawyer solicitation the active seeking out of prospective clients had previously been addressed by the Supreme Court in two companion cases, *In re Primus*[49] and *Ohralik v. Ohio State Bar Association.*[50] While *Bates* and *Zauderer* dealt with advertising through mass media, *Ohralik* and *In re Primus* involved the lawyer's in-person promotion of legal services. More important, the outcome of *Bates* and *Zauderer* rested on the rights of prospective clients to obtain information about available legal services, not on the rights of lawyers to express themselves. But these decisions made it unclear whether lawyers enjoyed the personal constitutional right of free expression.

In *Ohralik,* the client was a minor injured in an automobile accident, who, while visited by the lawyer in the hospital, was induced to sign an employment contract for the lawyer's services. The Court found the dangers of overreaching were too great not to allow the state to impose broad

48. Kaspar, *Attorney and Client—Constitutional Law—Attorney Advertising: The Expanding Horizons of Permissible Conduct,* 62 N.D. L. Rev. 575, 588 (1986).
49. 436 U.S. 412 (1978).
50. *Id.* at 447.

regulations on such behavior. On the other hand, the Court allowed First Amendment protection to the solicitation involved in *In re Primus*.[51] In that case, the lawyer targeted a mailing to a potential client. But in *Primus,* the client was poor, and the lawyer was offering the client free representation by the American Civil Liberties Union. The Court, noting that this was not "in-person solicitation for pecuniary gain,"[52] determined that this was a "form of political expression" entitled to First Amendment protection.[53] The lawyer's actions were therefore constitutionally protected, not as commercial, but as political, speech.

The outcome of both *Ohralik* and *In re Primus* made it clear that, in the view of the Court, states cannot absolutely prohibit all in-person solicitation where it is not for pecuniary gain. Even where the solicitation is for pecuniary gain, the state may not absolutely prohibit it. But such solicitation could be subject to stringent state regulations.

The Court of Appeals for the Eleventh Circuit followed *Ohralik* in a less egregious case involving two attorneys, Falanga and Chalker, who maintained a personal injury practice with five offices and many staff members. Most of their clients were poor and uneducated persons who were solicited through in-person, telephone, and direct mail solicitation after their names were obtained in two ways: First, a "public relations" agent asked doctors and chiropractors to recommend the attorneys to their injured patients and grieving family members in need of legal services. In exchange, the lawyers would take the health care professionals to lunch and provide them with free legal advice. Second, staff members would sift through police reports, obtaining names of person who had been injured or killed in automobile accidents. With this information, the lawyers would mail approximately 300 letters and brochures per week to accident victims. The Eleventh Circuit upheld various rules of the State Bar of Georgia against solicitation as not being in violation of the "First Amendment commercial speech rights of Falanga, Chalker and other similarly situated lawyers who approach unsophisticated, injured or distressed lay person[s]."[54]

51. 436 U.S. 412.
52. *Id.* at 422.
53. *Id.* at 428.
54. Falanga v. State Bar, 150 F.3d 781 (11th Cir. 198), *cert. denied,* 526 U.S. 1087 (1999).

The Supreme Court has ruled that states cannot categorically prohibit lawyers from soliciting business through truthful, non-deceptive direct mail targeted to potential clients known to face particular legal problems. In the case of *Shapero v. Kentucky Bar Association*[55] a Kentucky lawyer sought prior approval from that state's Attorney Advertising Commission of a letter that he proposed to send to potential clients who were about to have a foreclosure suit filed against them. The letter advised the client that "you may be about to lose your home," that "[f]ederal law may allow you to . . . ORDER your creditor to STOP," that "you may call my office . . . for FREE information," and that "[i]t may surprise you what I may be able to do for you."[56] Although the letter was not found to be false or misleading, the commission failed to approve the letter, relying on a state supreme court rule that barred advertisements "precipitated by a specific event . . . involving or relating to the addressee . . . as distinct from the general public."[57] Although this rule was subsequently deleted by the state supreme court, the rule was replaced by Rule 7.3, which prohibited all targeted direct-mail solicitation by lawyers for pecuniary gain.[58]

The United States Supreme Court reversed the decision of the state supreme court. In so doing, the Court distinguished between in-person solicitation and targeted direct-mail solicitation. With targeted direct-mail solicitation, the Court wrote, there is a much lower risk of improper lawyer conduct through coercive tactics.[59] The recipients of such advertising are not faced with the presence of a trained advocate or the pressure of having to give an immediate yes-or-no answer. They can simply put the letter aside, ignore it, or discard it. Moreover, any risks associated with a personalized letter can be minimized by requiring the lawyer to file the letter with a state agency having authority to supervise targeted mailings and penalize actual abuses. On remand, the Court directed the state court to consider whether the mailing was false or misleading by emphasizing trivial or uninformative

---

55. 486 U.S. 466 (1988).
56. *Id.* at 469.
57. *Id.* at 469–70.
58. *Id.* at 470–71.
59. *Id.* at 475.

facts, or by offering overblown assurances of client satisfaction.[60]

Against this developing constitutional background, the ABA amended both the Model Code and the Model Rules to include provisions governing the permissible content, format, and media of lawyers' communications. Actually, even as the *Bates* decision was being prepared by the Supreme Court, the ABA was revising the Model Code's advertising rules.[61] The amended Model Code prohibited a lawyer from communicating any information that is false, fraudulent, misleading, deceptive, self-laudatory, or unfair.[62] The Model Rules, adopted by the ABA to replace the Model Code after the Supreme Court rendered its decision in R.M.J., simply prohibit any "false or misleading communication about the lawyer or the lawyer's services."[63] Each state and the District of Columbia have also adopted rules that prohibit false, misleading, or deceptive communications.

In the past, it was not clear whether mail directed toward a particular recipient should be referred to as advertising, and subjected to minimal restrictions, or as solicitation, and subjected to greater restrictions. Before *Shapero,* the answer depended upon the practicing lawyer's state, the content of the mailing, and the identity of the addressees.[64] After *Shapero,* some of the prior restrictions on this form of client contact were eliminated, thereby permitting, for the first time, contact through direct mail with a potential client for pecuniary gain.[65]

Following the decision in *Shapero,* the courts provided guidance as to the proper form of lawyer advertising. Some jurisdictions left the precise nature of the advertising to the marketplace. Others established regulatory bodies to deal specifically with various forms of advertising. Still others left the form of advertising to the courts to be determined case by case. Several

---

60. *Id.* at 479.

61. M. SCHWARTZ & R. WYDICK, PROBLEMS IN LEGAL ETHICS 71 (2d ed. West 1988).

62. *See* MODEL CODE DR 2-101(A).

63. MODEL RULES OF PROF'L CONDUCT, R. 7.1

64. William C. Becker, Shapero—Direct *Mail Clarified,* 22 AKRON L. REV. 199 (1988).

65. For an analysis of the rule of Shapero, and the forms of in-person solicitation it may render permissible, see Note, *Professional Responsibility:* Shapero v. Kentucky Bar Association: *Guideline for a Constitutional Lawyer Solicitation Rule—Does* Shapero *Open the Door to In-Person Solicitation?* 42 OKLA. L. REV. 341 (1989).

of the decided cases have provided directions as to the legitimacy of various forms of advertising.

Summary

The need to educate members of the public as to the existence of legal problems and the resultant need for legal services, and methods for intelligent selection of counsel, has long been recognized. This need has been met by lawyer referral programs and by lawyer advertising and solicitation of clients. However, with the increased use of lawyer advertising and solicitation, rules have developed to govern the form, timing, and content of such communication.

As a type of commercial speech, lawyer advertising is protected under the First Amendment of the Constitution. As such, lawyer advertising is afforded an intermediate level of protection; advertising that is truthful and non-deceptive cannot be absolutely prohibited. Yet, even though states may not impose absolute prohibitions on all lawyer advertising, states may reasonably regulate the time, place, or manner of advertising as long as the regulations do not suppress or regulate the actual content of the advertising. States may absolutely prohibit false or misleading advertising or advertising that contemplates an illegal transaction. Thus, state regulations may require a warning or disclaimer on the advertisement, or ask that the lawyer forward a copy of the proposed advertisement to the appropriate state agency for approval before circulation.

Unlike advertising, in-person solicitation for pecuniary gain is not on a par with truthful advertising. The potential for overreaching and undue influence by the lawyer over the recipient "overwhelmed" by legal troubles requires that states be given the discretion to ban categorically all in-person solicitation for pecuniary gain. On the other hand, solicitation for pecuniary gain through targeted mailings cannot be categorically prohibited, although it can be subjected to stringent state regulations. The recipient of targeted mail advertising is not subject to the coercive personal presence of a trained advocate. The recipient can simply put the letter aside until later or completely ignore it. Any risk associated with targeted solicitation letters can be minimized by scrutiny by the reviewing agency.

The Model Rules now contain provisions that generally prohibit lawyer advertising only when the communication is false, fraudulent, or misleading. One form or another of these rules has been adopted by each state.

As forms of communication, the firm name, letterhead, and professional business card of a lawyer are subject to the general rules on lawyer advertising. The Model Rules have adopted a generally relaxed attitude toward communications concerning a lawyer's services and prohibit use of these forms of communication only when the content of the information conveyed is false or misleading. As long as there is an actual "Of Counsel" relationship, the lawyer or law firm can convey that fact in all communications. In some states, the phrase may be modified to reflect the lawyer's particular skills or areas of expertise. In most jurisdictions, a nonresident "Of Counsel" attorney or law firm must list his, her, or its jurisdictional limitations on the firm's letterhead.

Checklists for Issue Spotting

Is There an Actual Of Counsel Relationship?

If so, that fact may be included on all firm letterheads, professional announcement cards, shingles, law lists, and legal directories.

Is Of Counsel an Out-of-State Lawyer?

Are Of Counsel's jurisdictional limitations listed on the firm letterhead? Must Of Counsel be licensed to practice in the jurisdiction in which the firm is located before he or she may be listed on the firm's letterhead?

CHAPTER 10

The Of Counsel Agreement

In this chapter we consider the uses of various forms of the "Of Counsel" agreement. The form of the agreement is a function of (1) the business objectives of the parties; (2) the nature of the relationship; and (3) the form of business organization. The interplay of these parameters is illustrated by examples in the Appendices.[1]

At the outset, the "Of Counsel" agreement should make it clear that the "Of Counsel" attorney is neither a partner nor an associate of the firm. The name of an "Of Counsel" attorney who is a retired partner may be included in the firm name. But the partnership should give careful consideration to whether this is in the best interest of the firm as a whole. To avoid liability as an implied partner, the status of the "Of Counsel" attorney should be clearly communicated in the firm letterhead, professional announcement cards, shingles, directories, and law lists.

Terms of the Agreement

As the parties draft the various terms of the "Of Counsel" agreement, they should foresee as many problems as possible, and draft a detailed agreement

1. *See generally infra* at pp. 241–270.

to meet their precise needs. Typical of some of the problems with which the drafters must contend are

- *Compensation:* In Formal Opinion 90-357, the ABA Standing Committee on Ethics and Professional Responsibility stated that it took no position on the manner in which an "Of Counsel" attorney should be compensated. This is a matter of contract between the parties.
  The parties may use a flat hourly rate, a percentage of gross receipts for business that originates with Of Counsel, a percentage of net income after deducting expenses related to such business, a drawing account, a draw plus a splitting of fees on matters the "Of Counsel" attorney brings to the firm, or any combination of or variation on these approaches.

- *Perquisites:* The "Of Counsel" agreement should spell out in precise detail those items of expense to be borne by the firm rather than by the individual lawyer. For example, car allowance, cell phone expenses, health insurance, malpractice insurance, bar association dues, travel and entertainment expenses, group term insurance, contributions to 401(k) plans, etc.
- *Protection of trade secrets:* A law firm may wish to protect itself against the personal use or disclosure of trade secrets by an "Of Counsel" attorney. Alternatively, the "Of Counsel" agreement may incorporate this type of clause by reference to the general partnership agreement. Trade secrets include such things as client lists, financial information, business plans, etc.
- *Malpractice insurance:* Before entering into an "Of Counsel" agreement, both parties should be certain that proper arrangements have been made for malpractice insurance and the "Of Counsel" agreement should specify which party is responsible for maintaining the coverage.[2] Since a lawyer's potential liability as an "Of Counsel" attorney may be much less, if they are practicing less than full-time, the portion

---

2. If the parties desire an independent-contractor relationship, they should insert a clause detailing that, solely for purpose of the malpractice insurance coverage, the "Of Counsel" attorney should be treated as an employee.

of the premium attributed to the "Of Counsel" attorney for coverage may be less or may even be included in the firm's existing coverage at no additional cost.

- ***Other fringe benefits:*** In addition to coverage for malpractice insurance, "Of Counsel" agreements often provide for payment by the law firm of the "Of Counsel" attorney's professional dues and licensing, business expenses, health insurance, and the like. If the parties desire an independent-contractor relationship, they should specifically provide that the "Of Counsel" attorney is to be treated as an employee for the purposes of these benefits. The drafter should avoid using this rubric with reference to too many such characteristics of the agreement if the "Of Counsel" attorney wishes to retain independent-contractor status.
- ***Duties:*** The description of the "Of Counsel" attorney's duties and responsibilities relating to the firm, clients, and other parties will present some of the most difficult drafting problems surrounding the "Of Counsel" agreement. Contracts will vary greatly depending upon what the parties are seeking to accomplish. In the case of the retired partner, the parties may wish to specify the extent and manner in which the "Of Counsel" attorney will cut back on former duties as a partner. For example, they may agree that the "Of Counsel" attorney need no longer be required to take an active role in the litigation conducted by the firm. Or there may be a reduction in the number of hours that the "Of Counsel" attorney will typically be expected to be on the premises of the firm. Or there may be some indication that the "Of Counsel" attorney will retain a more active role in serving some clients rather than others. However the duties of the "Of Counsel" attorney are outlined, there must be some consonant relationship between these duties and the compensation and perquisites to be provided to the "Of Counsel" attorney.

Independent Contractor versus Employer-Employee Relationship

Although there may be some situations in which an employer-employee relationship will be indicated, drafters usually find that the relationship of independent contractor is most beneficial for both the "Of Counsel" attorney and the firm. In drafting the agreement, the drafter must sail between the Scylla[3] of the employer-employee relationship and the Charybdis of partnership. For some purposes, such as malpractice insurance, employee benefits, health insurance, and the like, the parties may wish to treat the "Of Counsel" attorney as an employee. At the same time, the parties must be careful about assigning duties to the "Of Counsel" attorney that would seem managerial, giving the semblance of power to make decisions for the firm. An absence of care in this drafting may cause the firm or the "Of Counsel" attorney to suffer unnecessary vicarious liability.[4]

The Internal Revenue Service has required some "Of Counsel" attorneys who are practicing as independent contractors to answer elaborate questionnaires designed to determine the extent to which one party has "control" over the other.[5] If the common law element of control is present, the relationship is that of employer-employee; if not, then the parties are independent contractors. Although no single factor is determinative, to the extent that some of the following questions are answered in the affirmative, the relationship of the firm with the lawyer may be deemed that of employer-employee, rather than independent contractors:

(1) Must the lawyer comply with the firm's instructions regarding the work?
(2) Does the lawyer receive training from or at the direction of the firm?
(3) Does the lawyer provide services that are integrated into the firm's business?
(4) Does the lawyer provide services that must be rendered personally?
(5) May the lawyer hire, supervise, and pay assistants for the firm?
(6) Does the lawyer have a continuing relationship with the firm?
(7) Must the lawyer follow set hours of work?

3. In Greek mythology, Scylla was a sea monster that lived underneath a dangerous rock at one side of the Strait of Messina, opposite the whirlpool from the monster Charybdis.

4. *See, generally,* Chapter 6, *supra.*

5. The issue of control has been the subject of much litigation in the determination of the coverage of typical fidelity bond. Cf. Auchincloss v. United States Fidelity & Guar. Co., 190 A.D. 6, 179 N.Y.S. 454 (1st Dept. 1919) and its progeny.

(8) Does the lawyer work full-time for the firm?
(9) Does the lawyer work on the firm's premises?
(10) Must the lawyer work in a sequence set by the firm?
(11) Must the lawyer submit regular reports to the firm?
(12) Does the lawyer receive regular amounts of compensation at set intervals?
(13) Does the lawyer receive payments for business or traveling expenses?
(14) Does the lawyer rely on the firm to furnish tools and materials?
(15) Does the lawyer lack a major investment in the facilities used to perform the services?
(16) Is the arrangement such that the lawyer cannot make a profit or suffer a loss from his or her services?
(17) Does the lawyer work for one firm at a time?
(18) Is the arrangement such that the lawyer does not offer his or her services to the general public?
(19) May the lawyer be fired by the firm?
(20) May the lawyer quit work at any time without incurring liability?

No single affirmative answer or even several affirmative answers is necessarily determinative of whether the firm is in fact in control of the lawyer. But the questions provide a guide for one drafting an "Of Counsel" agreement to ensure that a particular contract between a lawyer and a law firm will be construed as establishing an independent contractor, rather than an employer-employee, relationship. The drafter of the agreement should make certain that the majority of the above questions will be answered in the negative. This should not be too difficult since there are only one or two questions (for instance, the sixth question, dealing with the continuing relationship) that require an affirmative answer to appropriately designate the arrangement as an "Of Counsel" arrangement.

Tax Advantages and Disadvantages of the Independent-Contractor Status

As an independent contractor, the "Of Counsel" attorney may take business deductions "above the line" (that is, prior to determining adjusted gross income), on Schedule C of the attorney's Form 1040 federal tax return. The "Of Counsel" attorney then will have the option of itemizing non-business deductions or taking the standard deduction. This eliminates the two-percent floor on miscellaneous business deductions applicable to employees, since these amounts will be shown as part of the cost of doing business on Schedule C.

But the use of the independent-contractor, rather than employee, status does have one disadvantage. The Internal Revenue Code imposes the self-employment tax on the self-employment income of any U.S. citizen or resident alien who has self-employment income.[6] For 2012, the maximum taxable earnings amount for Social Security taxes was $110,100. There was no limitation on taxable earnings for Medicare taxes. Under an employee/employer relationship in 2012, the Social Security tax rate for the employee was 4.2 percent[7], the Social Security tax rate for the employer was 6.2 percent, and the Medicare tax rate was 1.45 percent for both the employee and the employer. However, the Social Security tax rate for the self-employed was 10.4 percent in 2012 and the Medicare tax rate was 2.9 percent. For the self-employed, one-half of these amounts is deductible. But since these amounts are treated as *a deduction,* rather than a *credit against tax,* the independent contractor's position is less advantageous than that of an employee. A self-employed person with $100,000 of earnings would pay net Social Security and Medicare taxes of $11,438.00, computed as follows:

Taxable	Tax Rate	Amount	Amount of Tax
Social Security	10.4%	$100,000.00	$ 10,400.00
Medicare	2.9%	$100,000.00	$ 2,900.00
Taxable income		$100,000.00	$ 13,300.00

6. Self-employment income is income that arises from the performance of personal services, but which cannot be classified as wages because an employer-employee relationship does not exist between the payer and the payee.

7. The Tax Relief, Unemployment Insurance Reauthorization, and Job Creation Act of 2010, reduced the 6.2% Social Security payroll tax rate by 2% on the portion of the tax paid by the worker in 2011 and the 12.4% self-employment Social Security tax rate. This reduction was extended through the end of February 2012 by the Temporary Payroll Tax Cut Continuation Act of 2011 and under the Middle Class Tax Relief and Job Creation Act of 2012, the reduction was extended through December 2012.

Taxable	Tax Rate	Amount	Amount of Tax
Less deduction of 50% of Social Security and Medicare taxes			$6,650.00
Taxable income, as adjusted			$ 93,350.00
Tax benefit attributable to Social Security and Medicare taxes, assuming a tax rate of 28%			$ 1,862.00
Taxes attributable to Social Security and Medicare:			$13,300.00 less $1,862.00, or $11,438.00.

By contrast, an employee would pay a 4.2 percent tax on the first $100,000 of earnings for purposes of the Social Security taxes, and a 1.45 percent tax on all earnings for Medicare:

Taxable	Tax Rate	Amount	Amount of Tax
Social Security	4.2%	$100,000	$ 4,200.00
Medicare	1.45%	$100,000	1,450.00
Taxes owed on Social Security and Medicare for an employee			$5,650.00
Additional cost for being an independent contractor:			$11,438.00 less $5,650.00, or $5,788.00*.
* Even in the absence of the 2% Tax Relief, there remains an additional cost for being an independent contractor, as both the employee and the self-employed would be higher.			

The law firm also gains substantial tax advantages from the independent-contractor relationship. It retains the use of the money that it would otherwise be required to withhold for the income tax payable by the lawyer who is classified as an employee. It files an information return, Form 1099, on which it reports the lawyer's earnings. Of Counsel files the Form 1040, including Schedule C, on which business income is reported. The independent contractor also files a Schedule SE, on which the taxes payable for Social Security and Medicare are calculated.

The Retired Partner

Many lawyers are not overly keen on retiring completely from the practice of law. Despite the lure of grandchildren, bridge, golf, travel, hunting, fishing, or other activities having no relation to the practice of law, few activities have the intellectual challenge — and joy — that law practice often affords. Yet continuing the high level of stress to which lawyers become accustomed may not be in the best interest of the lawyer's physical and mental well-being. There are, of course, workaholics who have no desire to change their pattern of living or to engage in some activity other than law practice. Some lawyers, particularly those in small law firms with weak retirement programs, may feel that they cannot afford to retire because they will have insufficient income to maintain the standard of living to which they have become accustomed.

What many retiring lawyers want is some form of activity related to the practice of law, with a substantial amount of free time to do those things that they have been unable to do during the more active years of their careers. For the lawyer who has retired, or is planning to retire, the "Of Counsel" agreement offers a solution to some of those retirement problems, and provides the firm with an opportunity to take advantage of the experience of a senior member of the bar.

If a lawyer has practiced with a firm large enough to establish some form of pension planning, and there is a general notion — if not an express contract — that members of the firm will retire upon reaching a certain age, the "Of Counsel" agreement becomes the principal vehicle for establishing a relationship between a retired lawyer and that lawyer's former law firm.

Although it would be possible to incorporate the "Of Counsel" agreement into a pension plan, or even into the general partnership agreement, the best practice is to have a wholly separate agreement dealing solely with the "Of Counsel" relationship.

In Formal Opinion 90-357,[8] the ABA ethics committee eliminated the earlier requirement that "Of Counsel" attorneys be compensated only for the legal work performed. A retired partner may now draw a pension or

8. *See supra* Chapters 3 through 5.

other retirement benefit, and still share in the firm's profits. As a result, the parties are free to agree upon such compensation arrangements as are mutually satisfactory.

Financial Planning and Retirement

It is beyond the scope of this book to deal with an "Of Counsel" attorney's estate planning and financial problems.[9] Yet certain areas, such as Social Security and Medicare, are so important for the semiretired lawyer that an abbreviated treatment of these matters is warranted.

Social Security

There are two components of Social Security taxes: (1) Old-Age, Survivors, and Disability Insurance (OASDI); and (2) Hospital Insurance (HI). OASDI pays for the typical Social Security benefits, and HI pays for Part A of Medicare—that is, hospital benefits for those who are covered.

The annual earnings limitation for persons under full retirement age (FRA) who are drawing Social Security was $14,640 for 2012. For persons with earnings in the year of reaching FRA, the 2012 limitation was $38,880. For persons who are younger than FRA, earnings in excess of the $14,640 limitation are subject to a $1 deduction from Social Security retirement benefits for each $2 of excess earnings. In the year a person reaches FRA, $1 in benefits will be deducted for each $3 in excess earnings, up to the month in which FRA is reached. There is no limit on earnings beginning the month an individual attains full retirement age, such that an "Of Counsel" attorney of full retirement age or better is free to earn an unlimited amount without reduction of their Social Security retirement benefits.

Social Security benefits are increased by a certain percentage (depending on date of birth), called delayed retirement credits (or DRC), if an individual delays their retirement beyond full retirement age. The yearly rates of

9. *See* Jay A. Soled, Estate Planning Strategies: A Lawyer's Guide to Retirement and Lifetime Planning (ABA 2002), for more extensive treatment of the financial issues outlined herein.

increase for DRC range from 5.5% to 8%. The benefit increase no longer applies when an individual reaches age 70, even if the individual continues to delay taking benefits. The effect of the DRC is to increase the Social Security retirement benefit amount of a person who delays retirement after reaching FRA. The DRC is potentially an additional benefit for the "Of Counsel" attorney who chooses to continue working past FRA.

Medicare

Medicare is the U.S. health insurance program for people age 65 or older, and certain people younger than age 65, such as those with disabilities and those who have permanent kidney failure. Medicare helps with the cost of health care, but it does not cover all medical expenses or the cost of most long-term care. An individual receiving Social Security retirement or disability benefits or railroad retirement checks, will be contacted by the Social Security Administration a few months before they become eligible for Medicare and given the information they need and, if the individual lives in one of the 50 states or Washington, D.C., they will be enrolled in Medicare Parts A and B automatically. However, because there is a cost associated with the Part B coverage, an individual has the option of turning it down. For individuals who are not receiving Social Security retirement, disability, or railroad retirement benefits, it is important to sign up for Medicare at age 65, even if delaying retirement, to avoid delays in Medicare coverage and/or additional costs for the same.

Medicare has four parts: (1) hospital insurance (Part A) helps pay for inpatient care in a hospital or skilled nursing facility following a hospital stay, as well as some home health care and hospice care; (2) medical insurance (Part B) helps pay for doctors' services and other medical services and supplies that are not covered by hospital insurance; (3) Medicare Advantage (Part C) plans available in many areas, through which some people with Medicare Parts A and B can choose to receive all of their health care services; and (4) prescription drug coverage (Part D).[10] Individuals who are eligible for the free Medicare hospital insurance (Part A) can enroll in

10. Detailed information about Medicare is available online at http://www.medicare.gov/publications, last visited Dec. 9, 2012.

Medicare medical insurance (Part B) by paying a monthly premium. Some beneficiaries with higher incomes will pay a higher monthly Part B premium. This premium is typically deducted from the beneficiary's Social Security benefits each month.

In addition to Medicare Parts A and B, many "Of Counsel" attorneys buy Medicare supplementary, or "Medigap" insurance. However, if the attorney already has other health insurance, they should get in touch with their insurance agent to see how their private plan fits with Medicare medical insurance before making any changes, especially if family members are covered under the same policy. And remember, just as Medicare does not cover all health services, most private plans do not either.

Taxation of Social Security Benefits

A portion of the retiree's Social Security benefits (SSB) may be included in gross income after retirement. Benefits include any Social Security payments plus any amounts withheld for Medicare Part B. For 2012, a person with total income in excess of $25,000, filing their federal tax return individually, or in excess of $32,000, filing jointly, will have to pay federal taxes on their Social Security benefits. However, the maximum amount of Social Security benefits subject to taxation is 85 percent.[11]

The Part-Time Lawyer

In contrast with the retired or retiring partner is the lawyer who becomes "Of Counsel" in order to practice law part-time. The reasons for this may vary: a specialty that provides the law firm with particular expertise; service of a client whose needs do not require a full-time lawyer; the attorney's desire to pursue additional vocations such as teaching, writing or politics; or a wish to spend more time at home with family. Whatever the reason, the "Of Counsel" arrangement can provide a vehicle whereby the lawyer can satisfy both the law firm's needs and personal ones.

11. Detailed information about income taxes and Social Security benefits is available online at http://www.ssa.gov/planners/taxes.htm, last visited Dec. 9, 2012.

Case Study: The Matrimonial Law Expert and the WIMPs Firm

Assume that you have established your reputation as an excellent matrimonial lawyer in Metropolis, a city of approximately 700,000 persons. Metropolis is the largest city in your state, which is predominantly rural with a population of 3.5 million. The next largest city has a population of 250,000. Twenty-five hundred lawyers are engaged in active practice in Metropolis. Of these, more than 80 percent are either solo practitioners or practicing in firms of no more than five attorneys. There are twelve law firms with fifty or more lawyers.

During the last twenty years, you have acquired the reputation of being the leading matrimonial lawyer in Metropolis and your state. You are an adjunct professor at the University's law school in Metropolis, where you teach a course in domestic relations one semester each year. You frequently appear as a lecturer in continuing legal education programs sponsored by the local and state bar associations and you have long been active in the Family Law Section of the ABA.

The prestigious law firm of Wills, Ingersoll, Martin, and Peters, P.S.C. (WIMPs) is one of the leading firms in Metropolis, with a long list of corporate clients whom they regularly service in all aspects of commercial and corporate law, trusts and estates, taxation and the like. But WIMPs has never developed a matrimonial law practice.

Recently, Josiah Martin, managing partner[12] at WIMPs, invited you to lunch to discuss the possibility of your joining the firm on such terms as the two of you might find mutually agreeable. Martin explained that the firm needs to develop the area of matrimonial practice, and they need someone like you who is experienced and knowledgeable in the field.

---

12. WIMPs is organized as a professional service corporation (P.S.C.). Technically speaking, it has *no* partners. But the principal stockholders of WIMPs, all of whom are lawyers, refer to themselves as partners and to Josiah Martin as their managing partner. In their corporate structure, Martin holds the title of president, and J. Cuthbert Wills serves as chairman of the board and chief executive officer. Ingersoll is secretary of the corporation; and Peters, its treasurer. As a practical matter, the firm is run by the executive committee, chaired by Wills and consisting of the four persons in the corporate name, plus three other senior partners.

Not all of Martin's partners are happy with the idea of having a matrimonial lawyer walking the halls of their prestigious firm. Martin's grandfather, who founded the firm, once remarked, "I'll never let some darn divorce lawyer inside this firm." But times have changed, and even some of Martin's partners have been divorced. "I hear there's a lot of money in matrimonial practice these days," Martin observes.

Martin is worried that some of his partners may be reluctant to have you come into the firm as a partner. "A lawyer like that should start at the bottom, like everyone else," I. Grumble Alot, a former senior associate who recently made partner, has stated to the firm's recruitment committee. Others are willing to accept you as a partner, as long as a portion of the net profit attributable to the business that you generate will be distributed among the partners at the end of the year.

In response to Martin, you indicate that you would like to come into the firm, but you want an opportunity to think about the possibility of joining in an "Of Counsel" capacity. Martin agrees and the following are some of your thoughts about the opportunity to become "Of Counsel" to WIMPs.

Formal Opinion 90-357 indicates that compensation arrangements between an "Of Counsel" attorney and a law firm can be whatever the parties desire.[13] You wish to retain as much of your earnings from fees as possible, but you recognize that WIMPs will be entitled to reimbursement for any costs expended by the firm on your behalf. What is the best arrangement to resolve these competing demands? Should WIMPs be entitled to share in a portion of your earnings? Should you seek to share in the firm's earnings? Should you base the amount you pay WIMPs for overhead on a percentage of your gross earnings? On a percentage of *their* gross earnings? Or should it be a flat fee, with payment for some direct costs, such as long distance telephone calls?

WIMPs will no doubt have different ideas about how you should be compensated. From the firm's perspective, it will want to know:

13. *See* Chapter 5 especially at pp. 92-95.

- What benefits can the firm expect from expanding its areas of practice to include matrimonial law (e.g., more business from existing clients, reduced chance of losing existing clients to other firms, new clients)?
- Are there more financially beneficial ways to enter into the field of matrimonial law, contrary to the opinion of the managing partner?
- Under the assumption that the firm invites you to join as "Of Counsel," what revenues will the firm receive as a result of your practice?
- What costs will accrue to the firm as a result of adding you as "Of Counsel"?

One of the advantages of practicing with a large firm is the opportunity to participate in what are often extensive fringe benefit programs. You will certainly want to take advantage of the firm's retirement and health care programs. Solely for these purposes, you will want the contract between you and WIMPs to treat you as an employee. In all other respects, you will want to be an independent contractor. As a solo practitioner for the past twenty or so years, you have tried, but not too successfully, to establish an effective retirement program. The demands placed upon you by virtue of raising a family have made it extremely difficult — and at times, impossible — to contribute to your own retirement plan, funded through the American Bar Retirement Association (ABRA).[14] You have begun to think more about retirement, and you want to take part in the excellent retirement program at WIMPs.

You also wish to participate in WIMPs' excellent health care program. While you presently have hospital and medical insurance coverage, the premium that you pay is higher than WIMPs would have to pay if you were under their policy. Moreover, the insurance coverage under their policy would be somewhat greater than the coverage under your own. WIMPs

14. Most pension plans for solo practitioners and small firms funded through ABRA are defined contribution plans (DCP) rather than defined benefit plans (DBP). In a DCP, a lawyer periodically contributes a percentage of earnings on a tax-sheltered basis, and takes an annuity that becomes taxable upon retirement. A DBP functions in the same manner, except that the amount contributed to the plan is determined by the goal that is set to produce a particular benefit upon retirement.

would agree to pay for your complete coverage, as long as the insurer agrees to include you under the firm's policy.

WIMPs has a number of other fringe benefits, such as the payment of your bar association dues, membership in a downtown club, and the like, but these are not at all critical in making your decision whether you should join WIMPs as an "Of Counsel" attorney.

One of the most important matters to be considered in your new arrangement with WIMPs is who will have the responsibility for paying for your malpractice insurance. If you become "Of Counsel" to WIMPs, it is expected that the firm will be vicariously liable for any of your errors or omissions, but you will not be responsible for those of the partners of WIMPs. The premium that WIMPs will have to pay for you to be included under their policy will not be as great as would be the case if you were a partner. This amount may, indeed, be even less than what you pay for malpractice insurance as a solo practitioner.

One of the reasons Josiah Martin is anxious for you to join WIMPs either as "Of Counsel" or as the equivalent of a junior partner is his belief not only that you will make it possible for the firm to develop a matrimonial practice, but that it will also cause some of the existing departments within the firm to grow. For example, Martin points out, divorce practice may well lead to the drafting of prenuptial agreements, which in turn may lead to additional estate planning work. This would give some additional strength to the estate planning department, which Martin believes has not been marketing itself as aggressively as it should. Martin foresees many symbiotic relationships between your practice as a matrimonial lawyer and other departments within the firm.

About eight years ago, when he first became managing partner, Martin established a very thorough intake screening system to guarantee that WIMPs would not represent any client that might present a conflict of interest.[15] Neither you nor Martin wants to be faced with problems of this sort. Accordingly, you agree to examine your respective client files closely for any potential conflicts that might arise by your becoming "Of Counsel" to the firm. Any doubts will be resolved in favor of the existence of a

15. *See generally* Chapters 7 and 8, *supra.*

conflict. Both of you will then consult with your respective clients, make a full disclosure, and obtain any necessary waivers. Martin assures you that any future conflicts will be easily avoided because of the screening system that has served the firm so well.

Neither you nor WIMPs has ever engaged in extensive lawyer advertising.[16] On occasion, you have purchased a slightly larger space in the yellow pages of your local telephone directory, but you have even abandoned that during the past two years. WIMPs has never advertised and doubts that it will ever need to. You both agree that it is very important that all of your stationery, business cards, website, and the like make clear the nature of the relationship between you and the firm. A major consideration for you in connection with choosing the "Of Counsel" status when you join WIMPs is to avoid liability for a potential securities fraud allegedly committed by one of WIMPs' partners.

With these considerations in mind, you and Martin work out an "Of Counsel" agreement that is satisfactory to all concerned. See Appendix C.

Of Counsel as a Vehicle for Firm Organization

Recent years have seen many changes in the organizational structures of firms and in the lives of the young men and women who have entered the profession. Today, many firms push the attainment of high billable hours and a high bottom line, sometimes at the expense of service to the client. As the profession has become more competitive, downsizing has increased. Simultaneously, law firms are seeking to eliminate unwarranted discrimination to minorities and women. Many law firms have come to recognize the importance of flexible work schedules, particularly for working parents with family responsibilities. Some have developed childcare centers to accommodate changing needs of families. Husbands who once spent weekends working in the office now stay at home caring for the family.

In this environment, some law firms have adopted organizational structures that depart from the simple partner-associate arrangement of the past.

16. *See generally* Chapter 9, *supra.*

These include the two-tiered partnership, various forms of employment (for instance, "permanent associates," "senior attorneys," "staff attorneys," and the like), reduced-hours arrangements, leaves, and sabbaticals. These arrangements serve a variety of professional, financial, family, and psychological needs.

One such structure is the law firm organized around a single lawyer who uses the "Of Counsel" agreement as the basis for the structure of the firm. Each lawyer with whom the principal works is "Of Counsel" to the principal (or the firm). Each of the contracting lawyers has a written agreement with the principal (or the firm). The resulting firm organization provides certain advantages not readily obtainable through traditional forms of organization and in technical ways, the position of these lawyers is different from that of their counterparts who are associates or junior partners in the typical law firm. For example:

- ***Employment status:*** The associate is an employee, while the "Of Counsel" attorney may be an employee or an independent contractor, depending upon the contract with the principal.
- ***Compensation:*** The associate is on salary, while the "Of Counsel" attorney will be compensated in accordance with the contract devised, which may include some fixed income, a percentage of gross receipts, a percentage of net earnings, or a mix of these various arrangements.
- ***Malpractice insurance:*** The firm's insurance would normally cover the associate, while the "Of Counsel" attorney may be self-insured or have coverage through the principal.
- ***Professional liability:*** The principal is liable for the errors and omissions of the associate as well as for the "Of Counsel" attorney, but neither the associate nor the "Of Counsel" attorney will be responsible for the tortious wrongs and contract violations of the principal.
- ***Overhead:*** The associate is not responsible for any portion of the firm's overhead expense, while the "Of Counsel" attorney will make an appropriate arrangement by contract to make such contributions to overhead as the parties deem appropriate.
- ***Taxes:*** Income taxes will be withheld by the firm on the associate's income, who will be treated as an employee, while the "Of Counsel"

> attorney treated as an independent contractor rather than as an employee will report gross income and business deductions on Schedule C of his or her federal Form 1040 tax return. The firm will file a Form 1099 with respect to any payments made under such an arrangement with an "Of Counsel" attorney, rather than a Form W-2 for wages paid to employees.

Some years ago, *Barrister*, the magazine of the ABA's Young Lawyers Division, published an article that stated that a law firm of fourteen lawyers provided the optimum job satisfaction for a young lawyer. Such a firm would have adequate resources for a successful law practice, but would not be so large as to cause the stress that sometimes characterizes the large law firm. The following paradigm illustrates how a lawyer might develop a law firm through the use of a series of agreements with "Of Counsel" attorneys.

Case Study: The Senior Solo with "Of Counsel" Attorneys

Lawyer, age fifty, is a general practitioner in the city of Metropolis. His practice continues to grow, so that he finds it necessary to seek outside help. Lawyer's success has long been attributed to his persuasive powers in front of a jury. He has acquired a reputation for an ability to obtain substantial verdicts in personal injury matters. He also achieved some success in criminal defense work, although he did not enjoy this aspect of the practice as much as tort litigation. As his practice expands, he finds it necessary to add personnel to his firm to develop his practice in areas of the law with which he was less familiar. One by one, he adds a young tax lawyer, a divorce lawyer, a commercial litigator, and an estate planner.

As a senior member of the Bar, all have great confidence in Lawyer. He has had many years of practice, is highly respected, and is noted for thoroughness and integrity. Other lawyers in the community would generally be proud to be associated with such a colleague. Young lawyers find that such an association enhances their own skills as well as their reputation.

At the time that these lawyers executed their respective "Of Counsel" agreements with Lawyer, they were not so well known that they could attract a substantial number of clients. But each was so expert in his or her field so that Lawyer's firm soon developed a reputation for total thoroughness and industry.

Lawyer has given each "Of Counsel" a free rein within his or her respective area, as long as each contracting lawyer carries out his or her responsibilities. Lawyer uses a variety of devices, depending upon the particular needs of the individual. The tax lawyer, for example, is given a leave of absence to gain an LL.M. degree in taxation. Since his return, the firm's tax practice has continued to grow.

The divorce lawyer is a single parent with two children (now aged fifteen and twelve). Following her divorce, she joined Lawyer's firm when she was thirty-five years old. She had entered law school at age twenty-seven, after a successful, but financially unrewarding, career in accounting. Upon graduating from law school, she joined a large law firm, where she remained for three years. The firm indicated that she would probably become an income partner, but that it was unlikely she would ever become an equity partner. Suspecting the existence of a glass ceiling, she left to join Lawyer. While her children were growing, she worked at home much of the time. She is now beginning to do more work at the office, as her two children become better able to care for themselves.

The commercial litigator is a single man with an arrogant attitude that is useful in dealing with adversaries, but less valuable in dealing with clients. He likes to work at night and drive around in his Porsche during the day, seeing clients. Lawyer recognizes his natural talents as a litigator, but wants to see him in the office more often, where he would be more readily available for consultation.

The estate planner is a hard-working former trust officer from a local bank. A studious type, he enjoys probate court work, as well as the planning and drafting trust and estate documents. Lawyer worries the estate planner may not be as effective with clients as he is with the law books.

Each "Of Counsel" attorney has an agreement with Lawyer. No two of these contracts are the same: Some allow for the payment of a fixed amount of overhead expense to Lawyer each month; others provide for the retention of a percentage of gross income by each "Of Counsel" attorney, and the payment of another percentage to the firm in lieu of overhead. Every year, Lawyer renegotiates the "Of Counsel" agreement with each lawyer.

The firm that is organized around a series of agreements with "Of Counsel" attorneys is not appropriate in some practice situations. The lawyer who is highly respected and an able leader may not be available to provide the necessary central focal point for the firm's organization. Such an arrangement may not have the cohesiveness of more traditional firm organization. This, however, is a function of the extent to which those executing the agreements have faith in the leader of the firm and the degree of independence and autonomy desired.

While consideration of the "Of Counsel" agreement as a vehicle for firm organization is not indicated in every law practice, for those seeking a high degree of flexibility in practice arrangements, it might well prove to be the most appropriate.

The foregoing examples illustrate a few possible situations in which contracting parties may find it desirable to use an "Of Counsel" agreement and some of the terms that can be addressed through an "Of Counsel" agreement under such circumstances. Obviously, substantial differences will exist among these agreements, depending upon the objectives sought. In the next chapter, we shall deal with the next step: planning and drafting the "Of Counsel" agreement.

CHAPTER 11

PLANNING AND DRAFTING

Rules of Professional Conduct impose few restrictions on the formation of a law partnership.[1] The agreement need not be in writing;[2] in fact, historically only about half of law partnerships have a written agreement.[3] The same appears to be true for "Of Counsel" attorneys.[4] But in view of the wide

1. One limitation, however, applies to partnership agreements: The agreement may not contain a restrictive covenant limiting the right of any partner to practice law after withdrawing from the partnership, except as a condition to payment of retirement benefits. *See* MODEL RULES OF PROF'L CONDUCT. 5.6:

> A lawyer shall not participate in offering or making:
>
> (a) a partnership, shareholders, operating, employment, or other similar type of agreement that restricts the right of a lawyer to practice after termination of the relationship, except an agreement concerning benefits upon retirement; or
>
> (b) an agreement in which a restriction on the lawyer's right to practice is part of the settlement of a client controversy.

Under this rule, an agreement that requires forfeiture of financial benefits if the withdrawing lawyer practices law within a particular locale would violate the rule and would be unenforceable as against public policy, the rationale being that such an agreement limits the public's ability to choose counsel freely. The only exception to such an agreement is any restriction incident to provisions concerning retirement benefits earned for past service with the firm.

2. It might be argued that the "Of Counsel" agreement also need not be in writing. But the law of partnership is well developed through both statutory and case law, while the law with respect to "Of Counsel" is still developing and may produce unexpected or undesirable results. The parties are therefore well-advised to shape their relationship by articulating their rights and duties in relation to one another, as well as with respect to third parties, in a written agreement.

3. M. ALTMAN & R. WEIL, HOW TO MANAGE YOUR LAW OFFICE § 8.01 (Matthew Bender 1988) [hereinafter ALTMAN & WEIL].

4. Informal surveys of Louisville and San Francisco "Of Counsel" lawyers have shown

variety of situations in which "Of Counsel" designations are used today, it would be unwise to leave any of these arrangements to oral agreements or the general understanding of the parties.

The failure of the law firm and the "Of Counsel" attorney to obtain written approval from the client and the court caused at least one "Of Counsel" attorney to lose his fee. The "Of Counsel" attorney had worked with the law firm on a case-by-case basis as requested. These single case retainers were always accomplished separately by agreement between the "Of Counsel" attorney and the law firm. In *In re Coin Phones*,[5] the law firm retained the "Of Counsel" attorney to represent the trustee in bankruptcy to recover assets on behalf of the debtor's estate in a Chapter 11 proceeding. Through the "Of Counsel" attorney's efforts, the law firm recovered in excess of $11 million. However, during an appeal of the litigation, the trustee obtained new counsel after it learned that the "Of Counsel" attorney had severed his relationship with the law firm due in part to a fee dispute. When the Chapter 11 proceeding was converted to a case under Chapter 7, the "Of Counsel" attorney sought a *nunc pro tunc* order for an award of legal fees from the bankruptcy estate, but the bankruptcy judge refused to issue the order on the ground that the "Of Counsel" attorney was not the attorney retained by order of the Court to represent the estate. Rather, he was an independent contractor who subcontracted with the firm that was in fact retained with court approval.[6] In affirming the bankruptcy judge, the district court stated:

> It was readily apparent to the Bankruptcy Judge and also is apparent to this Court that the sole reason for making the nunc pro tunc application was to seek a retroactive participation in the retainer because the "of counsel arrangements," or what-ever other association [Of Counsel] had with the [law firm], had come to end under circumstances which imply that there occurred a dispute over money. . . . We agree with the Bankruptcy Judge that if [Of Counsel] is entitled to

---

only about half had written "Of Counsel" agreements.

5. *In re* Coin Phones, Inc., 226 B.R. 131 (S.D.N.Y. 1998).

6. *Id.* at 133.

> additional compensation beyond that previously paid to him by the [law firm] or due to be paid, the source to which he must look is not the estate, but rather the [law firm].[7]

Much of the problem faced by the "Of Counsel" attorney and the law firm could have been avoided had

> [t]he court at the inception of the matter been asked to authorize the retention of both the law firm and the individual lawyer, each to be separately compensated directly from the estate. Hindsight suggests this might have been done, and perhaps should have been done, but it was not. It did not have to be done and the court was correct in not allowing [it] to be done retrospectively.[8]

In this chapter, we will explore the parameters of potential "Of Counsel" agreements, so that you may develop an agreement that will satisfy your needs before entering into the relationship.

Planning the Of Counsel Agreement

The parties must first consider what they hope to accomplish by entering into an "Of Counsel" agreement. A retiring partner, for example, often seeks to remain active without the burdens of a heavy practice to which he or she may be accustomed. If the firm has a well-established pension program, financial matters are normally secondary to other considerations.[9]

The law firm's objectives will normally be quite different from those of the "Of Counsel" attorney. What will be the incremental cost to the firm for placing a retiring partner in "Of Counsel" status? Will this cost be justified

---

7. *Id.*

8. *Id.* at 134.

9. The "Of Counsel" agreement should not be tied to the firm's pension program, or vice versa. "Of Counsel" agreements will vary in their terms from one lawyer to another, depending upon individual needs. But pension programs must be administered so that each retiring partner is treated fairly and equitably with respect to all those who have retired or will be retiring.

by the potential services the "Of Counsel" attorney may render, such as advice and counsel, instruction for younger lawyers, review of the work of partners and associates, and so on?

Is the lawyer's wish for "Of Counsel" status based on a reason other than retirement? For example, is an arrangement sought that will allow more time for pursuits other than the practice of law? Or is the lawyer a specialist looking for an association with a firm that will make it possible to pursue that specialty more effectively? Or is the "Of Counsel" position a way to demonstrate an ability as a practicing lawyer, with the possibility of joining the firm as a partner at a later date?

For each of these possibilities, the firm must consider its own needs and determine if these are in accord with the objectives of the prospective "Of Counsel" attorney. As a matter of form, the parties may find it helpful to include a preamble in the agreement in which they state their goals. For example:

> WHEREAS, John P. Doe ("Doe"), presently a partner in Jones, Smith & Doe, is planning to retire at the end of the present fiscal year, June 30, 2013, but desires to remain actively involved with the firm; and
>
> WHEREAS, Jones, Smith & Doe (the "firm") desires that the said Doe remain active within the firm following his retirement by being available for consultation and advice, and performing other related duties;
>
> NOW THEREFORE . . .

Essential Terms of the Of Counsel Agreement

While a written agreement may not solve all potential problems, lawyers will more likely feel bound by the terms of an "Of Counsel" agreement when it has been put down in writing and signed by both parties. The document may be a formal agreement or a simple letter agreement. In either event, the parties should not fail to consider the interests of third persons, since their rights will be affected by the agreement. Appendixes A through F present several "Of Counsel" agreement examples, based on different factual situations. The drafter will have to consider the circumstances of the individual situation to determine appropriate terms for a specific agreement.

Title and Status

Fundamental to the drafting of an "Of Counsel" agreement is whether the parties desire a relationship more akin to that of employer-employee or independent contractor. For example, the parties may wish to establish an independent-contractor relationship for purposes of control (or rather, lack thereof by the firm), but an employer-employee relationship for purposes of compensation. If the drafter's primary concern is to allow the "Of Counsel" attorney as much independence as possible, the language of the agreement should reflect the parties' intention to create an independent contractor relationship. If the parties then desire that the "Of Counsel" attorney participate in the firm's programs for malpractice and health insurance, these matters should be qualified by a phrase such as, "solely for the purposes of the firm's health insurance [or, malpractice] insurance program, [Of Counsel] shall be treated as an employee." The title and status of Of Counsel should be succinctly stated in the agreement. The independent-contractor relationship may be simply stated:

> Both [the firm] and [Of Counsel] desire that [Of Counsel] establish a continuing affiliation with [the firm] as an independent contractor rather than as a partner or associate.[10]

The parties' intention to create an employer-employee relationship can likewise be easily set out, as in the following sample provision:

> [Of Counsel] shall have the title of "Of Counsel" to [the firm]. Notwithstanding the foregoing, [Of Counsel] shall be neither a partner nor a special partner of the Firm but shall be considered an employee of the Firm.

---

10. Altman & Weil, *supra* note 3.

Once the parties have stated their desired title and status, the remaining provisions of the agreement should be consistent with the status indicated. For example, in a case in which the firm has been organized as a professional service corporation, the parties state their intention to create an independent-contractor relationship. The remaining provisions will be consistent with this intention in that the "Of Counsel" attorney will not be required to perform any specified number of hours of service to the corporation, and he will be compensated at an hourly rate for services he actually renders to clients of the firm.[11]

In another agreement, the parties might set forth their desire to establish an employer-employee relationship, but might insert provisions that are inconsistent with this relationship. The contract may, for example, provide that the "Of Counsel" attorney "have all the duties and responsibilities as if he were a partner of the firm" and be entitled to compensation "as if he were a partner of the firm." While such an agreement accomplishes the objective of giving the "Of Counsel" attorney the title and status he wants, it also might subject him to potential vicarious liability as a partner.

In some agreements, the parties state their desire to create an "Of Counsel" relationship, but also express their hope to enter into a different relationship when the "Of Counsel" agreement terminates.

This frequently occurs where an "Of Counsel" attorney is temporarily taken on as a "probationary partner." In one such agreement, a provision expressed the parties' intention to enter into such an arrangement by stating:

> This agreement will be for a term of XX months commencing on [specified date] (the "Term"). It is our expectation that a mutual decision regarding the "of counsel" attorney becoming an equity partner in the firm will be made at or prior to the conclusion of the Term.[12]

---

11. Appendix C §§ 4 and 5.
12. *See* Appendix A § 1.

Duties

Since the "Of Counsel" relationship contemplates a working relationship with the firm or other lawyer, an essential component of the "Of Counsel" agreement is the specific delineation of the "Of Counsel" attorney's duties. As the court pointed out in *Mutual of Omaha Insurance Co. v. Chadwell,*[13] an "Of Counsel" agreement that contains no express provisions for the actual rendering of services is of dubious value. In the *Chadwell* decision, the law firm had merely agreed to pay the "Of Counsel" attorney for his "long and outstanding service to the firm."[14] So, when the "Of Counsel" attorney's widow tried to collect on the firm's accidental death policy, the insurance company successfully argued that the husband was not a covered employee. His estate was therefore ineligible for employee benefits. Failing to define his expected duties while continuing to provide him with a fixed compensation meant that his status was nothing more than that of a retired partner receiving retirement benefits.

Duties of an "Of Counsel" attorney vary with each agreement. Much depends upon what the parties are seeking to accomplish. For example, one firm used an experienced senior lawyer primarily for the professional development of the firm's younger lawyers. This firm specifically provided that the "Of Counsel" attorney should:

- assist the firm in its continuing legal education program for its members and associates;
- review litigation files for the purpose of consulting on and recommending trial preparation, pleadings, strategy, and settlement;
- assist attorneys responsible for litigation files in pretrial discovery, motions, briefs, and trial;
- in his discretion, and with the agreement of the firm, assume responsibility for conducting discovery, motions, and trials, appellate proceedings, and related matters; and

13. 426 F. Supp. 550, 552 (N.D. Ill. 1977).
14. *Id.* at 552.

- engage in other activities relating to firm development and client development for the firm.[15]

Other arrangements may set forth the duties expected of the "Of Counsel" attorney in more general terms. For example, one agreement contained this provision:

> As "of counsel," he shall perform in the name of [the firm] such professional services as may be required by [the firm's] clients. [Of Counsel] shall foster the professional practice of [the firm] through the development of new clients and sources of business in a manner consistent with law and the applicable canons of professional ethics.[16]

Many "Of Counsel" agreements contain provisions that set a minimum number of hours that the "Of Counsel" attorney must bill to the clients of the firm. In one such agreement, the firm and the "Of Counsel" attorney agreed that during a one-year period he would "be required to bill to clients of the Firm a minimum of 1,500 hours." Another agreement provided that the "Of Counsel" arrangement "includes [Of Counsel's] full-time efforts."[17] Provisions such as these are not typical of most "Of Counsel" agreements. They are more analogous to provisions that would be found in an agreement between a law firm and an associate. Yet if the parties desire to provide for a minimum number of hours in their agreement, they should be careful to agree only to the number of hours that the "Of Counsel" attorney is certain to work. A minimum of 1,500 billable hours per year might be excessive for a senior lawyer who wants to wind down his or her law practice.[18]

Some agreements contain exclusive-services provisions that preclude the "Of Counsel" attorney from performing services outside the firm. A typical provision might be one that prohibits the "Of Counsel" attorney

---

15. Appendix C § 3.
16. ALTMAN & WEIL, *supra* note 3.
17. Appendix B § 2.
18. In 1988, the annual billable hours for an associate averaged just over 1,800. For a partner in that same year, the average annual billable hours were 1,731. *See* Thomas F. Gibbons, *Law Practice in 2001*, 76 A.B.A. J. 68, 71 (Jan. 1990).

from performing "professional services to any person, firm, corporation, or other entity for compensation or engage in any activity competitive with or adverse to [the firm's] practice during the term of this Agreement."[19] Or the agreement might restrict the "Of Counsel" attorney from accepting any position outside the firm without first giving written notice.

Compensation

A key consideration in the agreement is the manner of compensation selected by the parties. Formal Opinion 330 did not explicitly restrict the methods of compensation in the "Of Counsel" arrangement,[20] but it implied that the "Of Counsel" attorney should be compensated only for work actually performed.[21] Formal Opinion 90-357 swept these restrictions aside by making it clear that it is not relevant to the permissibility of the use of the "Of Counsel" designation what the compensation arrangements are. For example, the "Of Counsel" attorney may draw a salary or a salary plus a share of the profits. If the "Of Counsel" attorney is a retired partner, compensation may include payments from the firm's retirement plan. In some cases, the "Of Counsel" attorney may receive no compensation from the firm, any may even pay a portion of the firm's overhead.

Some commentators have insisted that "Of Counsel" attorneys should be compensated only for work actually and currently performed for the firm.[22] This is essential if the parties desire to treat the "Of Counsel" attorney as an independent contractor. But if they wish to establish an employer-employee relationship, they may deliberately choose to compensate the "Of Counsel" attorney with a fixed salary, whether weekly, monthly, or yearly. Difficult problems may arise if the parties wish to draft an agreement that will combine some features typical of the independent contractor (for instance, compensation directly related to the work performed) with those of an employee (for instance, a fixed salary, advance money, or annual bonuses).

---

19. ALTMAN & WEIL, *supra* note 3.
20. *See* Appendix K.
21. *Id.*
22. *Of Counsel: Revisited*, at 35 (Remarks of Don Jackson at the Annual Meeting of the American Bar Association, Senior Lawyers Division) (Aug. 8, 1988).

But if this is their desire, the basic philosophy of freedom of contract that characterizes 90-357 gives them the power to so provide.

A common method of compensation is for the "Of Counsel" attorney to receive a division of gross receipts for each case that he or she works on. In a typical arrangement, the parties may agree to divide the "Of Counsel" attorney's gross receipts on a fifty-fifty basis after first reducing those receipts by allocable overhead. One such agreement provided:

> [The firm] shall pay [Of Counsel] annually fifty percent (50%) of the amount by which [Of Counsel's] gross receipts in each calendar year for professional services rendered by [Of Counsel] exceed the Overhead Cost.
>
> In addition to the compensation paid to [Of Counsel] under [the above paragraph], [the firm] shall pay [Of Counsel] fifty percent (50%) of [the firm's] gross receipts in each calendar year for professional services rendered by [Of Counsel] to [the firm's] clients, except that if [Of Counsel's] gross receipts under [the above paragraph] in any calendar year are less than the Overhead Cost, [the firm] shall be obligated to pay [Of Counsel] only that portion of this compensation under this paragraph which exceeds the amount of the deficit.[23]

Where the "Of Counsel" attorney anticipates using the firm's support services, the parties may vary the proportions. One such agreement illustrates the varying proportions that may be included in the agreement:

> With respect to work performed by us or our associates, clerks, or paralegals for your clients, or new matters referred to us from your existing clients or from new business generated by you, we shall be allocated from gross receipts of fees as collected eighty-two and one-half percent (82 1/2%), and you shall retain seventeen and one-half percent (17 1/2%). With respect to matters generated by you and where work is performed by you, one hundred percent (100%) of the

23. ALTMAN & WEIL, *supra* note 3.

> sums collected shall be held for the benefit of your account.[24]

Another method is to compensate the "Of Counsel" attorney at an hourly rate. An example of this kind of arrangement appears in the following provision:

> The corporation shall pay [Of Counsel] as fees for his services at an hourly rate equal to eighty percent (80%) of the rate that his time is charged to any particular client or matter.[25]

These methods are commonly found where the "Of Counsel" attorney is an independent contractor, since the compensation is clearly related to the work actually done. This approach also works best when the "Of Counsel" is another firm.

Where the parties have an employer-employee relationship, it is common to compensate the "Of Counsel" attorney on a flat rate per week or month. The flat rate may sometimes be coupled with an annual or semiannual bonus. The following provision is typical:

> [Of Counsel's] base compensation shall be ____ Dollars ($____) per month ($ ____ annualized), payable semimonthly. . . . In addition to [Of Counsel's] base compensation, [Of Counsel] shall receive an amount equal to ten percent (10%) of [his] Aggregate Source Collections, as defined below, in excess of $50,000. . . . Aggregate Source Collections shall be the sum of Source Collections for all clients. This additional compensation shall be computed semiannually and paid to [Of Counsel] on or before [date]. . . .[26]

Still another possibility is to provide support services to the "Of Counsel" attorney at no cost.

---

24. Appendix B § 4 (paraphrased).
25. Appendix C § 5.
26. *See* Appendix A § 2.

The parties should consider any restrictions on compensation imposed by their state bar. Some states prohibit fee splitting with the "Of Counsel" attorney where it is not directly related to the work actually performed.[27] Other states allow an "Of Counsel" attorney to share fees with the firm or other lawyer without regard to services performed. Drafters should check the ethics opinions of the state in which the "Of Counsel" attorney and firm are located to determine whether their proposed compensation arrangement complies with their state's requirements.

As indicated in the discussion of *Coin Phones, supra,* much of the grief associated with compensation can be eliminated by careful drafting of the fee arrangement, emphasizing the *continuing* relationship between the law firm and the "Of Counsel" attorney. The "Of Counsel" attorney would also be wise to make a full disclosure to clients of any fee arrangements between the "Of Counsel" attorney and the law firm, and to obtain their approval for such fee arrangements to comply with ethical requirements. For example, Rule 2-200 of the California Rules of Professional Conduct provides:

> (A) A member [of the Bar] shall not divide a fee for legal services with a lawyer who is not a partner of, associate of, or shareholder with the member unless:
>
> (1) The client has consented in writing thereto after a full disclosure has been made in writing that a division of fees will be made and the terms of such division; and
>
> (2) The total fee charged by all lawyers is not increased solely by reason of the provision for division of fees and is not unconscionable as that term is defined in Rule 4-200.

In *Chambers v. Kay*,[28] this rule was tested with respect to co-counsel. The plaintiff and defendant were San Francisco attorneys who worked together on a sexual harassment case, resulting in a large award of compensatory and punitive damages and a significant award of attorney fees. Under their agreement, defendant owed plaintiff one-sixth of the 40 percent contingent

---

27. *See* Chapter 2.

28. 29 Cal. 4th 142, 126 Cal. Rptr.2d 536, 56 P.2d 645 (2002).

fee that defendant had recovered. When plaintiff sued defendant for breach of contract and *quantum meruit,* the trial court ruled that the agreement between the attorneys was unenforceable because it violated Rule 2-200. The California Supreme Court agreed, holding that the requirement for the client's written consent was essential "to protect the public and to promote respect and confidence in the legal profession."[29]

Although *Chambers v. Kay* dealt with a co-counsel agreement, prudence requires that the drafter fully inform the client of the fee arrangement between the law firm and the "Of Counsel" attorney and obtain written consent of the client. Several possible clauses, variations of which might be used to obtain the client's written consent through an engagement letter to the client, include:

> [Attorney] serves in an "Of Counsel" capacity to our firm and has done so for many years. He is neither a partner nor an associate. Some part of the legal fees in your case will be divided with him. In no event will your fees be any higher due to the amount [Attorney] receives or what other lawyers hired by the firm may receive. By agreeing to the engagement terms, you are consenting in writing to a division of fees with [Attorney].

A similar clause might be:

> Client understands that Firm will be using lawyers and experts. The lawyers will be hired by Firm at no additional cost to Client. In most cases they will be compensated by the hour, in some cases they may be compensated by both an hourly rate and a percentage of the fee. In some cases they may be hired on a contingency basis, and receive all of their compensation from the proceeds of the case. Expert fees must be paid by Client before they will assist in the case.

Still another possibility might be:

29. 42 Cal. 4th at 158.

> Client is informed and acknowledges that attorneys' fees, whether hourly or contingent, are not set by law but are negotiable between [Firm] and Client. [Attorney] is "Of Counsel" to [Firm], and his rate is $___ per hour. He is neither a partner nor an associate of the firm. Client understands that in accordance with the Rules of Professional Conduct there may be a division of fees between [Firm] and "Of Counsel."

Effect of Pension Plan Payments

Formal Opinion 90-357 removed the implication within Formal Opinion 330 that a retired partner whose sole income from the firm is the partner's pension or other retirement benefits could not properly be considered to be "Of Counsel."[30] Informal Opinion 710 had a similar implication. Read strictly, Formal Opinion 330 required that any compensation received by the "Of Counsel" attorney must be directly related to work actually and currently performed. By contrast, payments received by the retired partner from a pension or other retirement plan are deemed to be compensation for past, rather than present, services.

In many law partnerships, the partnership agreement provides that the partnership will purchase a retiring partner's interest upon retirement or withdrawal from the firm.[31] These agreements typically provide for a payout period of five to ten years, with the total amount being based on a percentage of the firm's earnings.[32] The retired partner essentially becomes a creditor of the firm and has a vested interest in the firm's continued prosperity.[33] Out of concern that the firm remain prosperous, the retired partner may choose to remain active in the firm by providing services in an "Of

---

30. *See* Chapter 2.

31. Corinne Maskaleris, *"Of Counsel"—Defined* at 21 (compilation from transcript of *Of Counsel: Revisited*, a program presented by the Senior Lawyers Division of the American Bar Association at the annual meeting, Aug. 6, 1988) (available from Senior Lawyers Division, ABA).

32. *Id.*

33. *Id.*

Counsel" capacity.[34] But now the lawyer has two simultaneous relationships with the firm: (1) as a creditor of the firm and; (2) in association with the firm as "Of Counsel."

Formal Opinion 90-357 specifically eliminates any implication of impropriety in this arrangement. Despite this, the parties should spell out the distinction between these two relationships. This might be done within the "Of Counsel" agreement, or the parties might prefer to execute two separate contracts to further define their respective obligations under each relationship. In one contract, the firm would recognize its obligation to disburse to the retiring partner payments over a period of time.[35] The second contract would acknowledge the parties' desire to enter into a new relationship wherein the lawyer's status is recognized as "Of Counsel" to the firm.[36] Separating the two relationships protects the "Of Counsel" attorney from claims of vicarious liability by litigious clients.[37]

Overhead

Since firms commonly provide the "Of Counsel" attorney with an office, secretarial service, desk, telephone, and other support services, agreements between the parties should provide for overhead expenses. In an independent contractor relationship, provisions should be made for the "Of Counsel" attorney to reimburse the firm for a fair share of the overhead costs.

A variety of arrangements can be used. In one arrangement, the firm charged the "Of Counsel" attorney a flat rate per month:

> [The firm] will charge you $8,667 at the beginning of each month as your share of expenses for that month. This will be a charge against fees received by you. This $8,667 charge will include your share of all office costs, including rent, secretarial, telephone, equipment use, library, reception, accounting, word processing, office supplies,

34. *Id.*
35. *Id.*
36. *Id.*
37. *Id.* at 22.

> messenger services, postage, Bar dues, parking, health, life, disability and E&O insurance in accordance with [the firm's] current office practice.[38]

Or, the parties may agree to a flat rate per year:

> "Overhead Cost" means $20,000 for [this] calendar year and the amount mutually agreed by the parties for each calendar year thereafter. If this Agreement is terminated during a calendar year, Overhead Cost shall be prorated to the date of termination based on the number of months this Agreement is in effect.[39]

Where overhead is set at a flat amount per year (for instance, $20,000), the parties usually agree to prorate the overhead costs and deduct the prorated amounts from the "Of Counsel" attorney's weekly or monthly compensation.

In other arrangements, the firm might deduct a certain percentage, such as 25 to 50 percent, from the "Of Counsel" attorney's gross receipts as a fair share of overhead. If the parties use a percentage as the basis for calculating the "Of Counsel" attorney's compensation, they should make it clear whether the percentage is to be based on the "Of Counsel" attorney's gross or net earnings. Whether the parties agree to a fixed percentage or a flat amount, the method for computing overhead expenses should be clearly spelled out in the "Of Counsel" agreement.

Fringe Benefits

Malpractice insurance is essential for any person practicing law, whether as a solo practitioner, a member of a law firm, or as "Of Counsel." A malpractice policy usually provides coverage for all principals of the firm, as well as all employees, including lawyer associates, legal assistants, secretaries, and other staff. Whether the "Of Counsel" attorney is an independent contractor or employee, both parties must make sure that the attorney is covered by the firm's malpractice policy. With the increase in the cost of

---

38. *See* Appendix B § 5.

39. Altman & Weil, *supra* note 3.

single coverage, protection under the firm's malpractice insurance group policy is likely to be an important fringe benefit for any lawyer. This benefit should be clearly set out in the "Of Counsel" agreement. The usual provision is that the insurance will be carried and paid for by the law firm.[40] In some cases, the firm may reimburse the "Of Counsel" attorney for obtaining a separate malpractice insurance policy. But this approach would likely cost more overall. A better practice is for the firm to purchase a policy that includes the "Of Counsel" attorney along with all lawyers in the firm. The "Of Counsel" attorney may then reimburse the firm for his or her portion of the coverage, if the partners so desire.

Most insurance carriers will cover "Of Counsel" lawyers, even though they are not in an employer-employee relationship with the firm. A few agreements provide for the "Of Counsel" attorney to reimburse the firm for any additional expenses incurred as a result of including the "Of Counsel" attorney in the firm's policy. Other agreements provide malpractice insurance coverage for the "Of Counsel" attorney at the firm's expense regardless of the legal nature of the relationship — whether employee or independent contractor — with the firm. In the typical agreement, coverage is provided as a fringe benefit:

> In addition, the Firm will afford and pay for malpractice insurance coverage for [Of Counsel] on the same basis, if at all, as such insurance protection is afforded to Equity Partners. . . .[41]

Some agreements also include a provision for indemnification, for example:

> The Firm shall provide errors and omissions insurance on behalf of the Firm and [Of Counsel] in the same manner as if [Of Counsel] were a partner or associate of the Firm. The Firm acknowledges and agrees that that [Of Counsel] is an employee for purposes of [the State Labor Code] that provides for indemnification of employees. [Of Counsel]

40. The cost to the firm for the additional malpractice insurance coverage for the "Of Counsel" attorney is normally substantially below that for a partner or principal, since the insurer's risk is much less.

41. *See* Appendix A § 4 (footnotes omitted).

> agrees to cooperate with the Firm [for liability of the Firm] arising out of or in any way connected with his activities on behalf of the Firm and further agrees to make himself available for purposes of the defense of any action.

Where the "Of Counsel" attorney is covered by the firm's policy, the scope of the coverage should be the same as it is for other members of the firm. The "Of Counsel" attorney should keep in mind that the policy will apply only to acts committed in performing duties within the scope of his or her contract. If the "Of Counsel" attorney also maintains an independent or solo practice, or practices with another firm as "Of Counsel" or in some other capacity, separate coverage should be obtained for torts committed in those other practices.

Other fringe benefits typically include the firm's payment of professional dues and licensing, reimbursement for business expenses, and coverage under the firm's group health insurance plan. The accepted practice is for the firm to pay for the "Of Counsel" attorney's licensing dues; this alone will not jeopardize the "Of Counsel" attorney's independent status.

But the same is not true if the firm pays the "Of Counsel" attorney's business and travel expenses or coverage under medical and other health insurance programs. The common law considers workers to be employees if the person or firm for whom they perform services agrees to pay the workers' expenses and other benefits. Most health insurance programs require that all covered persons be full-time employees of the firm, working a minimum number of hours per week, typically thirty hours. This requirement may defeat the "Of Counsel" attorney's status as an independent contractor. But the independent contractor status is preserved if the firm agrees to include the "Of Counsel" attorney under the firm coverage at the individual's own expense. One such agreement provided:

> If [Of Counsel] so elects, he will be covered under the Firm's medical, disability, life, and other insurance plans *at his own expense*, as is the case for the Firm's Equity and Contract Partners.[42] (Emphasis added.)

42. See Appendix A § 4.

Where the "Of Counsel" attorney is an employee, these benefits are provided to the "Of Counsel" attorney at the firm's expense, as in the following sample text:

> [Of Counsel] shall participate in and shall receive benefits under all formal and informal employee benefit plans, under-standings, arrangements, or programs now or hereafter generally made available to the Firm's associates and their families, including, but not limited to, any group health, life, dental, disability, or other insurance, or any pension or profit-sharing plans or arrangements, or any other type of benefit.

Right to Terminate

Most "Of Counsel" agreements include a termination clause giving each party the right to terminate for any reason upon prior written notice, after a specified number of days. In addition, most agreements contain provisions for automatic termination upon the "Of Counsel" attorney's death, disability, or disqualification from the practice of law, or the dissolution or insolvency of the firm.

Summary

Planning the "Of Counsel" relationship requires careful coordination of both parties' expectations. A carefully worded written agreement should give due regard to the duties expected of the "Of Counsel" attorney, as well as compensation, overhead, fringe benefits, and right to terminate. By careful drafting, the parties may incorporate into their agreement the best features of various relationships. Appendices A through F provide several different examples of typical "Of Counsel" agreements.

Checklists for Issue Spotting

Title and Status

Do the parties desire the "Of Counsel" attorney to be an independent contractor or an employee? Does the agreement clearly state their intentions and support the desired status?

Duties

Does the agreement describe the duties expected of the "Of Counsel" attorney? Does the "Of Counsel" attorney assist in the firm's continuing legal education programs? Does the "Of Counsel" attorney review briefs and memoranda? Is the "Of Counsel" attorney available for consultation and advice to the firm and its clients?

Compensation

(1) Does the agreement provide for fee splitting between the "Of Counsel" attorney and the firm without regard to the services performed by the "Of Counsel" attorney? If so, does that comply with state ethics rules?

(2) If an independent contractor relationship is desired, does the agreement provide that compensation shall be directly proportional to the services performed?

(3) If the "Of Counsel" attorney is a retired partner, is he or she entitled to payments from the firm's pension or other retirement plan? If so, does the agreement establish these two separate relationships of creditor and "Of Counsel" attorney?

Overhead

(1) If an independent contractor relationship is desired, does the agreement provide that the "Of Counsel" attorney will reimburse the firm or other lawyer for overhead expenses?

(2) If the "Of Counsel" attorney is to reimburse the firm or other lawyer for overhead, is the method of reimbursement clearly spelled out in the agreement?

Fringe Benefits

(1) Is the "Of Counsel" attorney covered by the firm's malpractice policy? If so, has the policy been analyzed to determine the extent of coverage?

(2) If an independent contractor relationship is desired, does the agreement provide for the reimbursement of the "Of Counsel" attorney's expenses, such as payment for business and travel expenses, professional dues, licensing, and health insurance?

(3) If the firm provides the "Of Counsel" attorney with health insurance, does the "Of Counsel" attorney satisfy the policy requirements for coverage?

Right to Terminate

(1) Does the agreement give each party the right to terminate the agreement and specify a notice period?

APPENDIX A

Of Counsel Agreement

[INDEPENDENT CONTRACTOR AND PARTNERSHIP]

This agreement is entered into as of [date], by and between JOHN Q. LAWYER ("Lawyer"), an individual, and XYZ, a general partnership (the "Firm"), regarding a Contract Partner/Of Counsel[1] relationship between Lawyer and the Firm.

1. This agreement will be for a term of ___ months commencing on [date] (the "Term"). It is the Firm's expectation that a mutual decision regarding Lawyer becoming an Equity Partner in the Firm will be made at or prior to the conclusion of the Term.[2]
2. Lawyer's base compensation shall be ____ Dollars ($__) per month ($____ annualized), payable semimonthly,[3] plus an automobile allowance of $____ per month. In addition to Lawyer's base compensation, Lawyer shall receive an amount equal to ten percent (10%) of Lawyer's Aggregate Source Collections, as defined below, in excess of $50,000.00. Source Collections with respect to any client shall be the product obtained by multiplying (i) the total fees and nonrefundable

1. *See* Chapter 5 for a discussion of setting out the "Of Counsel" attorney's title and status. the use of the term "Contract Partner/Of Counsel" in this contract creates an unnecessary ambiguity. It would be better practice to use the term "Of Counsel" and make it clear that an independent contractor relationship is intended.

2. *See* Chapter 4 for a discussion of probationary partners in the "Of Counsel" context.

3. *See* Chapters 2, 4, and 5 for a discussion of permissible methods for compensating "Of Counsel."

retainers collected by the Firm during the Term and for a period of thirty (30) days following the conclusion of the Term from that client by (ii) Lawyer's percentage share (between 0 percent and 100 percent) of source credit for that client, as mutually agreed to by you, the Intake Committee, and the Firm's Managing Partner. Aggregate Source Collections shall be the sum of Source Collections for all clients. This additional compensation shall be computed semiannually and paid to Lawyer on or before [date] (as to Aggregate Source Collections in excess of $50,000.00). For tax purposes only, Lawyer will be compensated as if he were an Equity Partner of the Firm.

3. Lawyer hereby agrees that he (like the Firm's Equity Partners) shall have no ownership interest in the work in process, accounts receivable, or goodwill of the Firm. Lawyer hereby agrees that if he leaves the Firm during or after expiration of the Term, he will use his best efforts thereafter to assist the Firm in collecting on the unpaid work in process and unpaid accounts receivable from those clients for which he was the original source or shared source attorney.

4. If Lawyer so elects, he will be covered under the Firm's medical, disability, life, and other insurance plans at his own expense,[4] as is the case for the Firm's Equity and Contract Partners. In addition, the Firm will afford and pay for malpractice insurance coverage for Lawyer on the same basis,[5] if at all, as such insurance protection is afforded to Equity Partners, and will pay for his parking and dues for the State Bar of Any state and other bar association dues on the same basis as for Equity Partners.

5. In light of the Firm's desire that Lawyer actively develop and promote the Firm's financial institutions and business practice, Lawyer will be reimbursed for reasonable and documented business expenses in accordance with customary Firm procedures applicable to Equity

4. This kind of provision preserves the status of an "Of Counsel" as an independent contractor. *See* Chapter 5.

5. In this provision, "Of Counsel" chose to reimburse the Firm for inclusion in the firm's malpractice policy. This provision indicates an independent contractor relationship, rather than an employer-employee relationship. *See* Chapter 5.

and Contract Partners. Further, the Firm will pay the membership dues for such trade associations set forth on Schedule A hereto.[6]

6. As a Contract Partner/Of Counsel, Lawyer is not required to contribute capital to the Firm, nor will he have any formal voting rights at any Partnership meetings. Otherwise, he will be welcome to participate in discussions and meetings of the Firm and of the Partnership, except as to Partnership meetings or portions of meetings where only Equity Partners may participate.[7]

In addition, Lawyer will be given copies of periodic Firm financial information normally distributed to Contract Partners. Lawyer will not share in or be liable for any profits or losses of the Firm, including any malpractice liability not arising from his acts. He will be designated as the billing attorney on clients for whom he is the source attorney, subject to the approval of his Department Head and the Firm's Managing Partner.

7. Section of the Firm's Partnership Agreement, a copy of which section is attached hereto and incorporated herein, shall be applicable to this Contract Partner/Of Counsel arrangement.

8. Lawyer may assign his rights and delegate his duties under this agreement to a professional corporation of which he is the sole shareholder and employee. In accordance with the foregoing, the parties hereby execute this Agreement as of the date first set forth above.

"Lawyer"

____

JOHN Q. LAWYER

"Firm"

XYZ, a general partnership

By: ________________

[Partner], Managing Partner

---

6. *See* Chapter 4.

7. This provision would prevent "Of Counsel" from being characterized as a partner of the firm. *See* Chapter 4.

APPENDIX B

Of Counsel Agreement

[INDEPENDENT CONTRACTOR AND PARTNERSHIP]

This Contract, made on ________, 20__, between JOHN Q. LAWYER ("Lawyer"), an individual, and XYZ (the "Firm"), establishes the parties' agreement that Lawyer will become associated with the Firm on an "Of Counsel" basis in the practice of law.[1]

1. This relationship will commence as of [date], and will continue indefinitely thereafter, with either party having the right for any reason, on thirty (30) days' written notice, to terminate the relationship.[2]
2. As of the commencement date, all legal services performed by Lawyer will be on behalf of the Firm. This arrangement includes Lawyer's full-time efforts and precludes legal services (including teaching and serving on a board of directors) being rendered for a fee to any party outside of this arrangement.[3] All fees will be billed through the Firm and collected by the Firm, with the exception of one preexisting relationship that Lawyer has with ABC Company. Lawyer agrees to use the Firm's basic accounting systems and billing systems to permit

1. While this provision indicates the parties' intention to create an "Of Counsel" relationship, it does not establish whether the "Of Counsel" attorney's status will be that of an independent contractor or that of an employee. *See* Chapter 5.

2. *See* Chapters 4 and 5 for a discussion of the parties' right to terminate and common termination clauses.

3. This provision tends to indicate that the "Of Counsel" relationship is intended to be an employer-employee relationship. *See* Chapter 4.

effective coordination with the Firm's office procedures. Lawyer shall have full judgment as to billing of matters for clients that Lawyer brings to the Firm, including arbitrarily discounting or writing off fees, and the manner in which bills are sent to clients. All funds collected will be deposited in the general account of the Firm. All fees billed by Lawyer shall be accounted for separately, and accrued to the mutual benefit of both parties pursuant to the terms of this Agreement. To the extent of funds held for the benefit of Lawyer in excess of allocated expenses, the same shall be distributed to Lawyer at such time and in such amounts as the Firm directs.

3. The Firm will include Lawyer at its expense in the Firm's E&O coverage effective with the commencement date of this relationship.[4] All costs required for Lawyer's clients will be advanced by the Firm, and all recovery of costs will accrue to the Firm. If any costs are not billed to and paid by Lawyer's clients, Lawyer will reimburse the firm for them.[5]

4. Lawyer has indicated that he anticipates over a period of time the need for partners, associates, clerks, or paralegals of the firm to assist with the performance of legal services to his clients from time to time.[6] Any associates, secretaries, and support personnel will be hired by the Firm, with input from Lawyer. With respect to work performed by the Firm or the Firm's associates, clerks, or paralegals for the clients of Lawyer, or new matters referred to the Firm from the existing clients of Lawyer or from new business generated by Lawyer, the Firm shall be allocated from gross receipts of fees (but not costs because of the agreement as set forth above), as collected eighty-two and one-half percent (82 1/2%), and Lawyer shall retain seventeen and one-half percent (17 1/2%). With respect to matters generated by Lawyer, one hundred percent (100%) of the sums collected shall be held for the benefit of Lawyer's account. From time to time, there may be matters

4. *See* Chapter 5 for a discussion of malpractice liability coverage for "Of Counsel" and its effect on his status.

5. *See* Chapters 4 and 5.

6. For a discussion of overhead expenses, *see* Chapter 4. *See also* Chapter 5 for a comparison of overhead expense provisions in the "Of Counsel" contract.

where the Firm will want Lawyer to assist the Firm because of Lawyer's particular background and expertise. With respect to matters referred by the Firm to Lawyer, either with respect to existing clients or new clients or new business generated by the Firm in an area where Lawyer can provide special expertise or assistance, Lawyer shall retain eighty-two and one-half percent (82 1/2%) for his time expended, and the Firm shall retain seventeen and one-half percent (17 1/2%) of fees as collected. The parties appreciate that there may be times when it is difficult to determine the origination of the client or client matter and the Firm will work with Lawyer to make those allocations fairly.

5. The Firm will charge Lawyer the amount of $____ at the beginning of each month as his share of expenses for that month. This will be a charge against fees received by Lawyer. This charge will include Lawyer's share of all office costs, including rent, secretarial, telephone, equipment use, library, reception, accounting, word processing, office supplies, messenger services, postage, Bar dues, parking, health, life, disability, and E&O insurance in accordance with the Firm's current office practice. It also includes the amount of $____ per month ($___ per year) reserve for promotional activities to be undertaken by Lawyer. This contemplates secretarial needs on the basis of up to one-half a full-time secretary with word processing and office overflow as backup.

6. Notwithstanding anything to the contrary above, expenses shall be as follows:

a. For the period from [date] through [date], $____ each month plus ___ percent (___%) of actual fees collected (in excess of the first $____) for legal services performed after [date].

b. For the period from [date] through [date], $___ each month plus ___ percent (___%) for legal services performed after [date], but not to exceed $____ per month, and with no accrual of the difference between $____ and $_____ per month.

c. After [date], $____ each month plus___ percent (___%) of actual fees collected (in excess of $____) but not to exceed $____ per month, with the difference between $____ and $_____ accruing and being carried forward on a month-to-month basis.

If this Agreement is terminated by either party, Lawyer shall have no personal obligation for any accumulated expenses, except with respect to ___ percent (___%) of any uncollected receivables for legal services performed by Lawyer after date of termination.

"Lawyer"

____

JOHN Q. LAWYER

"Firm"
XYZ, a general partnership

By: ________________
[Partner], Managing Partner

APPENDIX C

Of Counsel Agreement

[INDEPENDENT CONTRACTOR AND PROFESSIONAL SERVICE CORPORATION]

This Agreement is made on ____, 20__, between XYZ, P.C., a professional corporation ("Corporation") and JOHN Q. LAWYER, an individual ("Lawyer"). The parties mutually desire that Lawyer establish an "Of Counsel" relationship to the Corporation. Accordingly, the parties desire to set forth the terms and conditions by which that relationship shall be governed. Therefore, it is agreed between the parties as follows:

1. *Employment.* The Corporation shall retain and employ Lawyer as an independent contractor, not as an agent or employee, in an "Of Counsel" relationship to the Corporation.[1]
2. *Term.* The employment of Lawyer shall commence upon the date first set forth above and shall continue until such time as either party terminates the Agreement by thirty (30) days' advance written notice to the other.[2]
3. *Duties.* During the term of this Agreement, Lawyer, subject to his availability and upon the request of the Corporation, shall: (a) assist the Corporation in its continuing legal education program for its

1. This provision clearly sets out the parties' intention as to the "Of Counsel" attorney's status. *See* Chapter 5.

2. *See* Chapters 4 and 5 for a discussion of the right to terminate and its effect on the "Of Counsel" attorney's status, as well as for common termination clauses.

members and associates; (b) review litigation files for the purpose of consulting on and recommending trial preparation, pleadings, strategy, and settlement; (c) assist attorneys responsible for litigation files in pretrial discovery, motions, briefs, and trial; (d) in his discretion, and with the agreement of the Corporation, assume responsibility for conducting discovery, motions, and trials, appellate proceedings, and related matters; and (e) engage in other activities relating to firm development and client development for the Corporation.[3]

4. *Time Requirements.* Lawyer shall not be required to perform any specified number of hours of service to the Corporation.[4] However, he shall devote such time as may be necessary to handle and complete those matters which he undertakes for the Corporation or for which his services are engaged by clients of the Corporation, and otherwise discharge his duties as set forth in paragraph 3 of this Agreement.

5. *Compensation.* The Corporation shall pay Lawyer as fees for his services at an hourly rate equal to eighty percent (80%) of the rate that his time is charged to any particular client or matter.[5] Lawyer's time will be billed by the Corporation at the same rate as a senior shareholder's time is billed to a particular client or matter for similar services. With regard to any contingent fee matter or other matter for which it has been agreed with the client that billing will be at the conclusion of the matter, Lawyer's fees will be paid at such time as the matter is concluded. For the purposes of this Agreement, matters will be deemed "concluded" and fees determined to be due within thirty (30) days after a final bill has been submitted to the client or a binding settlement executed on behalf of the Corporation's client. However, except as to fees related to clients or matters that Lawyer originates and for which he is principally responsible, his fees shall not be contingent on payment of the bill or receipt of fees by the

3. This provision clearly sets out the duties of the "Of Counsel" attorney. This is important, particularly where the "Of Counsel" attorney is a retired partner of the firm and is receiving compensation from a firm retirement plan. *See* Chapters 2, 3, and 5.

4. This provision is intended to preserve the "Of Counsel" attorney's status as an independent contractor, consistent with the parties' intentions. *See* Chapters 4 and 5.

5. This provision satisfies some states' requirement that "Of Counsel" be compensated only for work actually performed. *See* Chapters 2, 4, and 5.

Corporation. With regard to time spent by Lawyer in connection with the Corporation's continuing legal education program, Lawyer will be paid at the rate of $___ per hour. As additional compensation, the Corporation shall:

A. Pay the dues for Lawyer's membership in the American Bar Association, the State Bar of [Anystate], and the [Anycounty] Bar Association.[6]

B. Cover Lawyer under the Corporation's group health insurance plan and pay all premiums related thereto;[7]

C. Pay non-reimbursed expenses arising in connection with attendance at American Bar Association Committee meetings;

D. Cover Lawyer under the Corporation's professional liability (i.e., errors and omissions) insurance policy and pay all premiums related thereto;[8] and

E. The Corporation may, in its discretion, pay to Lawyer such bonuses at such times and in such amounts as it deems appropriate.

6. *Expenses.* The Corporation shall reimburse Lawyer for all reasonable out-of-pocket expenses (including automobile mileage) incurred or advanced by Lawyer in connection with any client matter or entertainment or business promotion expense.[9]

7. *Records.* Lawyer shall keep records of all time spent and expenses incurred in the same manner and in the same form as is prescribed for members and associates of the Corporation. Such time and expenses shall be submitted to the Corporation's office manager on at least a semi-monthly basis, that being on the fifteenth (15th) day and the last day of each month or if that day falls on a weekend or holiday, on the business day just preceding that date.

8. *Billing.* It shall be the obligation of the Corporation to prepare and mail all bills to clients to whom Lawyer renders service or expends

6. *See* Chapter 5.
7. *See* Chapter 5.
8. *See* Chapter 5.
9. *See* Chapter 4.

costs in the manner and form generally utilized by the Corporation.[10] Lawyer shall receive a copy of all bills prepared by the Corporation for services rendered or costs advanced to clients originated by Lawyer for his review price bills being forwarded to the client.

9. *Payment.* All fees and reimbursement of expenses due Lawyer pursuant to Paragraphs 5 and 6 of this Agreement shall be paid by the Corporation to him on the fifteenth (15th) day of each month for all amounts determined to be due prior to the last day of the preceding month, and on the last day of each month for all amounts determined to be due prior to the fifteenth (15th) day of the same month.

10. *Taxes.* It shall be Lawyer's sole responsibility to pay such federal, state, and local taxes (including but not limited to income taxes and FICA taxes) as may be imposed or levied upon the income earned or derived by him under this Agreement.[11] It is expressly understood and agreed that the Corporation shall not withhold any such taxes from the compensation paid to Lawyer.

11. *Support.* The Corporation shall provide Lawyer with necessary and suitable office space, office supplies, office furniture, and dictating equipment.[12] In addition, the Corporation shall provide Lawyer with nonexclusive secretarial and clerical services. With regard to any client or matter originated by Lawyer, the Corporation will assign such attorneys and other personnel to assist Lawyer as may be necessary. The assignment of particular personnel to such matters shall be at the discretion of the Corporation, upon consultation with Lawyer, based upon the availability, qualifications, abilities, and experience of such attorneys or other personnel.

12. *Legal Directories.* During the term of this agreement, the Corporation shall, at its sole expense, cause Lawyer's name to be listed as "Of Counsel" on the Corporation's stationery, in the Martindale-Hubbell Directory, Any state and Any county Bar directories, telephone

10. For a discussion of integration of billing procedures and its effects on the status of "Of Counsel," *see* Chapter 4.

11. *See* Chapter 4 for a comparison of amounts of Social Security taxes paid by employees and independent contractors.

12. *See* Chapters 4 and 5 for a discussion of overhead.

directories, and in other listings or directories, in which the Corporation may from time to time list its name and the name of its members and associates of the Corporation.[13]

13. *Announcements and Cards.* The Corporation shall, at its sole expense, cause announcements of Lawyer's association with the Corporation to be printed and sent to such persons or organizations as the Corporation may designate. Further, the Corporation, at its sole expense, shall provide Lawyer with business cards indicating his association with the Corporation in the form and style generally utilized by the Corporation.

14. *Termination.* This Agreement may be terminated at the discretion of either party, with or without cause, upon the party wishing to terminate the Agreement and giving the other party at least thirty (30) days' advance written notice of the termination. If this Agreement is terminated, Lawyer shall be entitled to receive from the Corporation payment of all sums that may thereafter become due for services performed by during the term of this Agreement.[14]

15. *Death or Dissolution.* In the event of death during the term of this Agreement, all sums that are then payable to Lawyer or thereafter become payable to him for services rendered prior to his death, shall be paid to Lawyer's personal representative in accordance with this Agreement as though Lawyer were still alive. In the event of dissolution of the Corporation during the term of this Agreement, the Corporation shall pay all sums due or to become due to Lawyer under this Agreement pursuant to its plan for liquidation or dissolution.

16. *Binding Effect.* This Agreement shall be binding upon the heirs, personal representatives, administrators, executors, and assigns of each of the parties.

17. *Partial Invalidity.* It is expressly understood and agreed by the parties that should any paragraph or any provision or portion of this

---

13. *See* Chapter 8 for a discussion of permissible methods of communicating the "Of Counsel" relationship. *See* Chapter 9 for a discussion of how failing to properly communicate the "Of Counsel" relationship affects the "Of Counsel" attorney's liability.

14. *See* Chapters 4 and 5 for a discussion of the parties' right to terminate the agreement and common termination clauses.

Agreement be held invalid, illegal, or void, then and in such event, any paragraph, provision, or portion so held to be invalid, illegal, or void shall be deleted from this Agreement, and this Agreement shall be read as though such invalid, illegal, or void paragraph, provision, or portion was never included herein, and the remainder of such Agreement excluding such invalid, illegal, or void paragraph, provision, or portion shall nevertheless subsist and continue with force and effect.

18. *Governing Law.* This Agreement shall be construed in accordance with the laws of the State of [Anystate].

19. *Modification of Agreement.* No modification or amendment of this Agreement shall be binding unless executed in writing by all parties. No waiver of any provision of this Agreement shall be deemed a waiver of any other provision, nor shall any waiver constitute a continuing waiver.

20. *Effect of Headings.* The subject headings of the paragraphs and sub-paragraphs of this Agreement are included for purposes of convenience only, and shall not affect the construction or interpretation of any of the provisions of this Agreement. Executed the date first appearing above.

"Lawyer"

____

JOHN Q. LAWYER
XYZ, P.C.

By: _______________
[Name of Officer], its [Title]

ATTEST:
____________________, Corporate Secretary

APPENDIX D

Of Counsel Agreement

[INDEPENDENT CONTRACTOR AND PARTNERSHIP; ALTERNATE LANGUAGE FOR PARTNERSHIP AND PARTNERSHIP]

THIS AGREEMENT made this ___ day of ________, 20__, by and between JOHN Q. LAWYER ("Lawyer"), an individual licensed to practice in the state of [Anystate],[1] and X, Y & Z ("XYZ"), a partnership engaged in the practice of law in [Anytown], [Anystate];

WITNESSETH, THAT WHEREAS XYZ desires to establish a continuing affiliation with Lawyer as Of Counsel, as an independent contractor, rather than as partner or associate;[2]

NOW THEREFORE, in consideration of the mutual covenants and obligations hereinafter set forth, the parties agree as follows:

1. Term

This Agreement shall commence on [date], and continue in force until terminated pursuant to this Agreement. Either party may terminate this Agreement by giving the other sixty (60) days' written notice at any time after one year from the date of this Agreement. This Agreement

1. Some states require that an "Of Counsel" attorney be licensed to practice law in the same state as the affiliated firm or other lawyer. *See* Chapter 3.

2. Formal Opinion 90-357 precludes the "Of Counsel" relationship from being like that of a partner or associate. *See* Chapters 2 and 4; *see also* Chapter 5 for methods of clearly setting out the status of the "Of Counsel" attorney as an employee or independent contractor.

shall terminate immediately if Lawyer is disqualified from the practice of law in the State of [Any state].

2. Definitions

(a) "Overhead Costs"[3] means twenty (20) percent of Gross Receipts for the current calendar year, and the amount to which the parties mutually agree for each calendar year thereafter.

(b) "Gross Receipts" means all moneys received by XYZ from clients for professional services rendered by Lawyer and any additional moneys received by XYZ from clients for which Lawyer is the attorney who originated the business.

(c) "Expenses" means any amounts incurred by Lawyer or XYZ in connection with professional services rendered by Lawyer or any other attorney of XYZ to Lawyer clients.

3. Duties[4]

During the term of this Agreement, Lawyer shall perform professional services on behalf of XYZ and not for any other individual or entity.[5] Both Lawyer and XYZ will work toward the development of new clients and sources of business in a manner consistent with law and the Model Rules of Professional Conduct of the American Bar Association.

4. Compensation[6]

XYZ shall compensate Lawyer for all services rendered in the following manner:

(a) XYZ shall pay Lawyer fifty percent (50%) of all gross receipts received by XYZ for professional services rendered by Lawyer, payable monthly. The fifty percent (50%) of gross receipts retained by XYZ shall include Lawyer's share of Overhead Costs.

(b) In addition to the amounts received as income under 4(a) of this Agreement, XYZ shall pay Lawyer an additional ten percent

3. *See* Chapters 4 and 5 for a discussion of overhead and a comparison of methods of overhead expense provisions in the "Of Counsel" contract.

4. Provisions describing the "Of Counsel" attorney's expected duties are important, particularly where the "Of Counsel" attorney is a retired partner also receiving compensation from the firm's retirement plan. *See* Chapters 3 and 5.

5. An exclusive services provision tends to indicate a relationship akin to that of an employee. *See* Chapters 4 and 5.

6. *See* Chapters 2, 4, and 5 for a discussion of permissible methods of compensation.

(10%) of gross receipts received from XYZ in each calendar year from clients for which Lawyer is the attorney who originated the business.

(c) XYZ shall reimburse Lawyer for all reasonable expenses incurred in connection with the rendering of professional services.

(d) XYZ shall pay all professional dues, premiums for malpractice insurance,[7] and expenses incurred by Lawyer in connection with attending any and all professional seminars. Lawyer may be entitled to participate in any group health insurance plan provided he pays his share of the premium for such insurance.

(e) At the end of each calendar month, XYZ shall pay Lawyer seventy percent (70%) of the estimated Gross Receipts less Overhead Costs allocable to Lawyer.

(f) Within thirty (30) days after the end of each calendar month, XYZ shall furnish an accounting to Lawyer showing Gross Receipts and Overhead Costs allocable to Lawyer. XYZ shall pay Lawyer the remaining thirty percent (30 %) of any compensation due Lawyer for professional services rendered by Lawyer in the previous calendar month.

(g) Within thirty (30) days at the end of each calendar year, XYZ shall furnish Lawyer a complete accounting of all Gross Receipts and Overhead Costs allocable to Lawyer. XYZ shall pay Lawyer any balance of compensation to which he may be entitled by virtue of the annual accounting. Lawyer shall pay XYZ any amount which he has been paid in excess of the amount to which he is entitled.

(h) Within one calendar quarter following the termination of this Agreement or until Lawyer's compensation has been fully paid, whichever period is less, XYZ shall furnish Lawyer a complete accounting of all Gross Receipts and Overhead Costs allocable to Lawyer. XYZ shall pay Lawyer any balance of compensation to which he may be entitled by virtue of the final accounting. Lawyer shall pay XYZ any amount which he has been paid in

---

7. *See* Chapter 5 for a discussion of professional malpractice insurance.

excess of the amount to which he is entitled. Within the same period, XYZ and Lawyer shall arrange for the payment of any future amounts to which Lawyer may become entitled.

5. Billing

XYZ shall be responsible for billing clients for all professional services rendered by Lawyer. Payments received by XYZ shall be deposited in the firm's bank account.

6. Facilities and Services[8]

XYZ shall provide such facilities, office space, equipment, furniture, supplies, and services necessary to the performance of Lawyer's duties under this Agreement. XYZ shall furnish stationery with letterhead showing Lawyer's Of Counsel status and shall amend its directory listings to include Lawyer as Of Counsel.

7. Indemnification

Lawyer agrees to indemnify XYZ for any liability suffered by XYZ, its partners, employees, or agents arising from his acts or failure to act that is not covered by XYZ's professional indemnity insurance. This does not apply to a deductible or self-insured retention on a liability that is otherwise covered by XYZ's professional indemnity insurance. XYZ agrees to indemnify Lawyer for any liability which he may suffer arising from the acts or failure to act of XYZ's partners, employees, or agents, which is not covered by XYZ's indemnity insurance. This does not apply to a deductible or self-insured retention on a liability which is otherwise covered by XYZ's professional indemnity insurance.

8. Governing Law. This Agreement shall be interpreted, construed, and governed according to the laws of the State of [Anystate].

9. Integration. This Agreement contains the complete understanding of the parties and shall be binding upon their respective successors, heirs, or assigns.

10. Assignability. This Agreement is personal and the rights and obligations hereunder are not assignable.

11. Disclosure of Information

---

8. *See* Chapters 4 and 5 for a discussion of provisions that require an "Of Counsel" attorney to perform work on the premises of the employer and a discussion of overhead expenses.

Following the termination of this Agreement, in the absence of authorization, neither party shall disclose to or use for the benefit of any person, partnership, corporation or other entity, any files, trade secrets, or other confidential information obtained by either party during the term of this Agreement.

IN WITNESS WHEREOF, XYZ has caused this Agreement to be signed by its duly authorized partner, and Lawyer has executed this Agreement in the State of [Anystate] on the day and year first above written.

____

JOHN Q. LAWYER
XYZ, a general partnership

By: ________________
[Partner], Managing Partner

[The following alternate sample paragraphs illustrate how two partnerships might form an "Of Counsel" relationship. Other paragraphs should be adjusted accordingly and additional paragraphs included as needed.]

THIS AGREEMENT made this ___ day of _________, 20__, by and between A, B & C ("ABC"), a partnership engaged in the practice of law in [Anytown], [Anystate], and X, Y & Z ("XYZ"), a partnership engaged in the practice of law in [Anytown], [Anystate];

WITNESSETH, THAT WHEREAS ABC desires to establish a continuing affiliation with XYZ as Of Counsel, as independent contractors;

2. Definitions
   (a) "Gross Receipts" means all moneys received by XYZ from clients for professional services rendered by Lawyer and any additional moneys received by XYZ from clients for which Lawyer is the attorney who originated the business.
   (b) "Expenses" means any amounts incurred by Lawyer or XYZ in connection with professional services rendered by Lawyer or any other attorney of XYZ to Lawyer clients.
3. Duties; Conflicts

During the term of this Agreement, ABC shall perform professional services in the area of tax law on behalf of clients of XYZ, as well as for its own clients, and XYZ shall perform professional services in the areas of civil and commercial litigation on behalf of clients of ABC, as well as for its own clients. ABC and XYZ will conduct joint meetings on at least a weekly basis and will work toward the development of new clients and sources of business in a manner consistent with law and the Model Rules of Professional Conduct of the American Bar Association. ABC and XYZ shall each check for potential conflicts through their own internal system as well as through the system of the other firm before engaging a new client. ABC and XYZ shall work together to resolve any potential conflicts and shall decline representation or withdraw as required where conflicts exist.

4. Compensation

ABC and XYZ shall be compensated for services rendered to each other's clients in the following manner:

(a) XYZ shall pay ABC seventy-five percent (75%) of all gross receipts received by XYZ for professional services rendered by ABC, and reimburse ABC for all reasonable expenses incurred in connection with the rendering of such professional services, payable monthly.

(b) ABC shall pay XYZ seventy-five percent (75%) of all gross receipts received by ABC for professional services rendered by XYZ, and reimburse XYZ for all reasonable expenses incurred in connection with the rendering of such professional services, payable monthly.

(c) ABC and XYZ shall each be responsible for paying all professional dues, premiums for malpractice insurance, and continuing education expenses relating to their practice and attorneys.

5. Billing

ABC and XYZ shall each be responsible for billing their own clients for all professional services rendered by the other. ABC and XYZ shall cooperate with each other to provide details of services provided to clients of the other for purposes of each firm's client billing.

6. Facilities and Services; Communication to Clients

ABC and XYZ shall each be responsible for providing their own facilities, office space, equipment, furniture, supplies, and services necessary to the performance of such firm's duties under this Agreement. ABC and XYZ shall each use a letterhead approved by the other showing the other firm's Of Counsel status and shall amend its directory listings to include the other firm as Of Counsel. The engagement letters employed by each firm shall disclose the Of Counsel relationship between the firms and obtain consent for possible fee sharing in connection with the same.

APPENDIX E

Of Counsel Agreement

[LETTERHEAD OF LAW FIRM][1]
[MONTH, DAY, YEAR]

John J. Doe, Esq. 1000 Broadway Major City, ZZ 00000

Dear John:

As you will retire as a partner of our firm at the end of this fiscal year, the firm invites you to remain associated with us as Of Counsel, under the following terms.

1. Title. Your title will be "Of Counsel." The firm will be permitted to list your name in that capacity, as it deems fit, on letterheads, brochures, professional listings (such as Martindale-Hubbell), and other promotional materials.
2. Status; Health and Life Insurance Coverage. Your status will be that of an independent contractor, but we shall nevertheless take such steps as may be necessary to assure that you are eligible to remain, and remain, a member of the group covered by the firm's health and life insurance policy. In this connection, you will have the opportunity to purchase from the firm's health and life insurance carrier such coverage as the carrier offers at group rates, and at your own expense. If

1. Based on Appendix C to *Law Partnership: Its Rights and Responsibilities*, by George H. Cain, American Bar Association, 1996. That publication also contains a discussion of the case law interpreting noncompetition clauses in "Of Counsel" and law partnership agreements.

the firm, rather than you, is billed by the carrier, then the firm, in turn, will bill you for the amount that shall be reimbursable to the firm.

3. Duties of the Firm. In addition to offering the insurance coverage aforementioned, the firm will provide you with an office in the firm's [Anycity] facility, equivalent in size to an associate's office, as long as you make minimal use thereof. The firm will also provide secretarial assistance, limited to (a) handling of correspondence related to professional organizations of which you may be a member, (b) forwarding of mail to you, and (c) responding to telephone calls made to you. You will also have access to all the firm's office services (telephone, computer online service, facsimile, photocopy, and so forth). The firm will pay or reimburse you for the use of parking facilities in the building where your office is located. The firm will pay or reimburse you for the dues of the American Bar Association, the [state] Bar Association, and the [local] Bar Association. Reimbursement, if any, of your expenses for attendance at meetings of such organizations will require the firm's approval before you incur such expenses. You are invited to attend meetings of the partnership. Upon your request to the secretary of the Executive Committee, you will receive copies of agenda materials for such meetings.

4. Compensation. You will receive no compensation from the firm for your service as Of Counsel. In consideration of the provision of services mentioned in paragraph 3, above, you agree to assist the firm, to a reasonable degree, with client development efforts upon request by the firm, but not to exceed the expenditure by you of more than five hours per month. Should you incur any out-of-pocket expenditures for such activity (such as, for example, expenses for client entertainment or meals), you will be reimbursed by the firm therefor.

5. Retirement Benefit. No Competition. During your service as Of Counsel, the firm will pay to you the retirement benefit provided for Retired Partners under the firm's partnership agreement. As long as the firm is paying such benefit to you, you will refrain from the active practice of law. "Active practice of law" means the provision of legal service or advice to clients, whether or not for compensation; however, it does not include serving as an arbitrator or mediator in your

personal capacity and not as a representative of this firm (and off its premises), nor writing articles or making addresses to professional organizations. Should the firm request that you perform any legal services, by way of providing advice to other lawyers of the firm or to clients of the firm, the firm will first agree with you upon an appropriate method and amount of compensation, and will undertake to provide and pay for legal malpractice insurance for you. Except as stated in the preceding sentence, and except to the extent otherwise required by provisions of the partnership agreement, the firm will not provide you with any legal malpractice insurance.

6. Arbitration. Any dispute between us arising out of this agreement shall be settled by arbitration in the city of [Anycity], State of [Anystate], according to the commercial arbitration rules of the American Arbitration Association, before a single arbitrator who shall be a partner in a law firm with at least seven (7) partners, and who shall have been a member of the bar of the State of [Anystate] for at least thirty (30) years. Judgment upon any arbitration award may be entered and enforced in any court of competent jurisdiction. Notwithstanding the foregoing, either party to this agreement, by notice to the American Arbitration Association, may insist that the arbitration be conducted by three arbitrators and that the arbitrators be selected as prescribed in the partnership agreement of the firm.

7. Term. This agreement shall extend for a period of one (1) year from the date hereof, but shall be renewable from year to year for additional periods of one (1) year, upon your application to the Executive Committee of the firm, submitted at least sixty (60) days before the anniversary date hereof. The Executive Committee shall act upon the application within thirty (30) days after its receipt; but failing such action, this agreement shall be renewed on the same terms for the further period of one (1) year from the date hereof.

If the foregoing is satisfactory, please sign and return one counterpart of this letter to me to evidence our agreement. We look forward to your acceptance and to a continuation of our long and pleasant relationship.

Sincerely,
JONES & SMITH
By: ________________
A Partner

Acknowledged and Agreed:

____
John J. Doe

APPENDIX F

Of Counsel Agreement

[LETTERHEAD OF LAW FIRM]
[MONTH, DAY, YEAR]

John J. Doe, Esq. 1000 Broadway Major City, ZZ 00000

Dear John:

We are delighted that we have reached an understanding with you with regard to your affiliation with Law Firm XY&Z (the "Firm"). This letter will confirm in writing our understanding regarding your relationship with the Firm, and supersedes any other arrangement, whether or not reduced to writing, you may have had with this Firm. This letter also sets forth the terms of our offer.

Commencing on [date], you will have an Of Counsel position in the Firm. As Of Counsel, you will be expected to perform legal services on business generated by you and by other members of the Firm and to meet a commitment of a minimum of 1800 billable hours and 100 non-billable business development hours per fiscal year. You will be assigned to the Labor and Employment Practice Group. Your practice and activities will be under the direct supervision of Mr. John J. Smith, Esq.

Election to Partnership is accomplished by vote of the Partners, once each year, based upon recommendations of the Firm's Executive Committee. Based on existing Firm policy, you will considered for election to Partnership for the Firm's fiscal year beginning [date], or at such time as the Executive Committee considers it appropriate. Since at least at the outset, virtually all your practice will be devoted to [special client], the work you perform to increase the amount of [special client] business received by the Firm and to maintain the existing [special client] business will be taken into account and given great value in the process of your evaluation for Partner.

Following one year of employment, you may enter the Firm's Profit Sharing Plan on the next entry date of April 1 or October 1, provided you work over 1,000 hours. If you become a Partner, you would then be required to contribute 10% of Partner compensation to the Firm's Profit Sharing Plan. Those mandatory contributions would be withheld from your Partner compensation as paid.

You also will be eligible to make salary deferral contributions to the Firm's 401(k) Plan, at the first plan entry date following your first year anniversary (subject to the Plan's provision).

The Firm will expect you to devote all of your professional time and effort to the practice of law with XY&Z, and all legal fees or other forms of compensation related to your professional services, from whatever source, shall be the income of the Firm.

Our Firm has a commitment to civic and pro bono activities, and reasonable amounts of time devoted to bar association, civic affairs, and so forth are consistent with your practice with the Firm.

You will be compensated an annualized rate of $[salary figure] payable semimonthly. You will receive the following benefits:

1. Aggregate annual reimbursement of up to $1,000.00 for dues for country clubs, downtown luncheon clubs, athletic clubs, and other civic and social organizations that you may be interested in pursuing;
2. Comprehensive hospitalization and major medical insurance (Firm pays single premium only, effective on the 91st day of employment, but family coverage is available; Cafeteria Plan with "premium conversion" available for health insurance family premiums);
3. $150,000 group term life insurance, effective one month from date of hire;
4. Long-term disability insurance, effective date of hire;
5. $150,000 group term accidental death and dismemberment insurance, effective one month from date of hire;
6. Two weeks paid vacation annually;

7. Dues for American, [Anystate], and [Anycounty] Bar Associations and similar preapproved professional associations;
8. Bar exam and bar review classes as necessary to take the [Anystate] bar exam;
9. Continuing legal education, including tuition, travel, and other costs of attending preapproved specialized seminars;
10. Professional liability insurance;
11. Up to 90 days paid disability leave.

The Firm does not offer employment on a fixed term basis, and any representations in this letter or during our meetings with you should not be construed as a proposed contract for any fixed term. Either you or the Firm has the right to terminate our association for any reason.

The Firm will review your performance from time to time in the Firm's discretion, with the expectation that a formal review will be made approximately annually. Your rate of compensation may be adjusted, either up or down, in connection with any such review. The Firm reserves the right to adjust the formal review schedule based upon its fiscal year, interim evaluations, and scheduling of other professional personnel reviews.

You have disclosed to us any potential claims against you for any act or omission in the conduct of any business conducted by you in your professional capacity as a lawyer. You agree to and do hereby indemnify and hold this Firm and its present and future partners harmless from any responsibility or liability to contribute money to any judgment based on or settlement of any such claim (whether so disclosed or not). You understand that this Firm will not apply to our professional liability carrier for prior acts coverage for you, and therefore, any professional liability coverage for any claim arising from any act or omission in the conduct of any business conducted by you in your professional capacity as a lawyer prior to your joining this Firm as Of Counsel must be purchased by you individually. You will, of course, be covered by the Firm's professional liability insurance policy for any act or omission in your professional capacity occurring after the date you become Of Counsel.

We trust that this letter sets forth our mutual understandings with respect to your affiliation with our Firm as Of Counsel. If there are any questions regarding our arrangement, please contact me. Assuming this letter is satisfactory, please indicate your acceptance by signing and returning to me the enclosed copy of this letter. We certainly look forward to your joining us in the practice of law and to our mutual development of your practice.

Sincerely,
X,Y & Z Law Firm
By: Z, Managing Partner
Acknowledged and Agreed:

____

John J. Doe

APPENDIX G

Formal Opinion 90-357

(May 10, 1990)

Use of Designation "Of Counsel"; Withdrawal of Formal Opinion 330 (1972) and Informal Opinions 678 (1963), 710 (1964), 1134 (1969), 1173 (1971), 1189 (1971) and 1246 (1972)

The use of the title "of counsel," or variants of that title, in identifying the relationship of a lawyer or law firm with another lawyer or firm is permissible as long as the relationship between the two is a close, regular, personal relationship and the use of the title is not otherwise false or misleading.

In this opinion the Committee revisits the general subject of use of the title "of counsel." The subject was last comprehensively addressed by the Committee in Formal Opinion 330 (1972), and one or another aspect of the subject has also been addressed by the Committee in a number of informal opinions, both before and after Formal Opinion 330.[1] The reasons for considering yet again this much-visited subject are several. One is that there has been a proliferation of variants of the term "of counsel," and of arrangements that one or another such variant term has been used to designate, not all of which are addressed by the Committee's prior opinions.

1. Informal Opinion 678 (1963), Informal Opinion 710 (1964), Informal Opinion 1134 (1969), Informal Opinion 1173 (1971), Informal Opinion 1189 (1971), Informal Opinion 1246 (1972), Informal Opinion 1315 (1975), and Informal Opinion 84-1506 (1984). The present opinion supersedes both Formal Opinion 330 and the referenced informal opinions that preceded it, and those opinions are hereby withdrawn.

Another reason is that the Committee's prior opinions may be unjustifiably restrictive with regard to some relationships that are commonly designated by the term "of counsel." Finally, it is desirable to consider whether the supersession of the ABA Model Code of Professional Responsibility (1969, amended 1980) by the ABA Model Rules of Professional Conduct (1983, amended 1989) warrants any modification of the Committee's previously announced views, all of which had reference solely to the Model Code or to its predecessor, the Canons of Professional Ethics.

To address the last question first, it is the Committee's conclusion that there have been no changes involved in the transition from Model Code to Model Rules that have any substantive effect on the use of the term "of counsel." The Model Code included a specific reference to the title "of counsel" in DR 2-102(A)(4), relating to letterheads, and the term does not appear in the Model Rules; but there is no substantive significance to this difference. Moreover, the textual basis in both the Model Rules and the Model Code for determining whether particular uses of the title are or are not ethically permissible is in substance the same-a prohibition against misleading representations-although the particular provisions embodying this prohibition are different in form. Model Rule 7.5(a) provides, in part, that "[a] lawyer shall not use a firm name, letterhead or other professional designation that violates Rule 7.1"; and the latter Rule states in part that "[a] lawyer shall not make a false or misleading communication about the lawyer or the lawyer's services." Similarly, DR 2-101(A) of the Model Code provides that "[a] lawyer in private practice shall not practice under a . . . name that is misleading, deceptive . . . or unfair statement or claim"; DR 2-102(B) provides that "[a] lawyer in private practice shall not practice under a . . . name that is misleading as to the identity of the lawyer or lawyers practicing under such name"; and EC 2-13 states that "[i]n order to avoid the possibility of misleading persons with whom he deals, a lawyer should be scrupulous in the representation of his professional status." The essence of the ethical requirement under both the Model Rules and the Model Code is avoidance of misrepresentations as to the lawyer's status, and the relationship between lawyer and firm.

Of present concern are the representations implied by the use of the title "of counsel" on letterheads, law lists, professional cards, notices, office signs and the like: that is, its use in circumstances where there is a holding out to the world at large about some general and continuing relationship between the lawyers and law firms in question. A different use of the same term occurs when a lawyer (or firm) is designated as of counsel in filings in a particular case: in such circumstances, there is no general holding out as to a continuing relationship, or as to a relationship that applies to anything but the individual case.[2]

The issues that have been addressed in the Committee's previous opinions and that will be revisited here are, generally speaking, of two kinds, relating respectively to defining the relationship among lawyers and firms that the title "of counsel" is properly understood to evoke, and to identifying the resulting ethical implications of and limitations on its use.

As to the meaning of the title, it is appropriate to note preliminarily that, although "of counsel" appears to be the most frequently used among the various titles employing the term "counsel" it is by no means the only use of that term to indicate a relationship between a lawyer and a law firm. Other such titles include the single word "counsel" and the terms "special counsel," "tax [or other specialty] counsel" and "senior counsel."[3] It is the Committee's view that, whatever the connotative differences evoked by these variants of the title "counsel," they all share the central, and defining, characteristic of the relationship that is denoted by the term "of counsel," and so should all be understood to be covered by the present opinion. That core characteristic properly denoted by the title "counsel" is, as stated in Formal Opinion 330, a "close, regular, personal relationship"; but a relationship which is neither that of a partner (or its equivalent, a principal of a professional corporation), with the shared liability and/or managerial responsibility implied by that term; nor, on the other hand, the status

2. The distinction between use of the term "counsel" on the filings in a particular case on the one hand, and in general announcements implying a continuing relationship on the other, is significant because, as discussed below, its use in the latter connection is improper when it rests on no more than collaboration in a single case. *See* note 7 below and accompanying text.

3. This opinion does not endeavor to address other terms of similar import that do not include the word counsel, such as "consultant," "consulting attorney," and "corresponding attorney."

ordinarily conveyed by the term "associate," which is to say a junior non-partner lawyer, regularly employed by the firm.[4]

This core characteristic of the title "counsel" is shared by several kinds of relationships that in other respects vary in significant ways. There appear to be four principal patterns of such relationships, all of which in the Committee's view are properly referred to by the title "of counsel" (or one of its variants). Perhaps the most common of such relationships is that of a part-time practitioner who practices law in association with a firm, but on a basis different from that of the mainstream lawyers in the firm. Such part-time practitioners are sometimes lawyers who have decided to change from a full-time practice, either with that firm or with another, to a part-time one, or sometimes lawyers who have changed careers entirely, as for example former judges or government officials. A second common use of the term is to designate a retired partner of the firm who, although not actively practicing law, nonetheless remains associated with the firm and available for occasional consultation. A third use of the term is to designate a lawyer who is, in effect, a probationary partner-to-be: usually a lawyer brought into the firm laterally with the expectation of becoming partner after a relatively short period of time. A fourth, relatively recent, use of the term is to designate a permanent status in between those of partner and associate—akin to the category just described, but having the quality of tenure, or something close to it, and lacking that of an expectation of likely promotion to full partner status.[5]

In the Committee's view, the "Of Counsel" designation, or one of its variants, is appropriately applied to any of the four kinds of relationships just described. Prior opinions of the Committee may, however, be read as finding the term inapplicable to one or more of these relationships. For example, Formal Opinion 330 states that the relationship implied by "Of Counsel" would not be that of an employee of the firm, yet both the third

4. Formal Opinion 330 relied in part on one passage in the Model Code that comes close to providing a definition of the term, DR 2-102(A)(4), which provides in part that "A lawyer may be designated 'Of Counsel' on a letterhead if he has a continuing relationship with a lawyer or law firm, other than as a partner or associate."

5. Other terms sometimes used to designate this status are "senior attorney" and "principal attorney."

and the fourth of the relationships identified in the preceding paragraph involve, as a technical matter, the status of an employee. Insofar as Formal Opinion 330 may be read to conclude that neither the probationary partner model nor the permanent between-partner-and-associate model are permissibly designated "Of Counsel," that conclusion is disavowed. Additionally, Formal Opinion 330 may be read as limiting the permissible use of the term "Of Counsel" by retired partners of a firm, because of possible implications from language in that opinion that an "Of Counsel" lawyer must be compensated for such legal work as the lawyer does, but only for that legal work which, if strictly read, would exclude both a retired partner whose sole income from the firm is the partner's pension or other retirement benefit and counsel who share in some degree in the firm's profits. See also Informal Opinion 710. It is the Committee's view that, the other conditions just described having been met, it is not relevant to the permissibility of use of "Of Counsel" what the compensation arrangements are.[6] Similarly, some retired partners might be deemed to be excluded by the suggestion in Formal Opinion 330 that an Of Counsel's relationship to the firm must be "so close that he is in regular and frequent, if not daily, contact with the office of the lawyer or firm" (citing Informal Opinion 1134). Again, insofar as Formal Opinion 330 carries any implication that the contact must be so frequent as to verge on daily, the Committee now disavows it.

Nonetheless, the Committee remains of the view, as stated in earlier opinions, that it is not ethically permissible to use the term "of counsel" to designate the following professional relationships: a relationship involving only an individual case, see Informal Opinion 678, Formal Opinion 330;[7] a relationship of forwarder or receiver of legal business, see Formal Opinion 330; a relationship involving only occasional collaborative efforts among otherwise unrelated lawyers or firms, see id.; and the relationship of an outside consultant, see id.

---

6. The Committee expresses no view, however, on whether an arrangement under which the Of Counsel lawyer shares in the profits of the firm may expose the lawyer to malpractice liability as a partner.

7. The reference is not to the appearance of a lawyer or firm on the court filings of a particular case, but rather to representation of an "of counsel" relationship on firm letterhead, professional cards, and the like on the basis of collaboration on a single case. *See* text at note 2 above.

The characteristic of continuing and frequent professional contact bears particular emphasis in the context of use of the variant of the term of counsel" that indicates a field of concentration: "tax counsel," "antitrust counsel" and the like. Such terms, although in the Committee's view as permissible as other variants of the term "counsel," must like them be confined to relationships that in fact involve frequent and continuing contacts, and not merely an availability for occasional consultations.[8] There is, moreover, in the term designating a specialty, a clear representation that the of counsel lawyer in fact has a special expertise in the designated area; and, for the firm, that it also has, by reason of the of counsel relationship, that special expertise.[9] It bears emphasis also that the use of a title indicating a specialty counsel, like the other uses here discussed, involves mutual attribution of all disqualifications of both the lawyer and the firm-and not just attribution with respect to matters falling within the designated area of specialty.

The Committee's previous opinions have expressed the view that a lawyer cannot properly be of counsel simultaneously with multiple firms, because the necessary "close, regular, personal relationship" cannot exist on a plural basis. Thus, the Committee's initial view, expressed in Informal Opinion 1173, was that a lawyer could not be of counsel to more than a single firm; this was modified in Formal Opinion 330 to set a limit of two firms. On further consideration, the Committee finds the conclusion it reached on this subject in Formal Opinion 330 to be a doubtful one. The proposition that it is not possible for a lawyer to have a "close, regular, personal relationship" with more than two lawyers or law firms is not a self-evident one. A lawyer can surely have a close, regular, personal relationship with more than two clients; and the Committee sees no reason why the same cannot be true with more than two law firms. There is, to be sure, some point at which the number of relationships would be too great for any of them to have the necessary qualities of closeness and regularity, and that number may not be much beyond two, but the controlling criterion is "close and regular" relationships, not a particular number. As a practical matter,

8. The use of such terms may also be subject to ethical provisions of a particular jurisdiction limiting the use of terms designating specialization. *See* Model Rule 7.4(c).

9. As on other points mention in this opinion, the Committee expresses no view as to the malpractice liability implications of such representation of special expertise.

nonetheless, there is a consideration that is likely to put a relatively low limit on the number of "of counsel" relationships that can be undertaken by a particular lawyer: this is the fact that, as more fully discussed below, the relationship clearly means that the lawyer is "associated" with each firm with which the lawyer is of counsel. In consequence there is attribution to the lawyer who is of counsel of all the disqualifications of each firm, and, correspondingly, attribution from the of counsel lawyer to each firm of each of those disqualifications. See Model Rule 1.10(a). In consequence, the effect of two or more firms sharing of counsel lawyer is to make them all effectively a single firm, for purposes of attribution of disqualifications.

The Committee has also previously held that a firm cannot be of counsel to another lawyer or law firm, see Informal Opinion 1173; Formal Opinion 330. The reasoning here was that the term connotes an individual rather than a firm. This may be still so as a matter of current usage;[10] but semantics aside, the Committee's prior opinions do not suggest, and the Committee does not now perceive, any reason that a firm should not be of counsel to another firm. Moreover, the Committee held in Formal Opinion 84-351 (1984) that two law firms could ethically present themselves as "affiliated" or "associated" with each other, and in Informal Opinion 1315 (1975), the Committee gave its approval to arrangements whereby two firms effectively became "of counsel" to each other by each designating a partner of the other firm as "of counsel" to itself. As with multiple of counsel relationships of a single lawyer, the relationships between firms addressed in Formal Opinion 84-351 and Informal Opinion 1315 would of course entail complete reciprocal attribution of the disqualifications of all lawyers in each firm.

A final issue regarding permissible use of the title "of counsel" is presented by the question whether the name of a lawyer who is of counsel may also be included in the name of the firm to which the lawyer is of counsel. This question may arise in two different sorts of circumstance, which in the Committee's view lead to two different results. The first is where a name partner in a firm retires from active practice and, as is of course permissible, the firm

10. It may be noted that firms are quite conventionally identified as of counsel to other lawyers or firms on the signature page of court filings.

retains the lawyer's name in the firm name, see Model Code DR 2-102(B), cf. Model Rule 7.5(a) and Comment; but the retired partner also assumes of counsel status of the sort that has been described above. The second is a situation where the affiliation is altogether new, and where although the lawyer lends his or her name to the firm, the lawyer is not undertaking the responsibilities of a partner or principal.

The issue raised by both of these circumstances is whether they entail implicit representations to the public that are misleading. The Committee believes that in the case of a new or recent firm affiliation there is no escaping an implication that a name in the new firm name implies that the lawyer is a partner in the firm, with fully shared responsibility for its work. On the other hand, the Committee also believes that there is not a similar misleading implication in the use of a retired partner's name in the firm name, while the same partner is of counsel, where the firm name is long-established and well-recognized.[11]

To turn from consideration of the circumstances where use of the titles under discussion is or is not proper and address the ethical implications of and limitations on their use, the most important implication has already been averted to. There can be no doubt that an of counsel lawyer (or firm) is "associated in" and has an "association with" the firm (or firms) to which the lawyer is of counsel, for purposes of both the general imputation of disqualification pursuant to Rule 1.10 of the Model Rules and the imputation of disqualifications resulting from former government service under Rules 1.11(a) and 1.12(c); and is a lawyer in the firm for the purposes of Rule 3.7(b), regarding the circumstances in which, when a lawyer is to be a witness in a proceeding, the lawyer's colleague may nonetheless rep-resent the client in that proceeding. Similarly, the of counsel lawyer is "affiliated" with the firm and its individual lawyers for purposes of the general attribution of disqualifications under DR 5-105(D) of the Model Code. See Formal Opinion 330; Formal Opinion 84-351.

11. The Committee does not express a view as to whether, when the retired partner's name remains included in the firm name, the retired partner may on that account be exposed to malpractice liability as if he or she were still a general partner.

An additional ethical consequence of the relationship implied by the term "of counsel" is that in any listing, on a letterhead, shingle, bar listing or professional card, which shows the of counsel's lawyer's name, any pertinent jurisdictional limitations on the lawyer's entitlement to practice must be indicated. See Model Rule 7.5(d); Model Code DR 2-102(D).

APPENDIX H

Formal Opinion 93-377

(October 16, 1993)

Positional Conflicts

When a lawyer is asked to advocate a position with respect to a substantive legal issue that is directly contrary to the position being urged by the lawyer (or the lawyer's firm) on behalf of another client in a different and unrelated pending matter which is being litigated in the same jurisdiction, the lawyer, in the absence of consent by both clients after full disclosure, should refuse to accept the second representation if there is a substantial risk that the lawyer's advocacy on behalf of one client will create a legal precedent which is likely to materially undercut the legal position being urged on behalf of the other client. If the two matters are not being litigated in the same jurisdiction and there is no substantial risk that either representation will be adversely affect by the other, the lawyer may proceed with both representations.

The Committee has been asked to address the question whether a lawyer can represent a client with respect to a substantive legal issue when the lawyer knows that the client's position on that issue is directly contrary to the position being urged by the lawyer (or the lawyer's firm) on behalf of another client in a different, and unrelated, pending matter.[1]

1. For purposes of this Opinion, the Committee assumes that the issue on which conflicting

At the outset, it should be noted that the second paragraph of the Comment to Rule 1.9 of the Model Rules of Professional Conduct (1983, amended 1993) specifically states that a lawyer who recurrently handled a type of problem for a former client is not precluded from later representing another client in a wholly distinct problem of that type even though the subsequent representation involves a position adverse to the prior client.[2]

On the other hand, arguing a position on behalf of one client that is adverse to a position that the lawyer, or her firm, is arguing on behalf of another current client raises a number of concerns. For example, if both cases are being argued in the same court, will the impact of the lawyer's advocacy be diluted in the eyes of the judge(s)? Will the first decision rendered be persuasive (or even binding) precedent with respect to the other case, thus impairing the lawyer's effectiveness—and, if so, can the lawyer (or firm) avoid favoring one client over the other in the "race" to be first? And will one or the other of the clients become concerned that the law firm it has employed may have divided loyalties?

What, then, should a lawyer do when confronted with such a "positional conflict"? To answer this question, we must look to Model Rule 1.7, which states:

> (a) A lawyer shall not represent a client if the representation of that client will be directly adverse to another client, unless:
>
> (1) the lawyer reasonably believes the representation will not adversely affect the relationship with the other client; and
>
> (2) each client consents after consultation.
>
> (b) A lawyer shall not represent a client if the representation of that client may be materially limited by the lawyer's responsibilities to another client or to a third person, or by the lawyer's own interests, unless:

---

positions are to be taken is one of substantive law. Although procedural, discovery and evidentiary issues could in some circumstances raise the same problem as is here addressed, such issues almost invariably turn on their particular facts, and it is therefore rare that such issues will give rise to the type of conflict problem that is the subject of this Opinion.

2. The exceptions implied by the Comment's reference to a "type" of problem would include circumstances where the matter is the same as the one in which the lawyer represented the former client, or where confidences of the former client may be susceptible to misuse. See Model Rules 1.9(a) and 1.9(c)(1).

(1) the lawyer reasonably believes the representation will not be adversely affected; and

(2) the client consents after consultation. When representation of multiple clients in a single matter is undertaken, the consultation shall include explanation of the implications of the common representation and the advantages and risks involved.

These provisions are supplemented by a Comment that recognizes (but does not resolve) the issue addressed here:

A lawyer may represent parties having antagonistic positions on a legal question that has arisen in different cases, unless representation of either client would be adversely affected. Thus, it is ordinarily not improper to assert such positions in cases pending in different trial courts, but it may be improper to do so in cases pending at the same time in an appellate court.[3] (emphasis added)

The rationale of the last clause is not clear, but it may stem from the view that a ruling in one of the two appellate cases would in all likelihood constitute binding precedent with respect to the second case, under the doctrine of stare decisis, and it would therefore be highly unlikely that the lawyer would be able to win both cases.

Conversely, if there is a likelihood that the lawyer can win both cases—as, for example, where the two cases are "pending in different trial courts" or before different trial judges in the same judicial district—there is no ethical reason why the lawyer should not proceed.

Whether this be the rationale or not, the Committee does not believe that a distinction should be drawn between appellate and trial courts in this regard. After all, the impact of an appellate court decision on the second case would be the same even if the second case were still before the trial court in that particular jurisdiction. Moreover, even if both cases were in the trial court, but assigned to different judges, the decision in the first-decided case would, in all likelihood, carry at least some precedential

3. The Comment also states that "loyalty to a client" is impaired when a lawyer cannot consider, recommend or carry out an appropriate course of action for the client because of the lawyer's other responsibilities or interests. The conflict in effect forecloses alternatives that would otherwise be available to the client.

or persuasive weight in the second case. And if both cases should happen to end up before the same judge, the situation would be even worse. For although judges well understand that lawyers, at various stages of their careers, can find themselves arguing different sides of the same issue, the persuasiveness and credibility of the lawyer's arguments in at least one of the two pending matters would quite possibly be lessened, consciously or subconsciously, in the mind of the judge.

The Committee is therefore of the opinion that if the two matters are being litigated in the same jurisdiction, and there is a substantial risk that the law firm's representation of one client will create a legal precedent, even if not binding, which is likely materially to undercut the legal position being urged on behalf of the other client, the lawyer should either refuse to accept the second representation or (if otherwise permissible) withdraw from the first, unless both clients consent after full disclosure of the potential ramifications of the lawyer continuing to handle both matters.[4]

If, on the other hand, the two matters will not be litigated in the same jurisdiction, the lawyer should nevertheless attempt to determine fairly and objectively whether the effectiveness of her representation of either client will be materially limited by the lawyer's (or her firm's) representation of the other.

In addressing that key issue, the lawyer may usefully consider the following questions:

(a) Is the issue one of such importance that its determination is likely to affect the ultimate outcome of at least one of the cases?
(b) Is the determination of the issue in one case likely to have a significant impact on the determination of that issue in the other case?

---

4. Where there is such a conflict between separate representations, in the Committee's view the provision of Rule 1.7 that is potentially applicable is not paragraph (a), but paragraph (b). The former, in referring to a representation that is "directly adverse" to another client, contemplates litigating, or maintaining a position, in a given matter, on behalf of one client against a person or entity which is a client of the lawyer (or her firm) in another matter. The test under paragraph (b), on the other hand, is whether the representation of a client in one matter may be "materially limited" by the lawyer's responsibilities to another client in another matter, and the Committee views the impairment of a representation as a material limitation within the meaning of that paragraph.

(For example, does the issue involve a new or evolving area of the law, where the first case decided may be regarded as persuasive authority by other courts, regardless of their geographical location? Or: is the issue one of federal law, where the decision by one federal judge will be given respectful consideration by another federal judge, even though they are not in the same district or state?)

(c)Will there be any inclination by the lawyer, or her firm, to "soft-pedal" or de-emphasize certain arguments or issues—which otherwise would be vigorously pursued—so as to avoid impacting the other case?

(d)Will there be any inclination within the firm to alter any arguments for one, or both clients, so that the firm's position in the two cases can be reconciled—and, if so, could that redound to the detriment of one of the clients?

If the lawyer concludes that the issue is of such importance and that its determination in one case is likely to have a significant impact on its determination in the second case, thus impairing the lawyer's effectiveness—or if the lawyer concludes that, because of the dual representation, there will be an inclination by the firm either to "soft-pedal" the issue or to alter the firm's arguments on behalf of one or both clients, thus again impairing the lawyer's effectiveness—the lawyer should not accept the second representation. The reason is that, in such a situation, the representation of at least one client would be adversely affected if the firm were to proceed with both.[5]

If, on the other hand, even though there is a significant potential for the representation of one client to be limited by the representation of the other, the lawyer nonetheless reasonably believes that the determination in one case will not have a significant impact on the determination of that issue in the second case and that continuing to handle both matters will not cause her, or her firm, to "soft-pedal" the issue or to alter any arguments that

5. See *Fiandaca v. Cunningham*, 827 F.2d 825, 829 (1st Cir.1987), where the First Circuit held that, under New Hampshire Rule 1.7 and the Comment thereto (which are based on Model Rule 1.7 and Comment), a law firm has an ethical duty to prevent its loyalties to other clients from coloring its representation of the plaintiffs in this action and from infringing upon the exercise of its professional judgment and responsibility. Moreover, in such a situation it would seem clear that the law firm will not be able to provide the clients with the "competent representation" required by Rule 1.1.

otherwise would have been made, the lawyer may proceed with both representations, provided that both clients consent after full disclosure has been made to them of the potential ramifications (including the possibility that the law firm's adversary in one case might become aware, and be able to make advantageous use, of the briefs filed by the law firm in the other case).

Although the foregoing discussion is predicated on the assumption that the existence of the positional conflict is immediately apparent to the lawyer at the time she is asked to represent the second client, the Committee is of the opinion that the same analysis should be followed if such a conflict emerges after the second representation has been accepted and pursued. If that analysis leads to the conclusion that the law firm should not proceed with both representations, then the law firm must withdraw from one of them.[6]

Finally, although this Opinion began with a consideration of the provisions of the Model Rules, the Committee is of the opinion that the above-stated conclusions also hold true under the Model Code of Professional Responsibility (1969, amended 1980). Disciplinary Rule 5-105(A) states that a lawyer shall decline preferred employment if the exercise of his independent professional judgment in behalf of a client will be or is likely to be adversely affected by the acceptance of the proffered employment, or if it would be likely to involve him in representing adverse interests. (emphasis added)

Disciplinary Rule 5-105(C) provides that a lawyer may represent multiple clients if it is obvious that he can adequately represent the interest of each and if each consents to the representation after full disclosure of the possible effect of such representation on the exercise of his independent professional judgment on behalf of each. (emphasis added)

Hence, insofar as the issue here being considered is concerned, the result should be the same under the Model Code as under the Model Rules.

6. If possible, the lawyer should determine which of the representations would suffer the least harm as a consequence of the lawyer's withdrawal and then withdraw from that matter.

APPENDIX I

Formal Opinion 94-388

(December 5, 1994)

Relationships Among Law Firms

Lawyers have an obligation not to mislead prospective clients as to what the lawyer is able to bring to bear on the client's matter in terms of the size of the firm, the resources available to the firm or the relationship between the firm and other law firms with which it is associated. Words like "affiliated," "associated," "correspondent," or "network," without further explanation, can be misleading and, therefore, use of these terms, without a meaningful description of the nature of the relationship, violates Model Rule 7.1.

In certain instances, because of the nature of the relationship between law firms and without regard to whether the relationship has been disclosed, it may be necessary for a lawyer to decline a proffered representation because the representation would be materially limited by such a relationship; in addition, if the lawyer believes the representation will not be adversely affected, it may be necessary for the lawyer to disclose the relationship to prospective clients so that the clients can determine whether, despite the relationship, they wish to consent to the representation.

If a law firm licenses its name to other firms, all firms so licensed must, in fact, operate as a single firm and be treated as part of a single firm for all purposes under the Model Rules. Law firm relationships that result in the sharing of fees must comply with the requirements of reasonableness of the fee, disclosure to the client of the sharing arrangement, and division of the fees in accordance with services performed or assumption of responsibility. Lawyers must also avoid running afoul of Model Rule 7.2(c)'s prohibition on giving something of value for referrals.

The growth, development and diversity of the legal profession have spawned a proliferation of new ways of conducting the practice which have taken lawyers far beyond the sole practitioner and single office law firm models of an earlier era. Today law firms operate in multiple cities, form networks of law firms under a common firm name or trade name, and join forces and pool resources in any number of business arrangements. The Committee has received a number of inquiries relating to the ethical propriety of these relationships and the ethical requirements associated with them.

This opinion is intended to suggest some guidelines with respect to two fundamental ethical precepts which must be addressed in this context. The first is the obligation not to misstate what a law firm has to offer. The second is the obligation to assure that a client of one firm is aware of the relationship between that firm and any other firms with which it is involved insofar as the relationship may give rise to conflicts of interest, the sharing of fees, or certain other interactions that implicate the Model Rules of Professional Conduct. This opinion presumes that the actual formation of relationships between law firms will have occurred only where the law firms were able to comply with their obligations to existing clients with respect to all such matters.

I. Full Disclosure

A client should not be misled about the firm resources available to assist in the provision of services the client requires. For example, if the lawyer has given the client reason to believe that the firm has offices in multiple cities, that should in fact be the case. Similarly, if the lawyer has given the client reason to believe that in going to firm "A" the client will have available to work on its matter the resources of an affiliated firm "B," then firm "A" must, in fact, have access to the talent, expertise and experience of attorneys at firm "B."

This obligation not to mislead clients, potential clients or the general public, whether about the basic law firm associations or otherwise, derives from Model Rule 7.1, which prohibits communications by a lawyer regarding legal services that are false or misleading.[1] In addition, Model Rule 7.5(a) prohibits the use of a "firm name, letterhead or other professional designation that violates Rule 7.1,"[2] and Model Rule 7.5(d) provides that "lawyers may state or imply that they practice in a partnership or other organization only when that is the fact."[3]

The problem confronting the Committee is that a vast array of different words and phrases have been used to describe the relationships among law firms: "strategic alliance," "network," "affiliation," "association," "correspondent" are but a few that have come to the Committee's attention. Moreover, despite the Committee's attempt in Formal Opinion 84-351 to define what is meant when two firms say that that they are "associated" or "affiliated," various words, including those two, are being used to describe relationships ranging from something very close to an actual partnership to one involving occasional referrals.

This state of affairs has led the Committee to conclude that its efforts in Formal Opinion 84-351 to bring some order and meaning to the use of several common terms describing relationships between firms have not been successful. Any similar attempt simply to define what relationships are meant by such terms as "network," "alliance" or "correspondent" is likely to be similarly unavailing. It is critical, no matter what words are used to describe the relationship between firms, for clients to receive information that will tell them the exact nature of the relationship and the extent to which resources of another firm will be available in connection with the client's retention of the firm that is claiming the relationship.

The Committee concludes that the use of one or two word shorthand expressions is not sufficient to fulfill that requirement. Because the words

1. Rule 7.1 states in pertinent part, "A lawyer shall not make a false or misleading communication about the lawyer or the lawyer's services." The Comment to Rule 7.1 states, in part, that "This Rule governs all communications about a lawyer's services, including advertising permitted by Rule 7.2." See also DR 2-101(A), which provided that "[a] lawyer shall not . . . use or participate in the use of any form of public communication containing a false, fraudulent, misleading, deceptive, self-laundry or unfair statement or claim."

2. Similarly, DR 2-102(B) provides that "[a] lawyer in private practice shall not practice under . . . a name that is misleading as to the identity of the lawyer or lawyers practicing under such name. . . ."

3. DR 2-102(C) is substantially identical to Rule 7.5(d).

mentioned above and others have been employed to describe so many different relationships, and because the modern era has generated so many imaginative ways in which firms relate to one another (and with which they describe them), the Committee believes that the mandate of Model Rule 7.1 not to mislead or deceive can only be met if a full description of any relationships the firm may have used in marketing its services is provided to all prospective clients as to whom the lawyer reasonably believes the relationships may be relevant, and to all present clients to whom the lawyer reasonably believes the relationships may be relevant if at any time any of those relationships changes. Thus, for example, a firm that represents that it has a "special affiliation" with a Washington, D.C. firm that specializes in tax matters would probably conclude that complete disclosure of that relationship was required for most, if not all, of its tax and business clients, but not necessarily required for the firm's litigation clients, if the affiliation would be irrelevant for them.

This conclusion contemplates that if the clients or prospects for whom the relationship is relevant are told the firm is a member of a "network," in an "association" or is a "correspondent" of another firm, they will be given the following information:

a. whether any professional personnel from the other law firm(s) may be involved in providing the professional services.
b. whether any part of the fee the client pays will be shared with any of the other firm(s).
c. whether profits of the firm the client originally retained will be shared with the other firm(s).
d. whether the law firms in the relationship conduct common training programs and/or share strategies and/or expertise.
e. whether the firms in the relationship conduct any other common operations, or, by contrast, the relationship is simply a common marketing device.

The goal here would be to provide the client with sufficient meaningful information to avoid misleading the client about the nature of the relationship. Similar information would have to be provided for each of the other descriptive words mentioned in this opinion as well as the many other shorthand words and phrases that are used to describe inter-firm relationships.

In so concluding, the Committee does not mean to suggest that on letterhead and law lists like Martindale Hubbell the firm cannot simply state that it is "affiliated" with another or that it is a member of a particular "network." The full disclosure addressed here rather must be given to any prospective client to whom the lawyer reasonably believes the relationship may be relevant, preferably in writing, before the lawyer embarks on the work required by the engagement. Most firms will no doubt find it simplest to prepare an addendum to their standard retention letter that would include a description of the relevant relationship for this purpose.

II. Disclosure for Conflict of Interest Purposes

The dimensions of the second ethical precept implicated by law firm relationships are somewhat different. Rather than an issue of truth in representations regarding available resources, this issue concerns the need for full disclosure of potential conflicts of interest stemming from inter-firm relationships and, where appropriate, client waiver of objection to those conflicts. This obligation to address conflicts of interest, unlike the obligation outlined in Part I of this Opinion, exists without regard to whether the firm has disclosed that such a relationship exists.

Just as clients are entitled to know that their law firm does work on a regular basis for the firm representing their adversary, so, too, may they be entitled to know that their law firm and their adversary's law firm have other types of relationships. This disclosure obligation derives from Model Rule 1.7(b), which states, in pertinent part:

> (b) A lawyer shall not represent a client if the representation of that client may be materially limited by the lawyer's responsibilities to another client or to a third person, or by the lawyer's own interests, unless:
>
> (1) the lawyer reasonably believes the representation will not be adversely affected; and
>
> (2) the client consents after consultation.

The extent of the obligation to make disclosure in accordance with Rule 1.7 is peculiarly fact-dependent.

No opinion can begin to identify all the possible situations where the obligation to disclose may arise. Similarly, for the reasons described above, no hard and fast rules can account for all situations in which a particular word or words are used to describe the relationship. Whether conflicts have to be cleared between law firms and whether relationships have to be disclosed to prospective clients of either turns on the substance of the relationship, not the name the law firms choose to call it. But if a particular representation may be materially limited by an existing relationship, the lawyer must decline the representation unless the lawyer believes the representation will not be adversely affected and the client consents after consultation.[4]

It may be instructive to evaluate several examples along the continuum from that which clearly would not materially limit a representation (no relationship) to that which clearly does (full partnership). Near one end of the spectrum are situations where firms from time to time informally refer matters to one another where practicable. Even in cases where such relationships have resulted in multiple referrals there is no reason that the relationship would, as a general proposition, materially limit the representation. These casual referrals, or even periodic mutual backscratching, should not constitute the kind of interest that would trigger the determination required by Model Rule 1.7(b).

A more difficult question arises when both firms belong to a "network" (or otherwise characterized group) of firms which in fact share no clients, no confidences, no fees and no professional engagements but which do agree more or less formally to advertise their relationship and refer matters to each other on an ad hoc basis. Given the limited nature of such a relationship, it is the view of the Committee that this sort of limited network relationship without more, also would not call into play Model Rule 1.7(b).

4. The term "consultation," used in Rule 1.7(b)(2), is defined in the Model Rules terminology to denote "communication of information reasonably sufficient to permit the client to appreciate the significance of the matter in question." It is important in this context to recall that the Comment to Rule 1.7(b)(1) states that "when a disinterested lawyer would conclude that the client should not agree to the representation under the circumstances, the lawyer involved cannot properly ask for such agreement or provide representation on the basis of the client's consent."

A more regular practice of referral may, however, give rise to a need to clear conflicts if the relationship involves sharing of client fees.

A different series of questions is presented if there is a non-law related business relationship between law firms. For example, if one firm lends another significant working capital, or if two firms jointly buy a building they both will use, or if two firms enter into a joint venture to establish, for example, a title company, the resulting business relationship may give rise to a need to address the conflict question. In some instances the business relationship between the two firms will be so marginal or unimportant that Model Rule 1.7(b) will not come into play. On the other hand, there may be situations in which one firm's business connection with another will be so integral to its enterprise that it could materially limit its ability to oppose the other firm's clients. In this case, the firm's clients ought to have an opportunity to decide whether they wish to continue to be represented by a firm whose business partner is representing an adverse party against the client. At some point the lawyer's interest in the relationship with the other firm will be of sufficient moment that, even if the lawyer believes the representation will not be adversely affected, the lawyer must disclose the relationship to her client to enable the client to decide whether to agree to the representation.

Difficult questions are also raised when the professional relationship between the firms becomes more substantial than the network arrangement described above. As the two firms become more inextricably linked, the need to consider the conflict potential becomes more pronounced. As a general proposition the Committee concludes that where two law firms have a relationship in which they share profits, it is highly unlikely that one could represent a client whose interests are adverse to clients of the other firm without following the procedure prescribed by Model Rule 1.7(b). In such a case the lawyer must make a good faith determination that the representation will not be adversely affected and, if that determination can be made, secure the informed consent of the client if the representation is to go forward.

* * *

There is one other question in the conflict area raised by relationships between law firms. At some point the client of law firm A is entitled to know whether law firm B, with whom law firm A has a relationship, represents interests adverse to the client of law firm A. This is certainly so if a client, in going to law firm A, will have law firm B working on its matter. In this situation the client is the client of both firms, and is entitled to the full protections of Model Rule 1.7 as to both firms. A client is also entitled to know of conflicting commitments where, as described in Formal Opinion 84- 351, the relationship between the two firms is "close and regular, continuing and semi-permanent, and not merely that of forwarder-receiver of legal business." In that relationship one firm was "available to the other firm and its clients for consultation and advice." Quite apart from the name that is applied to that relationship, the Opinion correctly concluded that lawyers of the "affiliated" or "associated" firm will not simultaneously represent persons whose interests conflict with the client's interests, just as would be true of lawyers who occupy an 'Of Counsel' relationship with the firm.

The same expectation necessarily exists when two firms are "Of Counsel" to each other. Formal Opinion 90-357; Informal Opinion 1315 (1975). In each case, of course, if the lawyer believes the representation will not be adversely affected, the client can be asked to consent to the representation.

But even in situations short of a "close and regular, continuing and semi-permanent relationship," if the relationship of the two firms is sufficiently close, the client of firm A may be entitled to know whether firm B represents interests adverse to the client. Of course, the client of firm A, having been informed of firm A's "strategic alliance" with firm B and what that alliance means, may not wish to have the fact and nature of its representation by firm A circulated among the lawyers at firm B. Given these competing interests, in the view of the Committee it is enough if firm A informs its client of the nature of its relationship with firm B and permits the client to decide whether conflict clearance at firm B should occur.

III. Licensing of a Firm Name

The next question the Committee has been asked to address involves a law firm with a practice concentrated in a particular area which seeks to create a national network of firms, all of which will use the original firm's name under a licensing agreement by which the original firm will provide all marketing for the firms in the network. The Committee believes that, in contrast to the situation in which several firms are associated but retain their own identities, the use of the same name by all the firms in a network will effectively represent that they are all offices of one and the same firm. Such a representation is, quite clearly, a misrepresentation under both Rule 7.1 and Rule 7.5(a) if in fact all the firms bearing the same name are not part of the same firm.[5] If several entities are, or are held out as, a single firm, then their lawyers must meet not only the obligations regarding preservation of confidences and avoidance of conflicts, but also those arising under Rules that normally come into play only when lawyers are associated in the same firm.

Principal among such provisions are Rules 5.1(a) and (c), which deal with one lawyer's responsibility for the conduct of other lawyers.[6] These provisions provide:

> (a) A partner in a law firm shall make reasonable efforts to ensure that the firm has in effect measures giving reasonable assurance that all lawyers in the firm conform to the Rules of Professional Conduct.
>
> * * *
>
> (c) A lawyer shall be responsible for another lawyer's violation of the Rules of Professional Conduct if:
>
> (1) the lawyer orders or, with knowledge of the specific conduct, ratifies the conduct involved; or
>
> (2) the lawyer is a partner in the law firm in which the other lawyer practices, or has direct supervisory authority over the other lawyer, and knows of the conduct at a time when its

5. This opinion does not address the legal significance of identity as a single firm in terms of contract, tort, corporate or other law.
6. There are no direct counterparts to these provisions in the Model Code.

> consequences can be avoided or mitigated but fails to take reasonable remedial action.

Also pertinent are Rules 5.3(a) and (c), which involve a lawyer's responsibility for the actions of persons acting under his supervision and direction and provide:

With respect to a non-lawyer employed or retained by or associated with a lawyer:

> (a) a partner in a law firm shall make reasonable efforts to ensure that the firm has in effect measures giving reasonable assurance that the person's conduct is compatible with the professional obligations of the lawyer; and
>
> * * *
>
> (c) a lawyer shall be responsible for conduct of such a person that would be a violation of the Rules of Professional Conduct if engaged in by a lawyer if:
>
> (1) the lawyer orders or, with the knowledge of the specific conduct, ratifies the conduct involved; or
>
> (2) the lawyer is a partner in the law firm in which the person is employed, or has direct supervisory authority over the person, and knows of the conduct at a time when its consequences can be avoided or mitigated but fails to take reasonable remedial action.[7]

If all of the lawyers in the participating firms in a "network" of licensed firms using the same name meet all of the ethical requirements that would be applicable to them if they were all lawyers in a single firm, then, at least

7. There are no direct counterparts to these provisions in the Model Code.

Also of possible pertinence are Rule 5.4(a), prohibiting a "lawyer or law firm" from sharing legal fees with a non-lawyer, with certain exceptions, and Rule 5.4(b), which provides that "A lawyer shall not form a partnership with a non-lawyer if any of the activities of the partnership consist of the practice of law."

from the ethical point of view, there would be no impropriety in such an arrangement. Absent such compliance, there would, at a minimum, be a violation of Rule 7.1 and Rule 7.5(a).

IV. Financial Arrangements Between Related Firms

The final issue that the Committee has been asked to address concerns fee sharing and other financial arrangements between related firms, however the relationship is denominated. A fundamental proposition, of course, is that all of the firms in the relationship must comply with ethical requirements regarding the sharing of fees. This is so even where, as described above, the firms must be treated for conflicts purposes as if they are a single firm.

Under Model Rule 1.5(e)(1), fees may be shared only if they are divided in proportion to services performed or if, pursuant to written agreement by the client, each lawyer assumes joint responsibility for the representation.[8] The Model Code differs in that it requires that fees be divided in proportion to the services performed and the responsibility assumed by each. See DR 2- 107(A). A client whose fee is shared must receive a complete explanation of the sharing arrangement, and the arrangement cannot be implemented under the Rules if the client objects. See Model Rule 1.5(e); Model Code DR 2- 107(A) (stating that the client must consent "to employment of the other lawyer"); see also Formal Opinion 84-351 at n. 8. Moreover, the total fee must be reasonable. See Model Rule 1.5(e)(3); Model Code DR 2-106, EC 2-17.

Another ethical question raised in this context is whether one firm may finance another (e.g., by making loans) in a manner that is tied to referral business generated by the financed firm. In general, one firm may finance another and may receive referrals from the financed firm. Since, however, under Model Rule 7.2(c) a lawyer "shall not give anything of value to a person for recommending the lawyer's services," a firm that finances another firm cannot either receive referrals of business as a purported return on its investment or make the referrals as a quid pro quo for a return on its investment. Indeed, in general firms may not contract to refer business to

8. The Committee does not address in this Opinion whether sharing of profits among lawyers is subject to the same requirements as the sharing of fees.

one another: the exchange of binding promises would in itself constitute "giving something of value" for referrals in violation of Rule 7.2(c).[9] This principle holds even if the firms are "associated," "affiliated" or part of a "network." However, as long as there is no fixed relationship between the referrals amounting to a quid pro quo, firms may agree to consider each other for appropriate referrals.

Arrangements whereby financing from one firm is tied to referral business from another may also violate the ethical constraints on sharing fees with lawyers not in the same firm. In Informal Opinion 85-1514 (1985), the Committee explained that a professional corporation of tax law specialists could not ethically use preferred stock dividends or a limited partner distribution to pay an outside lawyer in an amount proportional to the corporation's earnings from clients referred to it by the outside lawyer. This arrangement would amount to a division of fees among lawyers not in the same firm, and therefore would have to comply with the requirements of Rule 1.5(e) outlined in part above. Other financial arrangements that tie a sum of money to the level of earnings from referrals are similarly impermissible. For example, one firm may not finance another firm in an amount proportional to earnings from referrals from the financed firm. Nor may a firm receive a return on an investment in another firm pegged to earnings that the financed firm derives from referrals from the financing firm.

Finally, where one firm is providing financing to another firm, but the two firms are then asked to represent opposing parties in a matter, Rule 1.7(b) applies, as discussed in Part II above.

---

9. Cf., e.g., In re Weinroth, 495 A.2d 417, 420–21 (N.J.1985) (an arrangement whereby a law firm provided a referral client a credit for future legal expenses and the client gave the referrer a fee constituted a violation of ethical rules because the law firm indirectly gave "value" for a referral); Board of Commissioners on Grievances and Discipline of the Ohio Supreme Court Op. 92-19 (Oct. 16, 1992) (one lawyer may not purchase client files and client lists from another attorney because, among other reasons, "any money paid by a purchaser for client files and lists would be in essence a reward to the seller for recommending the purchasing lawyer" under Ohio DR 2-130(B); Illinois State Bar Ass'n, Op. No. 92016 (Jan. 22, 1993) (a lawyer who practiced before the IRS could not ethically offer reduced rates to family members of an IRS agent in exchange for that agent's "doing what he could to further the career" of the lawyer because, among other reasons, the reduction in fees is something 'of value' " under Illinois Rule 7.2).

Conclusion

In conclusion, the Committee observes that neither the Model Rules nor the Model Code speaks directly to the ethical problems raised by relationships between law firms. Although such relationships may raise special concerns, particularly in the area of conflicts of interest, any relationship between firms is permissible as long as the attendant ethical obligations are met. These include the obligation to assure that any representations that have been made regarding the relationship are clear and not misleading, and the obligations to avoid conflicts and preserve confidences as may be entailed by the actual circumstances of the relationship. Related firms should also see to it their fee and referral arrangements do not conflict with applicable ethical rules.

APPENDIX J

American Bar Association CPR Policy Implementation Committee Variations of the ABA Model Rules of Professional Conduct

As of September 4, 2012

Rule 7.5 Firm Names And Letterheads

(a) A lawyer shall not use a firm name, letterhead or other professional designation that violates Rule 7.1. A trade name may be used by a lawyer in private practice if it does not imply a connection with a government agency or with a public or charitable legal services organization and is not otherwise in violation of Rule 7.1.
(b) A law firm with offices in more than one jurisdiction may use the same name or other professional designation in each jurisdiction, but identification of the lawyers in an office of the firm shall indicate

the jurisdictional limitations on those not licensed to practice in the jurisdiction where the office is located.

(c) The name of a lawyer holding a public office shall not be used in the name of a law firm, or in communications on its behalf, during any substantial period in which the lawyer is not actively and regularly practicing with the firm.

(d) Lawyers may state or imply that they practice in a partnership or other organization only when that is the fact.

Variations from ABA Model Rule are noted. Based on reports of state committees reviewing recent changes to the model rules. For information on individual state committee reports, see

http://www.abanet.org/cpr/jclr/home.html.

Comments not included.

Current links to state Rules of Professional conduct can be found on the ABA website: http://www.abanet.org/cpr/links.html

AL Effective 2/19/09

(a) Deletes "legal services" and adds reference to Rule 7.4 to end to paragraph;

(b) Changes "more than one jurisdiction" to "another jurisdiction;" adds "in Alabama" after "may use;" changes "the same name" to "the name;" changes everything after "name" to: *it uses in the other jurisdiction, provided the use of that name would comply with these rules. A firm with any lawyers not licensed to practice in Alabama must, if such lawyer's name appears on the firm's letterhead, state that the lawyer is not licensed to practice in Alabama.*

Adds (c): *A lawyer or law firm may indicate on any letterhead or other communication permitted by these rules other jurisdictions in which the lawyer or the members or associates of the law firm are admitted to practice.*

(a) is similar to MR (c) but deletes "actively and regularly;"

Does not adopt MR (d);

Adds (d): *The name of a lawyer holding a public office shall not be used in the name of a law firm, or in communications on its behalf, during any substantial period in which the lawyer is not practicing with the firm.*

AK Effective 4/15/09

(d) Replaces language after "organization" with "unless the relationship stated or implied in fact exists;"

Adds:

(e) The term "of counsel" shall be used only to refer to a lawyer who has a close continuing relationship with the firm.

AZ Effective 1/1/13

Same as MR

AR Effective 5/1/05

Same as [Model Rule] MR

CA Current Rule

[California's Rules of Professional Conduct are structured differently from the ABA

Model Rules. Please see California Rules :
http://calbar.ca.gov/calbar/pdfs/rules/Rules_Professional-Conduct.pdf]

CO Effective 1/1/08

Same as MR

CT Effective 1/1/07

Same as MR

DE Effective 7/1/03

Same as MR

District of Columbia Effective 2/1/07

Same as MR

FL Effective 5/22/06

Advertisements in the Electronic Media Other Than Computer-Accessed Communications

(a) Generally. With the exception of computer-based advertisements (which are subject to the special requirements set forth in rule 4-7.6), all advertisements in the electronic media, including but not limited to television and radio, are subject to the requirements of rule 4-7.2.
(b) Appearance on Television or Radio. Advertisements on the electronic media such as television and radio shall conform to the requirements of this rule.

(1) *Prohibited Content.* Television and radio advertisements shall not contain:

(A) any feature that is deceptive, misleading, manipulative, or that is likely to confuse the viewer;

(B) any spokesperson's voice or image that is recognizable to the public; or

(C) any background sound other than instrumental music.

(2) *Permissible Content.* Television and radio advertisements may contain:

(A) images that otherwise conform to the requirements of these rules; or

(B) a non-attorney spokesperson speaking on behalf of the lawyer or law firm, as long as the spokesperson is not a celebrity recognizable to the public. If a spokesperson is used, the spokesperson shall provide a spoken disclosure identifying the spokesperson as a spokesperson and disclosing that the spokesperson is not a lawyer.

GA* Effective 1/1/01

**Has not amended Rule since the most recent amendments to the ABA Model Rules*

(a) Deletes language after "violates Rule 7.1;"
Adds:

(e) A trade name may be used by a lawyer in private practice if:

(1) the trade name includes the name of at least one of the lawyers practicing under said name. A law firm name consisting solely of the name or names of deceased or retired members of the firm does not have to include the name of an active member of the firm; and
(2) the trade name does not imply a connection with a government entity, with a public or charitable legal services organization or any other organization, association or institution or entity, unless there is, in fact, a connection.

The maximum penalty for a violation of this Rule is a public reprimand.

HI* Effective 1/1/94

**Has not amended Rule since the most recent amendments to the ABA Model Rules*

(b) A law firm may use as, or continue to include in, its name the name or names of one or more deceased or retired partners of the firm in a continuing line of succession; provided that where none of the names comprising a firm name is the name of a current partner who is on the list of active attorneys maintained by the Hawai'i State Bar, there shall be at least one supervisor, manager, partner, or shareholder of the firm who is on the list of active attorneys maintained by the bar.
(c) The name of a professional law corporation or limited liability law company, limited liability law partnership or other such lawful organization shall include the words "A Law Corporation," "A Limited Liability Law Company," "A Limited Liability Law Partnership," or other appropriate designation, whenever applicable.
(d) A lawyer who assumes a judicial or public executive or administrative post or office shall not permit the lawyer's name to remain in the name of a law firm or to be used in professional notices of or public communications by the firm during any significant period in which the lawyer is not actively and regularly practicing law as a partner of the firm, and during such period other partners and associates of the

firm shall not use the lawyer's name in the firm name or in professional notices of or public communications by the firm.
(e) A law firm shall not be formed or continued between or among lawyers licensed in different jurisdictions unless all enumerations of the partners, associates, and "of counsel" lawyers of the firm on its letterhead and in other permissible listings make clear the jurisdictional limitations on those partners, associates, and "of counsel" lawyers of the firm not licensed to practice in all listed jurisdictions.
(f) Lawyers may state or imply that they practice in a partnership or other organization only when that is the fact.

ID Effective 7/1/04

Same as MR

IL Effective 1/1/2010

Same as MR

IN Effective 1/1/05

title is: Professional Notices, Letterheads, Offices, and Law Lists

(a) A lawyer or law firm shall not use or participate in the use of professional cards, professional announcement cards, office signs, letterheads, telephone directory listings, law lists, legal directory listings, or a similar professional notice or device if it includes a statement or claim that is false, fraudulent, misleading, deceptive, self-laudatory or unfair within the meaning of or that violates the regulations contained in Rule 7.1.
(b) A lawyer shall not practice under a name that is misleading as to the identity, responsibility, or status of those practicing thereunder, or is otherwise false, fraudulent, misleading, deceptive, self-laudatory or unfair within the meaning of Rule 7.1, or is contrary to law. In that it is inherently misleading, a lawyer in private practice shall not practice under a trade name. However, the name of a professional corporation or professional association may contain "P.C." or "P.A."

or similar symbols indicating the nature of the organization, and if otherwise lawful a firm may use as, or continue to include in, its name, the name or names of one or more deceased or retired members of the firm or of a predecessor firm in a continuing line of succession. A lawyer who assumes a judicial, legislative, or public executive or administrative post or office shall not permit his name to remain in the name of a law firm or to be used in professional notices of or public communications by the firm during any significant period in which he is not actively and regularly practicing law as a member of the firm and during such period other members of the firm shall not use his name in the firm name or in professional notices of or public communications by the firm.

(c) A lawyer shall not hold himself out as having a partnership with one or more other lawyers unless they are in fact partners.

(d) A partnership shall not be formed or continued between or among lawyers licensed in different jurisdictions unless all enumerations of the members and associates of the firm on its letterhead and in other permissible listings make clear the jurisdictional limitations on those members and associates of the firm not licensed to practice in all listed jurisdictions; however the same firm name may be used in each jurisdiction.

IA Effective 7/1/05

(a) A lawyer shall not use a firm name, letterhead, or other professional designation that violates rule 32:7.1. A lawyer or law firm may use the following professional cards, signs, letterheads, or similar professional notices or devices if they are in dignified form:

(1) A professional card of a lawyer identifying the lawyer by name and as a lawyer, and giving addresses, telephone numbers, the name of the lawyer's law firm, and any information permitted under rule 32:7.4. A professional card of a law firm may also give the names of members and associates. Such cards may be used for identification.

(2) A brief professional announcement card stating new or changed associations or addresses, change of firm name, or similar matters pertaining to the professional office of a lawyer or law firm, which may be mailed to lawyers, clients, former clients, personal friends, and relatives. It shall not state biographical data except to the extent reasonably necessary to identify the lawyer or to explain the change in the lawyer's association, but it may state the immediate past position of the lawyer. It may give the names and dates of predecessor firms in a continuing line of succession. It shall not state the nature of the practice except as permitted under rule 32:7.4. A dignified announcement of a change in location of office, the addition of a new partner, equity holder or associate, or a change in the name of a law firm may be published in one or more newspapers of general circulation over a period of no more than four weeks.

(3) A sign on or near the door of the office and in the building directory identifying the law office. The sign shall not state the nature of the practice, except as permitted under rule 32:7.4.

(4) A letterhead of a lawyer identifying the lawyer by name and as a lawyer and giving the lawyer's addresses, telephone numbers, the name of the lawyer's law firm, associates, and any information permitted under rule 32:7.4. A letterhead of a law firm may also give the names of members and associates, and names and dates related to deceased and retired members. A lawyer may be designated "Of Counsel" on a letterhead if the lawyer has a continuing relationship with a lawyer or law firm, other than as a partner or associate. A lawyer or law firm may be designated as "General Counsel" or by similar professional reference on stationery of a client if the lawyer or the firm devotes a substantial amount of professional time in the representation of that client. The letterhead of a law firm may give the names and dates of predecessor firms in a continuing line of succession.

(b) A law firm with offices in more than one jurisdiction may use the same name or other professional designation in each jurisdiction, but identification of the lawyers in an office of the firm shall indicate

the jurisdictional limitations on those not licensed to practice in the jurisdiction where the office is located.
(c) The name of a lawyer holding a public office shall not be used in the name of a law firm, or in communications on its behalf, during any substantial period in which the lawyer is not actively and regularly practicing with the firm.
(d) Lawyers may state or imply that they practice in a partnership or other organization only when that is the fact.
(e) A lawyer in private practice shall not practice under a trade name, a name that is misleading as to the identity of the lawyer or lawyers practicing under such name, or a firm name containing names other than those of one or more of the lawyers in the firm. However the name of a professional corporation, professional association, professional limited liability company, or registered limited liability partnership may contain "P.C.," "P.A.," "P.L.C.," "L.L.P." or similar symbols indicating the nature of the organization and, if otherwise lawful, a firm may use as, or continue to include in, its name, the name or names of one or more deceased or retired members of the firm or of a predecessor firm in a continuing line of succession.
(f) A lawyer who is engaged both in the practice of law and another profession or business shall not so indicate on the lawyer's letterhead, office sign, or professional card, and shall not be identified as a lawyer in any publication in connection with the lawyer's other profession or business.

KS Effective 7/1/07

(b) Deletes "or other professional designation."

KY Effective 7/15/09

(1) is similar to MR (a) but deletes language after "Rule 7.1;"

(2) is similar to MR (b) but deletes "or other professional designation;"

(3) is MR (c);

(4) is MR (d);

Adds:

(5) The name of a lawyer who is suspended by the Supreme Court from the practice of law may not be used by the law firm in any manner until the lawyer is reinstated. A lawyer who has been permanently disbarred shall not be included in a firm name, letterhead, or any other professional designation or advertisement.

LA Effective 3/1/04

The rule is similar to 7.5. It includes the following sentence at the end of (a): "A lawyer shall not use a trade or fictitious name unless the name is the law firm name that also appears on the lawyer's letterhead, business cards, office signs and fee contracts and appears with the lawyer's signature on pleadings and other legal documents."

(b) does not include the phrase "or other professional designation" includes a subsection (e) not in the MR: "If otherwise lawful, a firm may use as, or continue to include in, its name, the name or names of one or more deceased or retired members of the firm, or of a predecessor firm in a continuing line of succession."

ME Effective 8/1/09

Same as MR

MD Effective 7/1/05

Same as MR

MA Rules effective 9/1/08

(b) Deletes "or other professional designation."

MI* Rules effective 10/1/88

**Made only partial amendments effective 1/1/2011 since the most recent amendments to the ABA Model Rules (amended Rules 3.1, 3.3, 3.4, 3.5, 3.6, 5.5, and 8.5 and adopted new Rules 2.4, 5.7, and 6.6.*

Same as MR.

MN Effective 10/1/05

Same as MR

MS Effective 11/3/05

See 7.7 for MS version of MR 7.5

Submission of Advertisements

(a) Mandatory Submission. A copy or recording of any advertisement to be published shall be submitted to the Office of the General Counsel of the Mississippi Bar (OGCMB) as set forth in paragraph(c) below prior to its first dissemination.

(b) Exemptions. The following are exempt from this submission requirement:

(1) Any advertisement that contains no illustrations and no information other than that set forth in Rules 7.2 and 7.4;

(2) Any telephone directory advertisement;

(3) Notices or announcements that do not solicit clients, but rather state new or changed associations or membership of firms, changed location of offices, the opening of new offices, and similar changes relating to a lawyer or law firm;

(4) Professional business cards or letterhead;

(5) On premises office signage;

(6) Notices and paid listings in law directories addressed primarily to other members of the legal profession;

(7) Advertisements in professional, trade, academic, resource or specialty publications circulated to specific subscribing audiences rather than the general public at large that announce the availability of a lawyer or law firm to practice a particular type of law in many jurisdictions and that are not for the purpose of

soliciting clients to commence or join in specific litigation to be performed in Mississippi;

(8) Internet Web pages viewed via a Web browser, in a search initiated by a person without solicitation.

(9) Informative or scholarly writings in professional, trade or academic publications;

(10) A communication mailed only to existing clients, former clients or other lawyers;

(11) Any written communications requested by a prospective client;

(12) Any notices or publications required by law; and

(13) Such other exemptions as may be authorized by the OGCMB.

(c) Items to be submitted. A submission with to the OGCMB pursuant to paragraph (a) shall consist of:

(1) A copy of the advertisement or communication in the form or forms in which it is to be disseminated (e.g., videotapes, audiotapes, print media, photographs or other accurate replicas of outdoor advertising);

(2) A transcript, if the advertisement or communication is on videotape or audiotape;

(3) A statement of when and where the advertisement has been, is, or will be used; and

(4) A fee of twenty-five dollars ($25) per submission of advertisement or communication timely filed as provided in paragraph (a), or a fee of one hundred and fifty dollars ($150) for submissions not timely filed, made payable to The Mississippi Bar. This fee shall be used only for administration and enforcement of these Rules. A "submission of advertisement" is defined as each advertisement unless the same advertisement is to be republished in print and or electronic media utilizing the same script. An advertisement does not need to be resubmitted upon each dissemination so long as no changes to form or content are made following the previous submission.

(d) Optional Advisory Opinion. A lawyer may request an advisory opinion concerning the compliance of a contemplated advertisement or communication with these Rules in advance of disseminating the advertisement or communication by submitting the advertisement or communication and fee specified in paragraph (1) below to the OGCMB at least forty-five days prior to such dissemination. The OGCMB shall, upon receipt of such request, evaluate all advertisements and communications submitted to it pursuant to this Rule for compliance with the applicable requirements set forth in this Rule. If an evaluation is requested, the OGCMB shall render its advisory opinion within forty-five days of receipt of a request unless the OGCMB determines that there is reasonable doubt that the advertisement or communication is in compliance with the Rules and that further examination is warranted but such evaluation cannot be completed within the forty-five day time period, and so advise the filing lawyer within the forty-five day time period. In the latter event, the OGCMB shall complete its review as promptly as the circumstances reasonably allow. If the OGCMB does not send any correspondence or notice to the lawyer within forty-five days, the advertisement or communication will be deemed approved.

(1) Items to be submitted to obtain Advisory Opinion. A submission to OGCMB to obtain an advisory opinion pursuant to paragraph (d) shall consist of the same items as (c)(1)(2)(3) above, and an additional fee of fifty dollars ($50) per submission of advertisement or communication made payable to The Mississippi Bar. This fee shall be used only for the purposes of evaluation and/or review of advertisements and preparing the Advisory Opinion. A "submission of advertisement" is defined as each advertisement unless the same advertisement is to be republished in print or electronic media utilizing the same script.

(2) Use of finding. A finding by the OGCMB of either compliance or non-compliance shall not be binding in disciplinary proceedings, but may be offered as evidence.

(3) Change of circumstances. If a change of circumstances occurring subsequent to the OGCMB's evaluation of an advertisement

or communication raises a substantial possibility that the advertisement or communication has become false or misleading as a result of the change in circumstances, the lawyer shall promptly resubmit the advertisement or a modified advertisement with the OGCMB along with an explanation of the change in circumstances and a fee of twenty dollars ($20) per "submission of advertisement or communication."

(e) Substantiation. If requested to do so by the OGCMB, the requesting lawyer shall submit information to substantiate representations made or implied in that lawyer's advertisement or communication.

(f) Non-compliance. When the OGCMB determines that an advertisement or communication is not in compliance with the applicable Rules, the OGCMB shall advise the lawyer by certified mail that dissemination or continued dissemination of the advertisement or communication may result in professional discipline.

(g) Policies and procedures. The Mississippi Bar shall formulate the necessary policies and procedures to implement and enforce the provisions of this Rule and submit same to the Supreme Court for approval pursuant to Rule 3 of the Mississippi Rules of Discipline.

MO Effective 7/1/07

Same as MR

MT Effective 4/1/04

adds reference to "website" as an example of a professional designation.

NE Effective 9/1/05

replaces (a) with: (a) A lawyer shall not use a firm name, letterhead or other professional designation that violates Rule 7.1. A trade name may be used by a lawyer in private practice if: (1) the trade name includes the name of at least one of the lawyers practicing under said name. A law firm consisting solely of the name or names of deceased or retired members of the firm does not have to include the name of an active member of the firm; (2) the trade name does not imply a connection with a government entity, with a public or charitable legal services organization or any other organization, association or institution or entity, unless there is, in fact, a connection; and (3) the trade name is not otherwise in violation of Rule 7.1.

NV Effective 5/1/06

(b): adds "that has registered with the State Bar of Nevada under Rule 7.5A" after "more than one jurisdiction"

(c), adds to end: "This provision does not apply to a lawyer who takes a brief hiatus from practice to serve as an elected member of the Nevada State Legislature when the legislature is in session."

NH Effective 1/1/08

(b) Deletes language after "jurisdiction;"

Adds:

(c) Identification of the lawyers in an office of a law firm shall indicate the jurisdictional limitations on those not licensed to practice in the jurisdiction where the office is located.

(d) is MR (c);

(e) is MR (d).

NJ Effective 1/1/04

> (a) A lawyer shall not use a firm name, letterhead, or other professional designation that violates RPC 7.1. Except for organizations referred to in R. 1:21-1(d), the name under which a lawyer or law firm practices shall include the full or last names of one or more of the lawyers in the firm or office or the names of a person or persons who have ceased to be associated with the firm through death or retirement.
> (b) A law firm with offices in more than one jurisdiction may use the same name in each jurisdiction. In New Jersey, identification of all lawyers of the firm, in advertisements, on letterheads or anywhere else that the firm name is used, shall indicate the jurisdictional limitations on those not licensed to practice in New Jersey. Where the name of an attorney not licensed to practice in this State is used in a firm name, any advertisement, letterhead or other communication containing the

firm name must include the name of at least one licensed New Jersey attorney who is responsible for the firm's New Jersey practice or the local office thereof.
(c) A firm name shall not contain the name of any person not actively associated with the firm as an attorney, other than that of a person or persons who have ceased to be associated with the firm through death or retirement.
(d) Lawyers may state or imply that they practice in a partnership only if the persons designated in the firm name and the principal members of the firm share in the responsibility and liability for the firm's performance of legal services.
(e) A law firm name may include additional identifying language such as "& Associates" only when such language is accurate and descriptive of the firm. Any firm name including additional identifying language such as "Legal Services" or other similar phrases shall inform all prospective clients in the retainer agreement or other writing that the law firm is not affiliated or associated with a public, quasi-public or charitable organization. However, no firm shall use the phrase "legal aid" in its name or in any additional identifying language.
(f) In any case in which an organization practices under a trade name as permitted by paragraph (a) above, the name or names of one or more of its principally responsible attorneys, licensed to practice in this State, shall be displayed on all letterheads, signs, advertisements and cards or other places where the trade name is used.

NM Effective 11/2/09

Changed to Rule 16-705;

(a) Renamed to Paragraph "A. Use of trade or firm name;" Replaces "Rule 7.1"
with "Rule 16-701 of the Rules of Professional Conduct;"
(b) Renamed to Paragraph "B. Multi-jurisdictional law firms;"
(c) Renamed to Paragraph "C. Use of names of lawyers holding public office;"

(d) Renamed to Paragraph "D. Statements about associations."

NY Effective 4/1/09

Changes title to:

RULE 7.5: PROFESSIONAL NOTICES, LETTERHEADS AND SIGNS

(a) A lawyer or law firm may use internet web sites, professional cards, professional announcement cards, office signs, letterheads or similar professional notices or devices, provided the same do not violate any statute or court rule and are in accordance with Rule 7.1, including the following:

(1) a professional card of a lawyer identifying the lawyer by name and as a lawyer, and giving addresses, telephone numbers, the name of the law firm, and any information permitted under Rule 7.1(b) or Rule 7.4. A professional card of a law firm may also give the names of members and associates;

(2) a professional announcement card stating new or changed associations or addresses, change of firm name, or similar matters pertaining to the professional offices of a lawyer or law firm or any nonlegal business conducted by the lawyer or law firm pursuant to Rule 5.7. It may state biographical data, the names of members of the firm and associates, and the names and dates of predecessor firms in a continuing line of succession. It may state the nature of the legal practice if permitted under Rule 7.4;

(3) a sign in or near the office and in the building directory identifying the law office and any nonlegal business conducted by the lawyer or law firm pursuant to Rule 5.7. The sign may state the nature of the legal practice if permitted under Rule 7.4; or

(4) a letterhead identifying the lawyer by name and as a lawyer, and giving addresses, telephone numbers, the name of the law firm, associates and any information permitted under Rule 7.1(b) or Rule 7.4. A letterhead of a law firm may also give the names of members and associates, and names and dates relating to deceased and retired members. A lawyer or law firm may be

designated "Of Counsel" on a letterhead if there is a continuing relationship with a lawyer or law firm, other than as a partner or associate. A lawyer or law firm may be designated as "General Counsel" or by similar professional reference on stationery of a client if the lawyer or the firm devotes a substantial amount of professional time in the representation of that client. The letterhead of a law firm may give the names and dates of predecessor firms in a continuing line of succession.

(b) A lawyer in private practice shall not practice under a trade name, a name that is misleading as to the identity of the lawyer or lawyers practicing under such name, or a firm name containing names other than those of one or more of the lawyers in the firm, except that the name of a professional corporation shall contain "PC" or such symbols permitted by law, the name of a limited liability company or partnership shall contain "LLC," "LLP" or such symbols permitted by law and, if otherwise lawful, a firm may use as, or continue to include in its name the name or names of one or more deceased or retired members of the firm or of a predecessor firm in a continuing line of succession. Such terms as "legal clinic," "legal aid," "legal service office," "legal assistance office," "defender office" and the like may be used only by qualified legal assistance organizations, except that the term "legal clinic" may be used by any lawyer or law firm provided the name of a participating lawyer or firm is incorporated therein. A lawyer or law firm may not include the name of a nonlawyer in its firm name, nor may a lawyer or law firm that has a contractual relationship with a nonlegal professional or nonlegal professional service firm pursuant to Rule 5.8 to provide legal and other professional services on a systematic and continuing basis include in its firm name the name of the nonlegal professional service firm or any individual nonlegal professional affiliated therewith. A lawyer who assumes a judicial, legislative or public executive or administrative post or office shall not permit the lawyer's name to remain in the name of a law firm or to be used in professional notices of the firm during any significant period in which the lawyer is not actively and regularly practicing law as a member of the firm and, during such period, other members of the firm shall not use the lawyer's name in the firm name or in professional notices of the firm.

(c) Lawyers shall not hold themselves out as having a partnership with one or more other lawyers unless they are in fact partners.

(d) A partnership shall not be formed or continued between or among lawyers licensed in different jurisdictions unless all enumerations of the members and associates of the firm on its letterhead and in other permissible listings make clear the jurisdictional limitations on those members and associates of the firm not licensed to practice in all listed jurisdictions; however, the same firm name may be used in each jurisdiction.

(e) A lawyer or law firm may utilize a domain name for an internet web site that does not include the name of the lawyer or law firm provided:

(1) all pages of the web site clearly and conspicuously include the actual name of the lawyer or law firm;

(2) the lawyer or law firm in no way attempts to engage in the practice of law using the domain name;

(3) the domain name does not imply an ability to obtain results in a matter; and

(4) the domain name does not otherwise violate these Rules.

(f) A lawyer or law firm may utilize a telephone number which contains a domain name, nickname, moniker or motto that does not otherwise violate these Rules.

NC Effective 3/1/03

(a): replaces "otherwise" with "false or misleading," adds "Every trade name used by a law firm shall be registered with the North Carolina State Bar for a determination of whether the name is misleading." to end

Adds (c) A law firm maintaining offices only in North Carolina may not list any person not licensed to practice law in North Carolina as a lawyer affiliated with the firm unless the listing properly identifies the jurisdiction in which the lawyer is licensed and states that the lawyer is not licensed in North Carolina.

(d): same as MR (c) but adds "whether or not the lawyer is precluded from practicing law" to end

(e): same as MR (d) but adds "professional" before "organization"

ND Effective 8/1/06

Adds: (e) A lawyer may identify legal assistants on the lawyer's letterhead and on business cards identifying the lawyer's firm, provided the legal assistant's status is clearly identified.

OH Effective 2/1/07

(a): replaces material after first sentence with "A lawyer in private practice shall not practice under a trade name, a name that is misleading as to the identity of the lawyer or lawyers practicing under the name, or a firm name containing names other than those of one or more of the lawyers in the firm, except that the name of a professional corporation or association, legal clinic, limited liability company, or registered partnership shall contain symbols indicating the nature of the organization as required by Gov. Bar R. III. If otherwise lawful, a firm may use as, or continue to include in, its name the name or names of one or more deceased or retired members of the firm or of a predecessor firm in a continuing line of succession."

(b) A law firm with offices in more than one jurisdiction that lists attorneys associated with the firm shall indicate the jurisdictional limitations on those not licensed to practice in Ohio.

OK Effective 1/1/08

Same as MR

OR Effective 12/1/06

(a) A lawyer may use professional announcement cards, office signs, letterheads, telephone and electronic directory listings, legal directory listings or other professional notices so long as the information contained therein complies with Rule 7.1 and other applicable Rules.

(b) A lawyer may be designated "Of Counsel" on a letterhead if the lawyer has a continuing professional relationship with a lawyer or law firm, other than as a partner or associate. A lawyer may be designated as "General Counsel" or by a similar professional reference on stationery of a client if the lawyer or the lawyer's firm devotes a substantial amount of professional time in the representation of the client.

(c) A lawyer in private practice:

(1) shall not practice under a name that is misleading as to the identity of the lawyer or lawyers practicing under such name or under a name that contains names other than those of lawyers in the firm;

(2) may use a trade name in private practice if the name does not state or imply a connection with a governmental agency or with a public or charitable legal services organization and is not otherwise in violation of Rule 7.1; and

(3) may use in a firm name the name or names of one or more of the retiring, deceased or retired members of the firm or a predecessor law firm in a continuing line of succession. The letterhead of a lawyer or law firm may give the names and dates of predecessor firms in a continuing line of succession and may designate the firm or a lawyer practicing in the firm as a professional corporation.

(d) Except as permitted by paragraph (c), a lawyer shall not permit his or her name to remain in the name of a law firm or to be used by the firm during the time the lawyer is not actively and regularly practicing law as a member of the firm. During such time, other members of the firm shall not use the name of the lawyer in the firm name or in professional notices of the firm. This rule does not apply to periods of one year or less during which the lawyer is not actively and regularly practicing law as a member of the firm if it was contemplated that the lawyer would return to active and regular practice with the firm within one year.

(e) Lawyers shall not hold themselves out as practicing in a law firm unless the lawyers are actually members of the firm.
(f) Subject to the requirements of paragraph (c), a law firm practicing in more than one jurisdiction may use the same name in each jurisdiction, but identification of the firm members in an office of the firm shall indicate the jurisdictional limitations of those not licensed to practice in the jurisdiction where the office is located.

PA Effective 7/1/06

(a): adds at the end: If otherwise lawful a firm may use as, or continue to include in, its name, the name or names of one or more deceased or retired members of the firm or of a predecessor firm in a continuing line of succession.

RI Effective 4/15/07

Does not adopt MR (c) but adds instead:

(c) The name of a lawyer holding a public office during any substantial period in which the lawyer is not actively and regularly practicing with the firm, and the name of a lawyer who is disbarred or suspended from the practice of law for a period of at least six (6) months, shall not be used in the name of a law firm or in communication on its behalf.

SC Effective 10/1/05

Same as MR

SD Effective 1/1/04

adds as (e): The disclosure required in Rule 1.4(c)(1) or (2) shall be in black ink with type no smaller than the type used for showing the individual lawyer's names.

TN Effective 1/1/2011

Same as MR

TX* Effective 3/1/05

**Has not amended Rule since the most recent amendments to the ABA Model Rules*

(a) A lawyer in private practice shall not practice under a trade name, a name that is misleading as to the identity of the lawyer or lawyers practicing under such name, or a firm name containing names other than those of one or more of the lawyers in the firm, except that the names of a professional corporation, professional association, limited liability partnership, or professional limited liability company may contain "P.C.," "P.A.," "L.L.P.," "P.L.L.C.," or similar symbols indicating the nature of the organization, and if otherwise lawful a firm may use as, or continue to include in, its name the name or names of one or more deceased or retired members of the firm or of a predecessor firm in a continuing line of succession. Nothing herein shall prohibit a married woman from practicing under her maiden name.

(c) Replaces language before "shall not be" with "(c) The name of a lawyer occupying a judicial, legislative, or public executive or administrative Position;"

(d) A lawyer shall not hold himself or herself out as being a partner, shareholder, or associate with one or more other lawyers unless they are in fact partners, shareholders, or associates.

(e) A lawyer shall not advertise in the public media or seek professional employment by any communication under a trade or fictitious name, except that a lawyer who practices under a firm name as authorized by paragraph (a) of this Rule may use that name in such advertisement or communication but only if that name is the firm name that appears on the lawyer's letterhead, business cards, office sign, fee contracts, and with the lawyer's signature on pleadings and other legal documents.

(f) A lawyer shall not use a firm name, letterhead, or other professional designation that violates Rule 7.02(a).

UT Effective 11/1/05

Same as MR

VT Effective 9/1/09

Same as MR

VA Effective 1/1/04

(a) A lawyer or law firm may use or participate in the use of a professional card, professional announcement card, office sign, letterheads, telephone directory listing, law list, legal directory listing, website, or a similar professional notice or device unless it includes a statement or claim that is false, fraudulent, misleading, or deceptive. A trade name may be used by a lawyer in private practice if it does not imply a connection with a government agency or with a public or charitable legal services organization and is not otherwise in violation of Rule 7.1 and 7.2.
(b) A law firm shall not be formed or continued between or among lawyers licensed in different jurisdictions unless all enumerations of the members and associates of the firm on its letterhead and in other permissible listings make clear the jurisdictional limitations of those members and associates of the firm not licensed to practice in all listed jurisdictions; however, the same firm name may be used in each jurisdiction.

WA Effective 9/1/06

Same as MR

WV* Effective 1/1/89

**Has not amended Rule since the most recent amendments to the ABA Model Rules*

(b) Deletes "or other professional designation."

WI Effective 7/1/07

Same as MR

WY Effective 7/1/06

(b): replaces "other professional designation" with "a similar name"

(d): Lawyers shall clearly and accurately state the organizational structure of the organization in which they practice. Lawyers may not state or imply that they practice in a partnership, firm or other organization if that is not the fact. If lawyers use a name or designation that implies they are practicing in a partnership, firm or other organization, when, in fact, they are not, adding a disclaimer such as "not a partnership" or "an association of sole practitioners" shall not render the name or designation permissible under Rule 7.4.

APPENDIX K

FORMAL OPINION 330 (AUGUST 1972)

[This Opinion was withdrawn in connection with the adoption of Formal Opinion 90-357 in 1990. A copy of Formal Opinion 330 is provided for historical context only.]

The relationship indicated by term "Of Counsel" is a close, continuing, personal relationship between an individual lawyer and a law firm or lawyer, and the relationship is one that is not that of a partner, associate, or outside consultant. A law firm may not be "Of Counsel" to another lawyer or law firm. While a lawyer conceivably could be "Of Counsel" to two law firms or lawyers, one cannot simultaneously have more than a maximum of two "Of Counsel" relationships. The term "Of Counsel" may be used if it correctly describes the existing relationship, on letterheads and professional announcement cards and in law lists and directories.

Code of Professional Responsibility; DR 2-102(A)(1), (2), (3), (4) and (6); DR 2-1-2(C) and (D); EC 2-13.

This Committee has been requested to reconsider Informal Opinions 1173 (February 19, 1971) and 1189 (September 8, 1971), particularly with regard to whether professional corporations may be shown to be "Of Counsel" or "In Association With" another firm, lawyer, or professional corporation. The Committee has reconsidered those opinions and has determined that a Formal Opinion will be helpful in clarifying the matter. Clarification is in order because the Code of Professional Responsibility uses the term "Of Counsel" only in DR 2-102(A)(4) relating to letterheads, yet the problems concerning "Of Counsel" arise in connection with other professional notices.

Generally speaking, the Code regulates the conduct of lawyers without regard to whether a particular lawyer practices as a solo practitioner, a partner in a partnership, a member of a professional legal association, or as an associate of another. The provisions of the Code evidence a desire, however, that the particular relationship existing between or among lawyers be stated clearly so that the public will not be misled. See EC 2-13, cf. DR 2-102(C) and (D). EC 2-13 states:

> In order to avoid the possibility of misleading persons with whom he deals, a lawyer should be scrupulous in the representation of his professional status. He should not hold himself out as being a partner or associate of a law firm if he is not one in fact, and thus should not hold himself out as a partner or associate if he only shares offices with another lawyer.

Even though lawyers are thus admonished to be scrupulous in the representation of their professional status and relationships, terms such as "associate" and "Of Counsel" are not defined. The Ethical Considerations and Disciplinary Rules of the Code generally speak in terms of what a lawyer must or should do or not do. Occasionally reference is made to a law firm, which is said (in the Code's Definitions) to include a professional legal corporation. In some instances, reference is made to the partners or associates of a lawyer. Yet none of these status-indicating terms, other than "law firm" and "professional legal corporation," is defined in the Code. Accordingly, clarification is dependent upon a determination of the scope of "associate," "professional associates," and "Of Counsel" as these terms are used in DR 2-102(A)(1), (2), (4) and (6).

It has been said, "The word 'associate' has a variety of meanings. Principally through custom the word when used on letterheads of law firms has come to be regarded as describing those who are lawyer employees of the firm. Because the word has acquired this special significance in connection with the practice of law the use of the word to describe relationships other than that of employer-employee is likely to be misleading." In re Sussman, 241 Ore. 246, 405 P.2d 355 (1965). ABA Opinion 310 (1963) adds that "associates" may be used "to describe a situation in which the firm or the individual [lawyer] has other lawyers working for them or him who are not partners and who do not generally share in the responsibility and liability for the acts of the firm." Also see Opinion 219 (1941), holding that the use of "associates" negates the existence of a partnership in which they are partners.

The use of the term "Of Counsel" was considered in Informal Opinions 678 (1963), 710 (1964), and 1134 (1969). In Informal Opinion 678 it was said, "It is the impression of the members of this Committee that the term, 'Of Counsel,' shown on a firm's letterhead or shingle, is customarily used to indicate a former partner who is on a retirement or semi-retirement basis, or one who has retired from another partnership or the general private practice or from some public position, who remains available to the firm for consultation and advice, either generally or in a particular field." Opinion 678 concluded that it would be misleading to use "Of Counsel" where the relationship involved only an individual case.

Informal Opinion 710 permitted the name of a retiring judge to appear as "Of Counsel" to a firm that included his son, a former law partner. The opinion stated in part, "From your letter of inquiry we infer that you do not intend to become a partner in the new firm nor would you be an 'associate' inasmuch as you would not be an employee of the firm, although perhaps you would (1) share responsibility and liability with the firm in those cases in which you become 'Of Counsel' . . . or (2) be recompensed in those cases on an independent contractor basis, without sharing responsibility and liability with the firm."

Turning to Informal Opinion 1173, we find its basic holding to be consistent with the guidance gleaned from the authorities cited above. Informal Opinion 1173 correctly held that, under DR 2-102(A)(4), a Chicago law firm may not be shown as "Of Counsel" on the letterhead of a New York lawyer or law firm. It also held, and we reaffirm, that it would be improper to "permit a law firm ever to be designated 'Of Counsel,' in legal directories, [or] in shingles, letterheads or cards of another lawyer or law firm wherever located." DR 2-102(A)(4) states that "[a] lawyer may be designated 'Of Counsel' on a letterhead if he has a continuing relationship with a lawyer or law firm, other than as partner or associate." Without necessarily adopting the descriptive language in Informal Opinion 678, we recognize that DR 2-102(A)(4) uses "Of Counsel" in a manner not inconsistent with earlier usage and that the term relates to an individual lawyer. Thus the term cannot be used with regard to a law firm, whether it be a partnership or professional legal corporation.

Informal Opinion 1173 also held that "it is not proper . . . for any lawyer or law firm to be designated 'Of Counsel' to more than one lawyer or law firm. . . ." Upon reconsideration, we recognize that, while it would be highly unusual for a lawyer to be able to maintain simultaneously with two law firms the close, personal relationship indicated by the term "Of Counsel," it may not be impossible, however, for one to maintain such a relationship with more than two law firms. This conclusion requires a restatement of the nature of the relationship that is indicated by the description "Of Counsel."

The lawyer who is described as being "Of Counsel" to another lawyer or law firm must have a continuing (or semi-permanent) relationship with that lawyer or firm, and not a relationship better described as a forwarder-receiver of legal business; see DR 2-102(A)(4), and cf. DR 2-107(A). His relationship with that lawyer or firm must not be that of partner (or fellow member of a professional legal corporation) nor that of an employee; see DR 2-102(A)(4). His relationship with the lawyer or law firm must be a close, regular, personal relationship like, for example, the relationship of a retired or semi-retired former partner, who remains available to the firm for consulting and advice, or a retired public official who regularly and locally is available to the firm for consultation and advice; see Informal Opinion 678. While it would be misleading to refer to a lawyer who shares in the profits and losses and general responsibility of a firm as being "Of Counsel," the lawyer who is "Of Counsel" may be compensated on a basis of consultation fees; see Informal Opinion 710. He is compensated as a sui generis member of that law office, however, and not as an outside consultant. Generally speaking, the close, personal relationship indicated by the term "Of Counsel" contemplates either that the lawyer practice in the offices of the lawyer or law firm to which he is "Of Counsel" or that his relationship, for example by virtue of past partnership of a retired partner that has led to continuing close association, be so close that he is in regular and frequent, if not daily, contact with the office of the lawyer or firm; see Informal Opinion 1134. The term obviously does not apply to the relationship which is merely that of a forwarder and receiver of legal business. In short, the individual lawyer who properly may be shown to be "Of Counsel" to a lawyer or law firm is a member or component part of that law office, but his status is not that of a partner or an employee (nor that of a controlling member of a professional legal corporation).

Given this view of the relationship indicated by the term "Of Counsel," it follows that one lawyer possibly could have the requisite relationship with two firms simultaneously, for example, one with which he practiced for many years before his retirement and another at a location to which he has moved after retirement. It has been recognized that a lawyer may be a member of two law firms (see New York State Opinion 231); and there is no per se prohibition against one's being "Of Counsel" to two law firms, even though this would seem impossible if the lawyer were currently a partner in any other firm, and even though it may be difficult for the lawyers to avoid other ethical problems such as the problem of differing interests; see DR 5-105(D); cf. Informal Opinion 710. To the extent that one lawyer does in fact have the requisite relationships properly designated "Of Counsel" to more than one lawyer or law firm simultaneously, Informal Opinion 1189 is modified.

Informal Opinion 1189 considered the question whether the designation "Of Counsel" may be used in connection with directories, law lists, shingles, and cards. The problem was created because the term "Of Counsel" was used only in regard to letterheads, subdivision (4) of DR 2-102(A).

Where a relationship exists which may be described accurately as an "Of Counsel" relationship, we hold that the relationship may be designated on a professional announcement card (see subd. 2), on a shingle (subd. 3), and in a law list or legal directory (subd. 6).

Little difficulty is encountered with regard to professional announcement cards, for subdivision 2 of DR 2-102(A) permits the use of a card stating "changed associations . . . or similar matters. . . ." The change of a lawyer's status to "Of Counsel," or the addition to the firm's ranks of a lawyer whose status factually will be "Of Counsel," falls within the quoted language and is permissible.

Subdivision 3 of DR 2-102(A) in general language permits a lawyer or law firm to use a shingle. Neither this subdivision nor the statements of underlying policy in the Ethical Considerations indicate any reason to prohibit the use of the term "Of Counsel" to indicate the status of an affiliated lawyer if the term accurately indicates the true relationship of the lawyers.

Proper interpretation of subdivision 6 of DR 2-102(A) is more difficult. That provision states in detail what may appear in a listing in a reputable law list or legal directory. In part, subdivision 6 states, "The published data may include only the following: name, including name of law firm and names of professional associates. . . ." "Of Counsel" is not listed among the permitted items of information. It is our opinion, however, that "professional associates" as used in subdivision 6 is intended to refer not only to "associates" but also to the affiliated lawyer who is more accurately described as being "Of Counsel."

Although we held that a listing in a law directory may properly show, if the statement describes the professional status accurately, that a lawyer is "Of Counsel" to the lawyer or law firm, we find nothing in the list of permissible data to support a view that the listing of a lawyer or law firm may include a reference to another lawyer or law firm that works, either occasionally or regularly, in association with the listed firm, or to whom or from whom legal business is occasionally or regularly referred. We believe that it is not permissible to include the statement in a listing that another lawyer or law firm is "New York Counsel," "In Association With," "Correspondent," and so forth. Thus, we construe "names of professional associates" to include only an individual lawyer whose status is accurately described either as that of partner in a firm, an employee of a lawyer or law firm, a member of a professional legal corporation, or one who is "Of Counsel." This much is reasonably necessary in order to make clear the professional status of the lawyers affiliated with an office; but to permit more under the guise of listing the "names of professional associates" would be to permit a degree of advertising not contemplated by DR 2-102(A)(6). Informal Opinion 1189 is modified to the extent it is inconsistent with the views here expressed.

Table of Cases

A

B

C

D

E

F

K

L

M

N

O

P

R

W

Y

Z

Index

G

L

P

R

T

Y

Z